Understanding democracy

Democracy has moved to the center of systemic reflections on political economy, gaining a position that used to be occupied by the debate about socialism and capitalism. Certitudes about democracy have been replaced by a new awareness of the elusiveness and fluidity of democratic institutions and the multiplicity of dimensions involved. *Understanding Democracy: Economic and Political Perspectives* is a book that reflects this new intellectual situation. It consists of a collection of essays by well-known economists and political scientists from both North America and Europe on the nature of democracy, the necessary conditions for a stable democracy, and the relationship between democracy and important economic issues such as the functioning of the market economy, economic growth, income distribution, and social policies.

Understanding democracy

Economic and political perspectives

Albert Breton
University of Toronto

Gianluigi Galeotti
Università di Roma "La Sapienza"

Pierre Salmon
Université de Bourgogne

Ronald Wintrobe
University of Western Ontario

CAMBRIDGE
UNIVERSITY PRESS

PUBLISHED BY THE PRESS SYNDICATE OF THE UNIVERSITY OF CAMBRIDGE
The Pitt Building, Trumpington Street, Cambridge CB2 1RP, United Kingdom

CAMBRIDGE UNIVERSITY PRESS
The Edinburgh Building, Cambridge CB2 2RU, United Kingdom
40 West 20th Street, New York, NY 10011-4211, USA
10 Stamford Road, Oakleigh, Melbourne 3166, Australia

First published 1997

Printed in the United States of America

Typeset in Times Roman

Library of Congress Cataloging-in-Publication Data

Understanding democracy : economic and political perspectives / Albert
    Breton ... [et al.].
p. cm.
ISBN 0-521-58236-9 (hardback)
1. Democracy–Congresses.   I. Breton, Albert.
JC423.U485   1997
321.8–dc21   96-46376
                                                      CIP

A catalog record for this book is available from the British Library

ISBN 0 521 58236 9 hardback

Contents

Contributors

Peter Bernholz, Universität Basel, Switzerland
Albert Breton, University of Toronto, Canada
Margot Breton, University of Toronto, Canada
Luigi Campiglio, Università Cattolica di Milano, Italy
José Antonio Cheibub, University of Pennsylvania, USA
Gianluigi Galeotti, Università di Roma "La Sapienza," Italy
Michele Grillo, Università Cattolica di Milano, Italy
Russell Hardin, New York University, USA
Dennis Mueller, Universität Wien, Austria
Adam Przeworski, New York University, USA
Pierre Salmon, Université de Bourgogne, France
Ian Shapiro, Yale University, USA
Barry R. Weingast, Stanford University, USA
Ronald Wintrobe, University of Western Ontario, Canada

Introduction

Albert Breton, Gianluigi Galeotti, Pierre Salmon,
and Ronald Wintrobe

Renewed interest in democracy – in its virtues and limitations, in its relationships to liberty, security, and stability, and in its connections to a variety of
attributes such as its capacity to solve collective problems – has been motivated to a considerable degree by developments that have taken place over the
last fifteen to twenty years. Foremost among these developments is the fact that
a number of countries in the Americas and in Europe that had never experienced
democracy, or had not been ruled democratically for many years, recently opted
for that form of governance. Of considerable importance also is the fact that
many of the countries that have recently chosen democracy had, for decades,
functioned under the rules and conventions characteristic of planned collectivist
systems. This fact has posed the question of whether democracy is compatible
with economic collectivism or whether it requires the more or less simultaneous adoption of a capitalist market system. Conversely, inasmuch as people in
these newly democratic countries are primarily concerned with their economic
well-being, the question of whether the transition to a market economy is easier
or more difficult under democracy has also been pushed to the fore. Of equal
importance is the fact that the disappearance of economic collectivism as an
alternative to capitalism (for the time being at least) has fostered a reorienta-
tion of systemic thinking, on both sides of the ideological spectrum, toward the
subject of democracy in all its dimensions – the nature of the system, the way
it works or can be made to work, its prerequisites, its results, and so on.

The developments just noted are not the only factors that have provoked a
renewed interest in democracy. In countries that have had a long and enduring
familiarity with that form of governance, long-standing certitudes have been
challenged by the severe financial imbalances, persistent unemployment, un-
sustainable welfare policies, diminished ability of national governments to address many of the windfalls associated with globalization, and similar problems,

1

which have become more or less permanent features of the politico-economic landscape of recent decades.

Another factor that has stimulated and nurtured interest in democracy is the amazing economic success of a small group of developing countries whose leaders have rejected democracy not only in practice but in principle, that is, as an ideal. In the case of Singapore, Malaysia, Chile, China, and a few other countries, a high level of economic performance has indeed proved compatible with authoritarian government, leading their rulers to claim that democracy is unnecessary and even harmful. This has prompted questions related to whether democracy and economic performance are independent of each other or, going one step further, whether they are negatively related. Although similar questions have often received affirmative answers in the past, they have again become salient because the preoccupations they reveal coincide with unprecedented efforts at democratization in some parts of the world and with severe bouts of democratic melancholia in the West.

Different perspectives thus compete or at the very least coexist, moving democracy to the center of systemic reflections, a position occupied until recently by capitalism and socialism.

With these questions as a general background, early versions of the essays that follow were presented and discussed in the setting of a Villa Colombella Seminar.[1] As has been the rule for these seminars, the participants came from both sides of the Atlantic, were specialized in different disciplines, and were influenced by different ideological or doctrinal inclinations.

The analyses offered in the various chapters cover much ground, but all make a contribution to answering one or the other of the questions raised earlier in this Introduction. The papers fall into four categories, which correspond to four broad classes of questions about democracy, namely: (I) the relation between democracy, the market, and the law; (II) the relation between democracy and economic growth; (III) democratic deficiencies and possible improvements; and (IV) democratic expectations. These categories define the four sections of the book. We present here a brief guide to their content.

Part I is devoted to the relationship between democracy, the market, and the law (including constitutional law). Barry Weingast's contribution provides a unified approach to the problems of stable democracy, rule of law, and limits to

---

[1] Volumes based on papers presented at Villa Colombella Seminars were published (under the same editorship as the present volume) as follows: Villa Colombella Papers on Federalism (*European Journal of Political Economy*, Vol. 3, Special Issue, nos. 1 & 2, 1987); Villa Colombella Papers on Bureaucracy (*European Journal of Political Economy*, Vol. 4, Extra Issue, 1988); *The Competitive State: Villa Colombella Papers on Competitive Politics* (Kluwer, Dordrecht: 1991); *Preferences and Democracy* (Kluwer, Dordrecht: 1993); *Nationalism and Rationality* (Cambridge University Press, New York and Cambridge: 1995).

government. His analysis is developed around a model that highlights the coordination problems faced by citizens when they want to police the state. Even if all members of society agree on a definition of citizen rights, those rights might not be respected. But the problem is exacerbated when views about the appropriate role of the state and what constitutes a transgression differ. In this context, though formal rules such as constitutions or citizen rights can be defended only if an informal consensus exists in society about the need to defend them, such a consensus is not likely to come about if the informal views of citizens are not coordinated, and this coordination may require a focal point that only formal institutions can provide. Weingast thus shows the existence of a fundamental complementarity between informal social mechanisms and the formal institutions of democracy. In the perspective of the current so-called transition to democracy and/or markets, one implication of his analysis is that political, legal, and market systems interact too much to be designed independently.

From a different yet consistent perspective, Michele Grillo, in Chapter 2, analyzes representative democracy as an exchange relationship. Citizens concede the formal authority to make collective decisions to a leader chosen by means of a competitive contest. How are the promises made by this leader to be enforced? Grillo analyzes this problem with the help of the theory of incomplete contracting and, in particular, of the work done recently on the allocation of authority, formal and real, in organizations. An essential condition for the enforcement of an incomplete contract in this context, Grillo stresses, is that the authority that is conferred in the exchange is not the authority to alter the competitive conditions under which the allocation of authority is organized. In the political domain, this implies that the constitutional contract that is required for representative democracy to work must include the crucial condition that the elected leader be subjected as everybody else to the classical constitutional principle of *isonomia* (equality before the law). Grillo shows then that a constitutional contract that includes this principle is both efficient and self-enforcing.

The analysis of constitutional democracy proposed in Chapter 3 by Dennis Mueller starts from two premises: Government ought to exist to advance the common interests of citizens, and citizens are capable of designing institutions that achieve that goal. Given these premises, what sort of institutions would citizens design? The design of government institutions is analyzed by Mueller as a principal-agent problem. Officeholders must be given the authority and resources to provide the public goods that justify government's existence but be prevented from using that to advance their interests at the expense of the citizens they nominally serve. Mueller discusses how institutions of government such as the legislative branch, the executive branch, the judiciary, a federal governmental structure, and the language of the constitution itself – most importantly in its delineation of individual rights – might contribute to the solution of the problem. He also considers the questions of how the constitutional contract that joins all citizens under government should be written, ratified, amended and, with particular attention devoted to the judiciary, enforced.

In the last chapter of Part I, Peter Bernholz argues that only a market economy with secure property rights and competition can preserve the independence of a number of individuals that is sufficient to maintain democracy. But a free market is only a necessary condition for the existence of stable democracies in complex societies. It is not a sufficient condition because, if democracies concede nearly unlimited powers to simple majorities, decisions made by these majorities will tend to erode property rights and the rule of law and steadily increase government activity. According to Bernholz, this in time will lead to a decrease in efficiency, saving, investment, and innovativeness. As a consequence voters become disillusioned, which allows various ideologies and ideas (including economic and political theories) to contend for their support. If incorrect theories, promising easy solutions, win the day and if the economic and political systems are restructured according to their recommendations, the free market economy, and with it democracy itself, may be eroded if not abolished altogether. It follows from this argument that only a constitutionally or institutionally restricted democracy can be maintained in the long run.

Part II is concerned with the relationship between democracy (or dictatorship, which amounts to the same thing in this context) and economic growth. It is made up of three chapters. Chapter 5, by José Antonio Cheibub and Adam Przeworski, is a study of the effect of the size of government on economic growth. The authors argue that any defendable analysis of the relationship between the state and the private sector must include the assumption that the state contributes to production in one way or another – without the help of the state a market economy cannot work. Cheibub and Przeworski discuss four alternative ways of modeling and specifying the assumption that the state plays a productive role. From that theoretical discussion, they derive equations that they estimate against a large set covering many countries over several decades. Their main result is that the size of the government has been on average too small. This is equally true, on average, of democracies and of dictatorships. Cheibub and Przeworski consider as, at best, dubious the argument that retrospective voting induces government to perform better and thus are not surprised to find out that the size of government is not closer to the optimum under democracy than under dictatorship. But the negative result, they caution, only means that a "finer grain analysis," both of different democratic institutions and of different forms of dictatorship, is needed to identify the effect of politics.

In Chapter 6, Ronald Wintrobe discusses the now almost conventional idea that democratic governments inhibit growth because they favor excess redistributory activity or rent-seeking. His analysis proceeds by examining the equilibrium level of redistribution in a number of well-known models of democracy: the median voter-average income model, in which income is redistributed from the mean to the median; the pressure group model; and the probabilistic voting model. Wintrobe then asks what would happen to this equilibrium level of redistribution if a dictator took over the government. The analysis suggests that we would expect more redistribution under dictatorship than democracy. It can even be shown that, *ceteris paribus*, the more powerful the dictatorship the larger the redistribution it engages in. This suggests an alternative explanation for the performance of "capitalist-authoritarian" regimes like Pinochet's Chile or South Korea. They achieved a high rate of economic growth, Wintrobe claims, not because they did not redistribute but because they did. The redistribution, however, was toward groups specially interested in growth, such as capital owners, and thus its content was necessarily welfare enhancing.

In the last chapter of Part II, Pierre Salmon argues that recent models in which inequality has, as a consequence of majority voting and redistributive policies, a negative influence on economic growth reflect a conception of democracy that is questionable. In these models, income distribution is a decisive variable because decision making is modeled as if it took place under direct democracy, voters are assumed to be fully capable of predicting the redistributive consequences of policies, and slow growth in one country is assumed to be politically sustainable and without problems even when growth is rapid in neighboring countries. When these assumptions are reversed, redistribution policies, Salmon argues, have to be compatible with minimum growth constraints. These constraints depend on what obtains abroad, on the extent to which discrepancies between what happens abroad and what obtains in the country are perceived and affect discontent in the country, and on the extent to which discontent endangers the government. The last variable is related to the political system: *ceteris paribus*, minimum growth constraints are likely to be tighter in democracies in which office holding is highly contestable than they are in democracies run by "partitocracies," and tighter in the latter than in dictatorships.

The chapters of Part III focus on some imperfections or deficiencies observable in democracies and on the processes through which these imperfections or deficiencies are or could be mitigated. In Chapter 8, Gianluigi Galeotti is concerned with the evolution of public bureaucracies and of their control in democratic settings. Taking as fact the existence of a decline of democratic control over bureaus, Galeotti argues that, contrary perhaps to a widely held expectation, this decline is not necessarily accompanied by a rise of comparable magnitude in bureaucratic power. In other words, the evolution may be analyzed as a negative-sum game. The question of whether that negative-sum game shows up in different ways in parliamentary and in congressional systems has to be solved by comparing degrees of institutional competition, both at the political and the administrative levels. Under all systems, however, the demand and supply of bureaucratic rules conspire to generate complex administrative structures. When that general trend is combined with weak political competition and with passivity or unaccountability at the higher levels of bureaucracy – two traits more specific of the Italian experience according to Galeotti – we have, he claims, an anonymous fragmentation of responsibility that calls to mind the notion of a headless Leviathan.

In the next chapter, Albert Breton and Margot Breton incorporate a mechanism of political empowerment into a theory of democracy. This theory assumes the supply side of the governmental system to be competitive and responsive to citizens, but allows that, at any point of time, responsiveness is imperfect. Some groups or categories are disempowered. In the course of time, however, notably because the supply side of politics is fundamentally competitive, processes of empowerment, concerning specific categories, take place – which tends to eliminate or mitigate in turn particular instances of unresponsiveness. Breton and Breton analyze in detail how the mechanism of empowerment operates – insisting in particular on the crucial steps of conscientization and of change in the paradigm used by the public and by politicians to analyze particular states of disempowerment. The incorporation of empowerment as a force giving shape to the demand side of politics has a bearing on traditional questions in the theory of democracy such as the stability of autonomy of the preferences of citizens, the viability and stability of groups concerned with public goods, and the value given by citizens to more equality in the distribution of socioeconomic, cultural, and political power.

In Chapter 10, Luigi Campiglio, after having assumed that voting is an acceptable indicator or measure of political participation, is mostly concerned with the age distributions of voters and nonvoters. His main point is that the difference between the two distributions is reflected in policy outcomes. Inasmuch as young children do not have the right to vote and do not get their parents additional voting rights, whereas young enfranchised adults and other low-income categories have a lower turnout than the rest of the population, the median voter has a higher income, that is, closer to the average income, than would be the case if everybody was equally represented, and modern democracies can thus be said to be unintentionally biased against the young – as well as against low-income groups in general. Campiglio insists that this is not only a defect of contemporary democracies with respect to justice but that it also affects economic efficiency and growth negatively – by fostering a more violent society than would be the case if there were more universal political participation in the form of voting. In the course of the analysis, Campiglio also explores a number of ways the problems he highlights could be dealt with.

The two chapters of Part IV are concerned with general questions about democracy and what should or should not be expected from it. Ian Shapiro reviews the major theoretical debates and defends a view of democracy that occupies a middle ground between a wholly procedural definition and an exclusive concern with outcomes, between the treatment of democracy as an ideal type and a contextual approach, and between an assessment in purely instrumental terms and the view that democracy is inherently valuable. On the last issue, for example, his position is that democracy is a good, albeit a conditioning or subordinate good. Democracy should be seen as important in every domain of civil society but never as the most important thing. Two commitments are essential components of the democratic ideal: participation of all concerned in collective decisions and the right for everyone to oppose decisions they reject, implying a presumptive suspicion of all hierarchies. Shapiro analyzes in detail how these commitments should influence the shape of various civil institutions, not only the political institutions. He discusses in particular how tensions internal to the implementation of the democratic ideal and tensions between it and other valuable goods can be managed in such a way that institutions become, in the course of time, somewhat more democratic.

In the last chapter of the volume, Russell Hardin argues that there are harsh limits to the possibilities of democracy. Democracy can deal with problems whose solution entails only small gains and losses. It can also handle big issues on which there is broad consensus. But, he notes, most forms of government could handle such issues roughly as well. When issues are both conflictual and big – that is, involve decisions that produce not only marginal but major winners and losers – democracy can only work against a background of coordination on order. Without that essentially prior coordination, democracy is trammeled or irrelevant. Democracy is in Hobbes's family of mutual-advantage devices. This means that if people are to continue coordinating on it even when they are seriously harmed at one point of time by the decisions it produces, they must consider that it nonetheless serves their interests better than would attempts to move to an alternative. This is likely to be the case when there is a large capital stock that is at risk if order breaks down and if that capital stock is spread fairly broadly through the society. These conditions are likely to be satisfied in contemporary industrial countries, but Hardin documents the view that even in these societies issues that are big and divisive can place democracy at risk.

Natural experiments are a major source of progress in nonexperimental disciplines. Given the wealth of experiments that nature, on its own, has made available to them in recent years, social scientists are fortunate indeed. Summaries neglect much that is worthwhile in papers. In the foregoing summaries, the extent to which the exceptional opportunities provided by nature have been put to good use by the chapters' contributors does not come through as well as it might. A reading of the chapters will reveal the truth of this affirmation.

At the same time, it must be noted that the scope of the volume itself is limited in various ways. Not all aspects of democracy are covered, and some issues that constitute the standard focus of scholars in public choice, for instance the obstacles democracies meet in balancing budgets, are addressed only tangentially. On the other hand, some questions are considered extensively. A case in point is the comparison, on various dimensions, of democracies and autocracies that is central to the chapters in Part II and that is discussed also in some other chapters. The reader will also discover links between papers found in different parts of the volume. For instance, Bernholz's point that democracy must be complemented by institutions that limit the domain of majoritarian politics is closely related to the analysis developed by Hardin in the last chapter of the volume. There are also features of the book that some readers might consider to be limitations or shortcomings but that were always intended. Let us mention two. Supporting evidence, in the form of quantitative data or of historical facts, is provided in many parts of the book but not in all chapters and not always in the form of comprehensive, rigorous empirical tests. On a subject such as this one, in which the theory itself is much in need of development, we do not consider purely theoretical, conceptual, or even tentative discussions to be inappropriate. A second feature is that a variety of viewpoints are expressed. No common understanding of democracy underlies – or emerges from – the views expressed in the various chapters, but we must stress that this reflects the state of knowledge in the disciplines of politics and economics on this question, and consensus could only be obtained by restricting the contributors to one or another school of thought, something we thought highly undesirable. Some of the reasons that no single interpretation of democracy seems possible for the time being are discussed in Shapiro's contribution.

Understanding democracy, that subtle and elusive institution, belongs to the class of achievements that recede as one advances and becomes aware of the multiplicity of the dimensions involved. This implies that one's understanding has improved relative to what it was before, that one's efforts have been worthwhile. We hope that readers of this volume will come to the same conclusion.

We wish to thank Giorgio Brosio, Francesco Forte, Luisa Giuriato, Elena Granaglia, Jean-Dominique Lafay, and George Tridimas for acting as discussants and for their participation in the seminar. We are grateful to the Lynde and Harry Bradley Foundation and to the Consiglio Nazionale delle Ricerche for their continuing financial generosity. We are also thankful to the Laboratoire d'Analyses et de Techniques Economiques (UMR CNRS 5601) and the Maison des Sciences de l'Homme for their support.

Democracy, the market, and the law

CHAPTER 1

Democratic stability as a self-enforcing equilibrium

Barry R. Weingast

Liberty lies in the hearts of men and women; when it dies there, no constitution, no law, no court can save it . . . .*

1   Introduction

The purpose of this essay is to develop an approach explaining democratic stability. To focus our attention, we begin by investigating the limits on sovereign or state power. We assume that all citizens have preferences, opinions, and values about these limits and about what acts violate them. This allows each citizen to classify state actions into two mutually exclusive categories: those they consider *legitimate* and those they consider a fundamental *transgression* of their rights. Notice that we define these concepts for an individual, not for the society. No automatic mechanism is assumed to create a societal consensus about such values. Citizens may have widely different views about these limits and about fundamental transgressions. Moreover, apart from their preferences about specific limits, citizens may also have varying views about *citizen duty*, that is, what they believe citizens should do in the face of a transgression.

The model is based on two assumptions about the relationship between a sovereign and his citizens. First, a necessary condition for an individual citizen to support the sovereign is that he not transgress what that citizen believes are his or her fundamental rights. Second, remaining in power requires that the

Senior Fellow, Hoover Institution, and Professor, Department of Political Science, Stanford University. The author gratefully acknowledges Robert Bates, Alessandra Casella, Larry Diamond, Paul Milgrom, Gabriella Montinola, Adam Przeworski, Kenneth Schultz, Ian Shapiro, and Kenneth Shepsle for helpful conversations. This paper draws on the author's larger study in Weingast (1996b).
*Learned Hand, "The Spirit of Liberty," in Hand (1952, pp. 189–90).

11

sovereign retain a sufficient degree of support among the citizenry. Without the necessary support, the sovereign loses power.

These assumptions have significant implications for sovereign behavior. If, on a particular issue, there exists a consensus in society about what constitutes the legitimate boundaries of the state, these assumptions imply that the sovereign will avoid actions that violate these boundaries. The reason is simple: If he ignores such boundaries, he will be deposed. On the other hand, if citizens hold different values about the legitimate boundaries of the state, the sovereign can take actions that some citizens consider fundamental transgressions as long as not all citizens consider them so. These assumptions also imply that, when citizens agree on the appropriate boundaries of the state, those boundaries are *self-enforcing*, that is, it is in the interest of the sovereign to respect them.

One advantage of the model is that it provides a unifying approach to a series of separate but important themes and findings in the literature on democracy. First, it reveals why democratic stability requires not only the formal institutions of democracy – elections, representation, legislatures – but the appropriate set of citizen attitudes about these institutions. For political officials to respect these institutions, citizens must be willing to withdraw their support from those officials who seek to violate these institutions. Citizens must be willing to do so even if they are the intended beneficiaries of the violation. Citizen reaction is thus central to maintaining self-enforcing limits on public officials, including adherence to the fundamental institutions of democracy such as voting rights and elections.

The model thus provides the theoretical underpinning for a range of important but seemingly disconnected topics in the literature. Two major themes are treated. First, the approach emphasizes the importance of citizen attitudes, beliefs, and values for the political foundations of democracy (e.g., Almond and Verba, 1963; Dahl, 1966, 1971; Lipset, 1960; Putnam, 1993). Nonetheless, the model shows that these attitudes are not exogenous, nor are they alone sufficient for democratic stability. Second, this perspective provides a theoretical basis for understanding why deeply divided societies are far less likely to maintain stable democracies (e.g., Horowitz, 1985; Rabushka and Shepsle, 1972).

I also extend the approach to a series of additional topics: the role of pacts in the initiation of democratization (e.g., Burton, Gunther, and Higley, 1992; Karl, 1986; O'Donnell and Schmitter, 1986, ch. 4); the critical interaction of institutions and expectations in what Lijphart has called the "politics of accommodation" (Lijphart, 1968); Przeworski's (1991) model of self-enforcing democracy in the face of electoral defeat; and Putnam's (1993) concept of "social capital."

Several of these findings are illustrated by the Missouri Compromise of 1820, an elite pact that helped maintain American democracy for another generation. The crisis over the admission of Missouri revealed that both Northerners and

Southerners were vulnerable to a national government dominated by the other section. To mitigate the problem of vulnerability, the Missouri Compromise created the "balance rule" (Weingast, 1996c), the notion that the number of Northern and Southern states would remain equal, thus granting each section a veto over national policymaking.

The Missouri Compromise illustrates our theme of the interaction of informal values and preferences with formal institutions, the latter serving as a focal point to help align and coordinate the informal views of citizens so that the more formal institutions of democracy and the state can remain stable. Thereafter, citizens could react in concert and were thus able to police state behavior.

This paper proceeds as follows. Section 2 develops the model and shows the consequences of the various equilibria, revealing the range of characteristics a society may exhibit. Section 3 applies the model to the problem of democratic stability and provides the basis for integrating several disparate components of the literature. Section 4 illustrates the approach by discussing the Missouri Compromise. The concluding discussion develops the implications of the approach for the maintenance of democracy, the emergence of a civil society, and the rule of law.

2   The model

I develop the approach in two stages. The first stage studies the pure coordination problem induced by sovereign transgressions. This model ignores politics and the potential for alliances between the sovereign and a subset of constituents. The second stage embeds the problem of citizen coordination within a political context.

Stage 1: Pure coordination

Consider a game that concerns the interaction of the polity and economy. The players are a sovereign, S, and two groups of citizens, A and B. The economy produces the social surplus. All players share in the surplus, but the quantity produced and its distribution depend on the political choices resulting from the interaction of the players. We assume not only that a set of economic and political rights has been specified, but that these rights are compatible with economic prosperity. Whether they are enforced – and hence whether prosperity occurs in practice – depends on the interaction of the players.

The sovereign holds political power and may choose to respect citizens' rights or violate them. This power allows him to confiscate some economic rents or other forms of wealth. It also generates an economic loss, reflecting the potential destruction of assets and the poor incentive effects generated by insecure property rights. The sovereign does not hold power indefinitely, however.

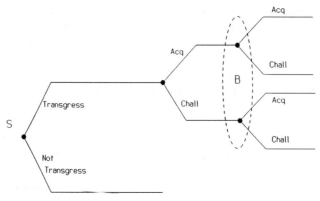

Figure 1.1. Sovereign-constituency coordination game.

In order to remain in power, he needs the support of a sufficient subset of the citizens.[1] This reflects the notion that there exist rivals with citizen support who challenge a sovereign without a minimal degree of support. Thus citizens hold some potential power over the sovereign in that they may withdraw their support. When a sufficient number of citizens do so, the sovereign is deposed. Specifically, the model assumes that the sovereign's survival requires the support of at least one of the citizens groups but not both.[2]

The sequence of play in the model is shown in Figure 1.1. The Sovereign moves first and must choose whether or not to transgress the rights of his citizens. Once S has chosen, A and B move simultaneously.[3] Each may choose to acquiesce or to challenge the sovereign. Challenging is costly; moreover, each may challenge even if the sovereign has not transgressed. If both A and B challenge, the sovereign is deposed and any attempted transgression by the sovereign is rebuffed. If only one group of citizens challenges S, the challenge fails and the transgression succeeds. Of course, if both A and B acquiesce, the transgression succeeds.

The payoffs from this game are given in Table 1.1. Power is valuable to the sovereign, and he gains 2 from retaining it. Total payoffs are maximized when no transgressions are attempted and neither group challenges: the sovereign

---

[1] Widespread evidence exists for this assumption (see, e.g., Ames, 1987). Even oppressive, authoritarian regimes require the support of a small group of citizens.

[2] Notice that this does not assume that the sovereign requires the support of a majority, however. The groups may be of unequal size, with the support of the smaller, minority group being sufficient to maintain the sovereign in power.

[3] The simultaneous move between A and B is shown in the figure as A moving first followed by B, but, as indicated by the dashed ellipse or "information set" around B's two nodes, B does not know A's decision when he must choose.

Table 1.1. *Payoffs for the sovereign-constituency coordination game*

S Moves first	Induced subgame between A&B (payoffs: S,A,B)

receives 2, and each group, 8. Successful transgressions are also valuable to him and increase his payoff by 6, a gain of 3 from each citizen group. Though a transgression benefits the sovereign by 3 from each group, it costs each 6, reflecting the economic costs and dislocations associated with transgressions. Challenging costs each challenger 1 regardless of whether it is successful.

Outcomes are determined by the strategy combinations chosen by the three players. If S attempts a transgression and both A and B acquiesce, the transgression succeeds and the payoffs are 8 to S (two for retaining power and three confiscated from each group) and 2 to both A and B (eight minus the loss of six from a transgression). If S attempts to transgress against A and B and both challenge, the transgression fails and the sovereign loses power, resulting in payoffs of 0 to the sovereign (he loses power and hence his payoff of two) and 7 to each group (eight minus the costs of challenging).

The structure of the game induces a problem of coordination among the citizens. If all act in concert, they are able to police the sovereign and prevent transgressions. On the other hand, if they fail to act in concert, the sovereign can transgress the rights of citizens and survive. As in all coordination games, how one citizen group reacts to a transgression depends upon how it anticipates the other citizen group will react. If it is assured the other will challenge, then it is best off challenging as well. But if it believes that the other group will acquiesce, then it is better off acquiescing as well.

This behavior reflects the two pure strategy equilibria of the game. In one, the sovereign transgresses the rights of citizens and both acquiesce in spite of the sovereign's behavior. This is an equilibrium because of the coordination problem. From the perspective of one citizen group, given that the other is acquiescing, it is best off by acquiescing as well: Challenging is costly and will do no good. Moreover, the sovereign has no incentive to change his behavior since he benefits from successful transgressions. Limits on the sovereign are not respected in this equilibrium.

In the other equilibrium, the sovereign honors rights in society and neither group challenges, thus maximizing social surplus. In this equilibrium, both groups challenge whenever the sovereign attempts a transgression. Given the behavior of the others, neither citizen group has an incentive to alter its behavior. Nor does the sovereign. Limits on the sovereign are self-enforcing in this equilibrium.

This game reveals a natural impediment to policing the behavior of the state. Even when all members of the society agree on the definition of citizen rights, those rights might not be respected. Because the sovereign benefits from transgressions against his citizens, the sovereign is potentially tempted to violate citizen rights. Preventing transgressions, in turn, requires that citizens react in concert against the sovereign. The model reveals that limits on the state are self-enforcing when the citizens coordinate their reactions to defend those limits. As in all coordination games, even though all players are better off when all challenge following a transgression, they will not automatically do so.

Stage 2: Adding a political coordination problem

The model in stage 1 is particularly simple. If coordination were the sole problem facing citizens, citizens would be likely to surmount it much as they easily overcome the coordination problem of which side of the road to drive on. Distributional issues complicate the problem considerably. Stage 1 affords no differentiation between the two groups. A transgression against one is a transgression against the other. This implies that there is no diversity of opinion about the nature of the appropriate boundaries of the state and hence about what actions constitute a transgression.

Stage 2 expands the first game to allow for two additional effects. First, the sovereign need not transgress the rights of all citizens simultaneously. Second, transgressions have distributional implications in that some of the benefits of a transgression are shared with a subset of citizens in exchange for their support. This has a natural interpretation because transgressions against one group in society often directly benefit another. For example, violating one groups' right of representation to the legislature allows the other to dominate and hence to capture a greater share of the benefits. The purpose of this second model is to add a political element to the problem, one in which typical distributive concerns arise.

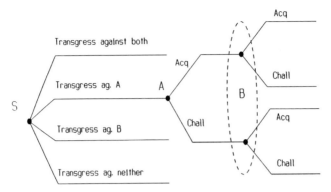

Figure 1.2. The sovereign-constituency transgression game.

As before, the sovereign faces two groups of citizens, A and B; he must retain the support of at least one group in order to retain power. The sequence of actions in this game is shown in Figure 1.2. S moves first and may choose to attempt to transgress against both A and B, against A alone, against B alone, or against neither. After S moves, A and B move simultaneously. Each may choose to acquiesce or to challenge the sovereign. Challenging is costly. If both A and B challenge, the sovereign is deposed, and any transgression attempted by the sovereign is rebuffed. If only one group of citizens challenges S, the challenge fails and any attempted transgression succeeds. If both A and B acquiesce, any attempted transgression succeeds.

The payoffs from this game are given in Table 1.2. Social surplus is maximized when no transgressions or challenges are attempted, yielding 2, 8, and 8, respectively. Power is valuable to the sovereign, and he loses 2 if he is deposed. Successful transgressions are also valuable and net a total of 3 each. When S successfully transgresses against one group, he keeps 2 of the 3 and shares 1 with the other group. If S transgresses against both, he keeps 6, the entire amount extracted. A transgression against either group costs that group 6. As before, fifty percent of all confiscated surplus is destroyed. Challenging costs each challenger 1 regardless of whether it is successful.

Outcomes are determined by the strategy combinations chosen by the three players. If S attempts to transgress against both A and B and both acquiesce, the transgression succeeds and the payoffs are: 8 to S, 2 to A, and 2 to B. If S attempts to transgress against both A and B and both challenge, the transgression fails and the sovereign loses power, resulting in payoffs of 0, 7, 7.

This game complicates the coordination problem by adding an aspect of the prisoners' dilemma. Although more complex than the standard prisoners' dilemma, the structure of this game resembles the latter in that responding to transgressions is costly for each citizen group. Consider the set of incentives

Table 1.2. *Payoffs for the sovereign-constituency transgression game*

S Moves first	Induced subgame between A&B (payoffs: S,A,B)

facing the citizens if S attempts to transgress against B. B naturally prefers that both challenge. Notice, however, that no matter what strategy B plays, A prefers to acquiesce; that is, A has a dominant strategy and will always acquiesce in the face of a transgression against B. Knowing this, B will also acquiesce.

This structure of interaction allows the sovereign to transgress some citizens' rights and survive.[4] In the one-shot game, there are three pure strategy equilibria, and the Pareto optimal strategy combination with no transgressions is not among them. Which equilibria occurs depends in part upon the reaction functions of

[4] Throughout we use the concept of subgame perfection as an equilibrium concept, defined as follows: A *strategy* is a specification of the action a player will take at every branch of the game tree. An *equilibrium* is a set of strategy combinations such that no player has an incentive to deviate given the strategies of others. The equilibrium is *subgame perfect* if it remains an equilibrium when restricted to every subgame.

the citizens groups to a transgression. The worst outcome for the citizens – where the sovereign transgresses against both – is an equilibrium. This occurs if citizens acquiesce whenever they are the target of a transgression. Because neither A nor B has an incentive to deviate, this is an equilibrium. Acting alone and taking the behavior of the others as given, one citizen group cannot change the outcome by challenging but it will increase its costs.

The two other equilibria are "asymmetric" and occur when S targets only one citizen group. These equilibria are supported when A and B challenge S if and only if *both* are the targets of a transgression. Suppose S targets B in every period and A and B respond as just suggested. Then S has no incentive to deviate: Transgressing against both leads to being deposed, transgressing against A instead of B is no better, and transgressing against neither leaves him worse off. Furthermore, neither citizen group has an incentive to deviate. For A, this conclusion is obvious. For B, it follows because B can do no better. Given that it alone is the target and that A will not challenge, B's challenging will not change the outcome but will increase its costs. Hence B is better off acquiescing if it alone is the target.

These equilibria can be interpreted in terms of their implied notion of citizen duty, that is, the implicit specifications embedded in a strategy about how a citizen should respond to a transgression. For example, the asymmetric equilibria where S successfully transgresses against B is supported by notions that citizens should respond to the most egregious violations by S, that is, when he targets both groups. The other equilibrium – in which the sovereign successfully transgresses against both – corresponds to the idea of passive obedience to the sovereign, perhaps because the sovereign serves by "divine right." Notice that two other concepts of citizen duty cannot be supported in equilibrium, namely, that a citizen responds whenever he is the target or that a citizen responds whenever *any* citizen is the target. Both fail owing to the dominant strategy feature of the game: When S attempts to transgress against only one citizen group, the other is always better off acquiescing. Taking this into account, the targeted citizen group is better off acquiescing. Thus the outcome of the one-shot game is particularly grim because the rights of all citizens cannot be supported.

The situation is more complicated when this game is repeated, that is, when the interaction between the sovereign and citizens is ongoing. Given the structure of payoffs, the "folk-theorem" applies, implying that virtually any outcome can be sustained as an equilibrium of the repeated game (Fudenberg and Maskin, 1986). In particular, any of the equilibria of the one-shot game is an equilibrium of the repeated game. The existence of multiple equilibria is a problem for prediction, an issue we return to below.

The folk-theorem implies that the Pareto optimal outcome can be sustained. The key to this result, as with the single-shot game, concerns the behavior of each citizen group when the sovereign attempts to transgress against the other.

The difference is that repetition not only provides the opportunity for citizens to punish the sovereign, but to punish one another. The Pareto optimal outcome is supported by both groups challenging the sovereign when the sovereign attempts to transgress against either. The reason why that behavior can be supported under repeat play is that, as in the repeated prisoners' dilemma, the players can use "trigger" strategies to punish one another for failure to cooperate. For example, if A fails to challenge the sovereign when the latter attempts to transgress against B, then B can retaliate by failing in the future to challenge the sovereign whenever the sovereign attempts to transgress against A. Once this behavior by B is triggered, the sovereign can transgress successfully against A.

In the context of an attempt by S to transgress against B, B's use of the trigger strategy confronts A with the following strategy choice. It can acquiesce today, avoiding the cost of 1, and then face losing 3 in all future periods; or it can challenge today, costing 1 today but maintaining 3 in all future periods. Clearly, when A does not discount the future too heavily, it will prefer the latter so that B's trigger strategy induces A to challenge the sovereign when the latter attempts to transgress against B alone.

The notion of citizen duty embedded in this equilibrium is complex. It holds that citizens should react to any transgression, regardless of the target. It further holds that those citizens who fail to fulfill that duty should themselves be punished. An important property of this equilibrium is that it supports a *consensus*: All citizens hold the same views about citizen duty. It thus reflects a Lockean principle of active resistance to the sovereign in the face of transgressions.

Unfortunately, the Pareto optimal outcome is not the only equilibrium. Although it is normatively attractive, this equilibrium will not inevitably occur. The game might instead yield any of the three equilibria of the one-shot game, allowing successful transgressions against some or all citizens. In these equilibria, the sovereign may transgress the rights of some citizens while retaining the support of others. These are stable patterns of behavior, and none of the players, acting alone, can alter them.

The notion of citizen duty embedded in the asymmetric equilibria differs from that in the Pareto optimal equilibrium. It holds that an individual citizen should punish the sovereign for the most egregious actions – transgressions targeted against all citizens – but not for transgressions aimed only at a subset of other citizens. The asymmetric equilibria cannot support the notion of citizen duty in which they punish one another for failing to police transgressions.

Implications

The presence of multiple equilibria inevitably raises the question of "equilibrium selection," that is, which equilibrium will occur. Often game theory affords little insight into this question. In some cases, however, the characteristics of a society can be used to suggest which equilibrium will result (Ferejohn, 1990).

The sovereign-transgression game presents members of a society with a massive coordination problem. In this context, Ferejohn's argument implies that it is unlikely that a society will resolve this coordination problem in a wholly decentralized manner. To see this, consider a society in which there is a diversity of preferences over outcomes. This will result from a variety of factors. First, citizens' economic circumstances differ considerably – some are wealthy elites; others, successful commercial agents or economic entrepreneurs; others, farmers who own their land; still others, peasants who work land they do not own. Second, there are individuals who are likely to be members of different groups that provide their members with a range of "cultural beliefs" (Greif, 1994). These include religious or ethnic groups, labor unions, guilds, and other economic, political and social organizations. Members of these groups come to share a set of experiences and beliefs that differ from members in other groups.

Under these circumstances, citizen views about the appropriate role of the state and about what actions constitute a transgression are likely to differ widely.[5] Because there is no automatic mechanism to produce a consensus on these issues, the most natural equilibrium of the game is the asymmetric one. The diversity of preferences, opinions, cultural beliefs, and values provides an impediment to the development of the Pareto optimal equilibrium. This diversity thus makes it more likely that the game will result in one of the asymmetric equilibria in which the sovereign transgresses the rights of some while retaining the support of others.

The model shows that it is costly for the citizens to police the sovereign. When their views about the nature of the state and of citizen duty diverge, it is possible for the sovereign to form a coalition with one group of citizens against another, allowing the sovereign to transgress boundaries considered fundamental by other citizens. This problem is exacerbated by the political aspects of the problem, namely, that some citizens may benefit from transgressions against others. In the asymmetric equilibria of the model, the sovereign in effect forms a coalition with a group of constituents, transgressing the rights of others for mutual gain.

These results extend in a natural way to more than two groups (although the problems of multiple equilibria are exacerbated). A large number of diverse groups – each with different experiences, interests, and values – exacerbates the impediments to coordination and hence to the ability to police limits on the state. Though the model implies that most societies will face impediments to

---

[5] As North (1993) argues, different circumstances for individuals imply that their "local" experiences will differ, and hence they will develop different "mental models," that is, beliefs about how the world functions and hence about what characteristics ought to characterize the state.

developing the necessary means to coordinate, societies will nonetheless differ in their degree of diversity and hence in their ability to overcome the coordination problems. In some societies, there may be total disagreement whereas in others, relatively limited disagreement. The approach implies that transgressions can be prevented over the range of agreement among citizens. The larger this range, the more extensive and, perhaps, comprehensive are the limits on the state that can be enforced.

The approach thus shows that policing a state or sovereign requires that citizens coordinate their reactions. It is therefore possible for a constitution or a pact to serve as a coordinating device. In the face of multiple coordination equilibria, these devices can serve to coordinate citizens' strategy choices so that they attain a specific equilibrium, for example, the Pareto optimal outcome.[6]

This model provides one approach to the fundamental problem of maintaining limited government, that is, a government that observes an agreed-upon set of citizen rights and boundaries on its behavior. It shows that limited government is not a natural equilibrium and is unlikely to emerge solely by the decentralized action of individuals. The inherent diversity in society prevents the required degree of consensus from emerging. And without a degree of consensus, citizens cannot police limits.

For limited government to survive in practice, citizens need a coordinating device such as a constitution. The model reveals that only limits of a specific kind of constitution can prove binding in practice, namely, those that are *self-enforcing* (Ordeshook, 1992; Przeworski, 1991; Weingast, 1995). Limits are self-enforcing when it is in the interest of the state or sovereign to abide by them. In terms of the model, this occurs when the constitutional provisions are held in sufficiently high esteem that citizens are willing to defend them by withdrawing support from the state when it attempts to violate them. Thus a constitution must have more than philosophical or logical appeal. It must be viewed by citizens as worth defending.

As a final observation, notice that the construction of a consensus does not imply that all citizens need to arrive at the same values or to agree on the most preferred definition of state boundaries. It instead means that citizens must agree on a set of strategies. In particular, they need to agree on the set of state actions that should trigger a reaction by the citizenry. Because they have different preferences about what limits are most appropriate, agreement on a unique best set is virtually impossible. Most citizens must therefore accept something less than their first best. What they gain by such compromises, however, is the ability to police the state. When citizens act in this way, they can all be better off. Social consensus thus has a special meaning in this approach.

---

[6] This point is made generally by Hardin (1989) and Ordeshook (1992) and, in the current context, by Weingast (1995).

3 Democratic stability

I now turn to the question of why some societies are able to maintain stable democracies. A remarkably diverse set of works relate to this question. In this section, we discuss a range of approaches developed in the last forty years, showing how the framework developed above amplifies them and provides a unifying approach.

The role of consensus in democratic stability

The answer given in the first two decades or so of the post-World War II era focused on the role of citizen consensus.[7] Almond and Verba (1963), for example, argued in part that citizens in stable democracies are characterized by a set of widely shared attitudes and views which they call the "civic culture." These attitudes and views focus on the role of government, legitimacy, and the duty of citizens. Citizens in stable democracies possess a relatively common set of understandings about the appropriate boundaries of government and about their duty in the face of violations of these boundaries. In contrast, Almond and Verba characterized unstable and nondemocracies by an absence of a system of shared beliefs about limited government, the sanctity of individual rights, and the duties of citizens to protect and preserve them.[8]

Because of inevitable differences of opinions in any democracy, tolerance and "mutual security" are a necessary requirement for democratic stability. Mutual tolerance also goes hand in hand with support for limited government. The latter reflects the institutional limits on power, protecting minorities and those out of power; the former reflects an aspect of the informal norms supporting and preserving the institutional system.

These results can be interpreted within the framework of our model. The model shows that two interrelated and complementary factors account for democratic stability. The first is a set of political institutions, rights of citizens, etc., that define the boundaries of government action. The second is a shared set of beliefs (Converse, 1964) among the citizenry that those institutions, rights, and boundaries are both appropriate and worth defending.

As the model demonstrates, citizens cannot police political rights if their notions of those rights fundamentally differ. In those circumstances, the state

---

[7] The discussion that follows emphasizes only one aspect of this rich literature.

[8] Dahl (1966, 1971) and Lipset (1960, 1963) also emphasize the importance of citizen consensus supporting democracy, including the role of tolerance of the beliefs and ideologies of others. Referring to the United States, Dahl (1966, p. 34) concludes that the degree of consensus supporting the system has remained sufficiently high that oppositions have nearly always sought power within the system and not undertaken to destroy or subvert it.

can undermine the fundamental pillars of a democratic society – for example, the right of some or all citizens to vote – and still survive. Moreover, as argued above, this diversity underpins the most natural equilibrium of the game. The massive coordination problem implies that without the construction of a coordination device, citizens are unlikely to police boundaries on the state.

Our model thus provides an explanation for the findings reported above. The equilibria of the game correspond closely to the phenomena they studied. For the phenomenon studied by Almond and Verba, Dahl, and Lipset, the model shows why a set of common attitudes and understandings about legitimacy is crucial to the success and maintenance of democracy.[9] They are intimately related. Without these common attitudes and the tolerance it implies, the universalistic standards of democracy and limited government could not be maintained.

And yet, as the model also demonstrates, stable democracy does not simply occur because some countries happen to have the relevant shared set of beliefs and others do not. It is equally plausible, as Barry (1970, ch. III) among others observed, that societies with stable democracies foster a set of common beliefs among the citizenry. Although Barry intended his remarks to undermine Almond and Verba's perspective, our view shows that his insight and critique were correct but that his conclusion was not.

The relationship between citizen views and democratic stability is not a causal one; the former cannot be treated as an independent variable with the latter as the dependent one (Lijphart, 1980). Both are instead properties of an equilibrium. Societies that have not been able to resolve their coordination dilemmas are characterized by a diversity of citizen attitudes and the lack of democratic stability. Those that have resolved such dilemmas have both democratic stability and a relative consensus among the citizenry. The critical step in establishing democratic stability is the resolution of the coordination problem.

The importance of the behavior implied by the various equilibria of the model is illustrated by the contrast between political behavior in a stable democracy like the United States and in the unstable ones of South America. This contrast is especially important because the formal institutions of democracy in South America often reflect a striking similarity to those in the United States, notably, a presidential system with separation of powers. These two cases illustrate the differences in political reaction to potential violations of established institutions and limits on government.

A revealing example from the United States concerns the reaction to Roosevelt's proposal to "pack the court" in the mid-1930s. Throughout the first four years of the Roosevelt administration, the Supreme Court maintained its historic interpretation of the Constitutional restrictions on the federal government.

---

[9] The model also suggests how to integrate some of the more recent and parallel findings of Putnam (1993), which emphasize "social capital."

Relying on this interpretation, it struck down many of the central components of the New Deal. In reaction, Roosevelt devised a plan to yield a more pliant court by expanding it. A series of new and favorable appointments would allow him to construct a pro-New Deal majority on the court.

For several reasons, Roosevelt never pressed the court-packing plan. Among them – and critical for our purposes – was the public reaction to this plan. Not only did his political opponents oppose his plan, so too did many of his supporters. It was viewed by large numbers of citizens, including many of the intended beneficiaries, as an illegitimate political strategy. Because it constituted a direct assault on the constitutional principle of the separation of powers, support for this plan was dubious at best. Put simply, citizen reaction to this proposed violation was an important reason for its abandonment.[10]

This example illustrates one of the central results of the model: Maintaining limits on the state requires that political leaders find it in their interests to abide by them. To support this behavior by leaders, constituents must withdraw their support in the face of extraconstitutional and contraconstitutional proposals, even when they are the intended beneficiaries of such proposals. The United States Constitution proves binding in practice, despite the absence of an exogenous enforcement mechanism, because of the deep respect for it among the citizenry, specifically, because citizens are willing to react to proposed violations. Knowing that reaction, political leaders rarely propose violations. Citizen reaction thus implies that the institutional restrictions are self-enforcing. The nexus of political behavior is thus mutually reinforcing, that is, it is an equilibrium.

In contrast, such behavior is less likely in Latin America. Many Latin American states are characterized by cycles of democracy, coups, dictatorship, and redemocratization. Coups not only remain a potential political phenomenon but also reflect a fundamental difference between democracy in the United States and Latin America. The states of the latter are not characterized by a common set of attitudes about the appropriate role of government. During hard times – for example, poor economic performance due to mismanagement or corruption – a surprisingly large portion of the citizenry are willing to support extra-constitutional means of political change.[11]

The absence of the necessary degree of legitimacy and support among the

---

[10] According to Friedman (1984, p. 188), "the court-packing plan was attacked from all sides as a threat to the independence of the justices and to the whole American system. The plan was hastily abandoned and soon died."

[11] Baloyra (1986), in his study of Venezuela, found that in 1983 over half of the respondents (53 percent) could conceive of situations where military coups are justified. After the recent, failed coup attempt in November 1992, the *New York Times* reported that "forty-four percent of Venezuelans responding to a poll last month said they would support a coup to remove [President] Pérez from office." (James Brooke, Latin Democracy Lives In Rockets' Red Glare, *New York Times*, December 6, 1992, p. E3.)

citizenry for the constitution and constitutional means of political change implies that constitutional constraints are not self-enforcing. Because citizens are not always willing to defend their constitution, political actors need not always adhere to it. Obviously, this nexus of behavior involves a complex series of political and economic phenomena, notably, mistrust in government, endemic corruption, and the lack of belief that the government can bring about and maintain prosperity for the bulk of the citizenry.[12]

This pattern of phenomena – citizens unwilling to defend the constitution, endemic governmental corruption, and the support for coups – is mutually reinforcing because it is an equilibrium. Thus, the beliefs and potential actions of the citizenry in the United States and Latin America fundamentally differ. In the former, citizens punish leaders for proposed violations to the Constitution, whereas, in the latter, citizens support such violations under particular circumstances.

Relationship to Przeworski's approach to self-enforcing democracy

Przeworski's (1991) important book studies a critical problem for democracy: Incumbents lose elections. This fact raises a fundamental question, why would a losing party accept its loss instead of attempting to subvert the democratic process in order to retain power? Przeworski's answer is that for democracy to be sustained it must be self-enforcing, that is, it must be in the interests of the losers to accept their loss.

An incumbent party that has just lost an election has two options: It may either accept its loss or it may attempt to subvert the democratic process in order to remain in power. The incumbent's payoffs associated with these outcomes are L and S, respectively.[13] For there to be a potential compliance problem, it must be that $S > L$.

What will the loser do? If it considers solely its immediate interests, it would clearly attempt to subvert because $S_0 > L_0$ (the subscripts indicate time period, set at 0 for the initial decision). Yet, democratic institutions provide the opportunity for winning tomorrow. If the defeated incumbent complies in this round, its expected payoff from the next round is $C_1 = pW + (1 - p)L$, where p is the probability that it wins the next election. This provides the formula for compliance. Today's losers will comply when the expected gains from accepting

---

[12] In a prescient comment, *The Economist* summarized the recent failed coup attempt by noting that "many Venezuelans distrust their rulers so deeply that, for them, getting rid of [President] Perez would be like killing the leaves of a weed, leaving the roots to thrive and grow again." (*The Economist*, Venezuela: The President's Two Lives, December 5, 1992, p. 46.)

[13] Note the S reflects the expected value of this strategy and hence includes the risk of the punishment following failure.

the loss exceed those from subverting, that is, when the following inequality is satisfied:

$$L_0 + C_1 > S_0 + S_1.^{14} \qquad\qquad (*)$$

Przeworski's (1991) perspective can be used to derive further implications about democratic stability by deriving two comparative statics results about the likelihood of compliance from inequality (*). Both follow from observations about characteristics of successful constitutions. The first holds that "Constitutions that are observed and last for a long time are those that reduce the stakes of political battles" (p. 36). The institutional restrictions of successful constitutions provide credible guarantees of the rights of individuals and limits on governmental decision making. This affects the above calculus by lowering the costs from losing. Or, in terms of the formula for compliance, it raises, L_0, making compliance more likely.

Przeworski's (1991, p. 36) second observation is that

> successful democracies are those in which the institutions make it difficult to fortify a temporary advantage. Unless the increasing returns to power are institutionally mitigated, losers must fight the first time they lose, for waiting makes it less likely that they will ever succeed.

Thus the institutions of successful democracies limit the degree to which those in power can subvert the system to increase their own prospects of winning the next election. In terms of the formula of compliance, this prevents tomorrow's incumbents from substantially lowering p, again making compliance by today's defeated incumbents more likely.

These results closely parallel those developed in the framework above. The first comparative statics result relates to limited government. By reducing the stakes of power – in particular, the costs of losing – a consensus supporting limited government with universalistic democratic standards applied to all makes compliance by elected officials more likely. Second, the approach emphasizes that limited government is policed in part via actions of citizens who punish leaders that propose to subvert the democratic system. This punishment lowers the value of subversion to the incumbents and hence, in terms of inequality (*), lowers both S_0 and S_1.

This discussion also shows that citizen behavior and elite behavior are strongly interrelated, for mass citizen reaction is a critical component of the incentives facing elites. Because preservation of the democratic system requires that elected officials abide by that system, citizen reactions provide a necessary contribution to democratic stability. Diamond (1994, p. 3) provides an excellent summary of this logic:

---

[14] Following Przeworski, this analysis ignores for simplicity the terms beyond period 1.

Elites choose democracy instrumentally because they perceive that the costs of attempting to suppress their political opponents exceed the costs of tolerating them (and engaging them in constitutionally regulated competition)...

Democratic stability in deeply divided societies

Deeply divided societies raise a series of problems for democracy (Horowitz, 1985; Rabushka and Shepsle, 1972). In divided societies, members of different ethnic, linguistic, religious, or racial groups typically have different views about all aspects of government, policy, and the public sector, including the appropriate limits on the state. These divisions represent an impediment to solving the society's coordination problem. Most plural societies therefore reflect the equilibrium in which there is an absence of shared beliefs about the appropriate boundaries of the state.

When the primary basis for political organization reflects ethnic divisions, the type of consensus necessary for democratic stability is difficult to devise and support.[15] As Rabushka and Shepsle emphasize, plural societies typically "lack consensus" and are states in which subnational cultural groups – as opposed to the state – serve as the primary basis of citizen loyalty. They found that "plural societies are qualitatively distinct from homogeneous ones... [and] that plural societies are inherently prone to violent conflict" as opposed to peaceful, democratic resolution of their differences (Rabushka and Shepsle, 1972, p. 12). Plural societies are thus less likely to sustain stable democracies.

Horowitz (1985, p. 8), in his classic treatise, describes divided societies in similar terms:

> ...almost any issue, any phenomenon, can suddenly "turn ethnic" or "turn communal"... Characteristically, issues that elsewhere would be relegated to the category of routine administration assume a central place on the political agenda of ethnically divided societies.

Politics of the openly divided societies is organized along ethnic lines. Mutual accommodation and toleration are difficult to secure, let alone maintain.

The plural societies studied by Horowitz and Rabushka and Shepsle reflect the equilibrium of the sovereign-transgression game in which citizens fail to

---

[15] Recent work emphasizes that linguistic, ethnic, religious, and racial divisions need not be the primary basis for political organization in a society, nor do these divisions represent an individual's primary loyalty (e.g., Bates, 1983; Horowitz, 1985). Indeed, Laitin's (1988, 1992, 1994) recent work emphasizes that these patterns are often endogenous, especially for linguistic groups. The literature on nationalism supports the same conclusion (see, e.g., Anderson, 1991; Gellner, 1983).

coordinate their behavior. Universalistic limits on the government – ones that apply equally to all ethnic groups – are difficult to maintain for several reasons. First, significant differences in values among members of different groups impede the resolution of the coordination problem to arrive at a unique set of fundamental rights and limits on the state. Second, as in the asymmetric equilibrium of the game, one of the groups may actually benefit from this equilibrium because it gains by exploiting the other. Third, even when all groups may seek to end repression, it may be difficult to devise a credible plan or pact, especially when revenge might motivate future action.[16] All these factors contribute to political instability in plural society. Not only do they make democracy difficult to sustain, but the absence of credible limits on the state allows mutual hostility to erupt into violence conflict (Weingast, 1996a).

Constructing trust in plural societies: Nonetheless, not all plural societies are openly divided in the manner described by Horowitz (1985).[17] Several plural societies in the developed West, such as Belgium and Switzerland, have developed stable democracies, and the reason underlying this stability is instructive. In both cases, a set of constitutional provisions has been devised that limits the effect of plural divisions.[18] In terms of the model, these institutional provisions reflect the construction of a solution to the coordination problem so that limits on the state can be sustained in equilibrium. In the presence of credible limits on the state, ethnic groups can trust one another and support mutual tolerance.

The solution to the coordination problem is accomplished through a variety of institutional means, such as the decentralization of political power to more homogeneous units and the imposition of express limits on majorities at the national level.

> Both Belgium and Switzerland have a written constitution: a single document containing the basic rules of governance... [that] can only be changed by special majorities.... [In Belgium] any bill affecting the cultural autonomy of the linguistic groups requires not only the approval of two-thirds majorities in both chambers but also majorities in each linguistic group.... (Lijphart, 1984, pp. 29–30.)

Both institutional devices decrease the likelihood that one ethnic or religious group will use political control to discriminate or subjugate the other.[19] In

---

[16] Pacts are treated in a separate subsection below. More generally, Weingast (1996a) analyzes the problem of establishing credibility of agreements in the face of potential or past violence.

[17] The material in this subsubsection draws on Weingast (1996a).

[18] See, e.g., Lijphart (1984). See also Tsebelis's (1990, ch. 6.) instructive analysis of Belgium.

[19] Horowitz's (1985) discussion of the inception of federalism in Nigeria reveals a similar finding.

contrast, Lijphart (1984, p. 23) emphasizes that in "plural societies, ... majority rule spells majority dictatorship and civil strife rather than democracy."

Lijphart's (1968, p. 23) characterization of the "politics of accommodation" in the Netherlands is particularly revealing. Identifying four political subcultures, he argues that this "fourfold division of Dutch society is manifested in virtually all politically and socially relevant organizations and group affiliations." Dutch politics, in other words, reflect important aspects of a classic plural society.[20]

Despite the plural nature of Dutch society, Dutch democracy and limited government remained relatively stable during this period. The reason, Lijphart emphasizes, was not due to a consensus over fundamental values or appropriate public policy. Instead, the consensus underlying stability involved two factors: first, the rules of the game that provide for significant autonomy among these groups; second, that the system be maintained:

> In the Netherlands, both the degree and extent of political consensus are very limited but *one vitally important element of consensus is present: the desire to preserve the existing system.* Each bloc tries to defend and promote its own interests but only within the confines of the total system and without the threat of secession or civil war. (Lijphart, 1968, p. 78.)

The rules of the game, in turn, include a series of unwritten, informal, and implicit strictures. From our perspective, the most important include: (1) an agreement to disagree; (2) that politics is not like warfare and that no group attempts to dominate or repress another; and (3) that large numbers of politically divisive issues be settled in a manner proportionate to the size of the relevant groups (Lijphart, 1968, ch. 7).[21]

The stability underlying the "politics of accommodation" reflects four factors. First, it emphasizes the importance of a consensus regarding the rules. This consensus holds that the rules must be defended and that appeals to violate them must be opposed, even by the intended beneficiaries of the violation. Second, it shows that despite the potentially divisive nature of this plural society, democratic stability is possible. Third, the proportionality features of the system reflect the lessons of the model. Though arbitrary, proportionality represents a constructed focal point from which deviations are easy to police. Fourth, it emphasizes an important feature of the theory, namely, the interaction of informal

---

[20] Cleavages are not "cross-cutting," but are "mutually reinforcing," and "congruent," "[C]lass and religious cleavages separate self-contained 'inclusive' groups with sharply defined 'political subcultures'..." (Lijphart, 1968, pp. 14–15).

[21] Lijphart also notes the importance of a consensus on the prohibition of any attempt to mobilize mass publics within a given bloc against the system or a policy advocated within the system's rules.

norms on the one hand and formal political institutions and the rules of the game on the other. The latter are important for creating the relevant focal equilibrium, that is, the types of limits on state action that must be defended. The former reflect the component of the equilibrium necessary for its maintenance.

As described by Lijphart, Dutch society remained stable because any attempt to destroy it by a particular group was likely to make that group worse off. Not only was the group unlikely to succeed at dominating the ensuing politics, but the attempt would disrupt, and possibly destroy, the system. Elites did not make such attempts because citizens, aware of the consequences of attempted subversion, would punish leaders who advocated them. Furthermore, the consensus-producing aspects of the system, fostered in part by the proportionality constraints, imply that no group would be cut out of the system. Proportionality further contributed to the democratic stability because, as discussed in the previous subsection, it lowers the stakes of political action. Taken together, these arguments imply that the system's constraints are self-enforcing.[22]

Summary: The model above provides new insights into the difficulties facing most plural societies. Differences among groups imply that most plural societies face fundamental barriers to resolving their coordination problems. Openly divided societies are characterized by the asymmetric equilibrium of the game in which at least one group is discriminated against or subjugated.

Where plural societies have been able to rise above these divisions, they do so by constructing explicit and self-enforcing constraints on the government that protect the various groups. The construction of self-enforcing limits on the state not only supports mutual tolerance and trust among groups but is what distinguishes divided societies in the West from those of Africa or Asia. These constraints go significantly beyond the granting of equal rights to all citizens. They also encompass institutions that allow for diversity of policy and programs rather than a single national policy or program imposed on all. In both modern Belgium and Switzerland, power is decentralized to more homogeneous groups while, at the same time, national majorities are prohibited from imposing uniform policies.[23]

As the model above suggests, credibility is central to these societies. Institutionalized limits on the state become self-enforcing when members of all plural divisions are willing to punish leaders who seek to violate their society's

---

[22] The long-term success this type of institution depends on the stability of the groups involved, a factor in Dutch politics, post-WWII Lebanon, and the accommodation of the North and South in antebellum United States (see Weingast, 1996a).

[23] In the antebellum United States, federalism helped maintain a national government strongly limited in scope. This allowed major variations in economic rights across the states, especially rights with regard to slaves (Weingast, 1996a).

restrictions. This conclusion is consistent with the evidence provided by Horowitz (1985), who carefully distinguishes behavior in the divided societies of the West from the openly conflictual societies he studies. In the West, he reports the following:

> A survey of Switzerland that tapped levels of identity found that, in spite of ethnic differences, about half of all respondents identified themselves as Swiss. . . . Supraethnic identities tend to have a salience in the West that they do not generally have in Asia and Africa. (Horowitz, 1985, pp. 18–19.)

Precisely these behavioral differences are expected under the two different equilibria of the model. In a society characterized by institutionalized mutual toleration and trust, limited government can be sustained. Citizens across the different groups have the appropriate incentives to promote and protect the system. Members of particular groups thus have the luxury to develop supraethnic identities. The system fosters this identification because it not only protects ethnic groups but serves the interests of citizens across groups. In contrast, under the asymmetric equilibrium, the absence of such institutionalized toleration and trust means that group conflict prevents such identification.

The consolidation of democracy

One of the central distinctions in the literature is between the initiation and the consolidation of democracy. The *initiation* of democracy reflects the onset of the procedural aspects of democracy such as regular elections with secret ballots and accountability of elected officials (O'Donnell and Schmitter, 1986, ch. 2). Also included are a set of citizen rights and corresponding limits on state action. Burton et al. (1992, p. 4) define a *consolidated* democracy as "a regime that meets all the procedural criteria of democracy and also in which all politically significant groups accept established political institutions and adhere to democratic rules of the game." Democracy's two characteristics are as follows: First, elites must share a consensus about political institutions and norms of political behavior. Second, there must be "extensive mass participation in elections and other processes that constitute procedural democracy."

The perspective developed above provides considerable insight into the consolidation of democracy. First, the model's requirements for an equilibrium supporting stable democracy are clearly consistent with the two characteristics noted by Burton et al. Second, my perspective adds an additional characteristic for consolidated democracy, notably, the importance of credibility and self-enforcement. That, in turn, requires an additional constraint on mass publics: that citizens be willing to punish elites who seek to deviate from those democratic institutions and procedures, even when they are the intended beneficiaries. It is precisely this additional condition that helps solve the problem of self-enforcement identified by Przeworski (1991), namely, that losers of elections be willing to turn over power.

In contrast, Burton et al. (1992, p. 31) emphasize that

> The dynamics of political conflict in unconsolidated democratic regimes are qualitatively different [from consolidated ones]. Important and powerful elites deny the legitimacy of the existing regime, and they seek to overthrow it. ... [B]ecause they also perceive rival political parties as conditional in their support for democracy and equivocal in their commitment to democratic rules of the game, political competition and conflict are fraught with suspicion and distrust.

This contrast between consolidated and unconsolidated regimes reflects the patterns following from two different types of equilibria noted in the theory. In unconsolidated regimes, there is no acceptance of the legitimacy of the state or its institutions and procedures. Violence and intimidation may be commonplace, and major political parties often advocate the overthrow of the government. There are no guarantees of respect for limits of governmental action. Mutual mistrust is the consequence. Consolidated regimes, in contrast, reflect a consensus at both the elite and mass levels on the rules of the democratic system and attendant limits on governmental power. In these regimes, elected officials respect limits on government, and thus those limits are self-enforcing. Finally, consolidated regimes reflect an established and accepted consensus about the fundamental limits on the state.

Elite pacts

Another important phenomenon emphasized in the recent literature is elite pacts (Burton et al. 1992; Karl, 1986; O'Donnell and Schmitter, 1986, ch. 4). Such pacts represent a particular form of agreement among elites to modify the rules of the political game. In O'Donnell and Schmitter's (1986, p. 37) words, an elite pact is

> ... an explicit, but not always publicly explicated or justified, agreement among a select set of actors which seeks to define (or, better, to redefine) rules governing the exercise of power on the basis of mutual guarantees for the "vital interests" of those entering into it.

Karl (1986, p. 198) articulates the purposes and effects of pacts:

> ...pact-making promulgates regime norms and state structures that channel the possibilities for economic change in an enduring manner. In Venezuela. ... the set of negotiated compromises embodied by pacts establishes political "rules of the game" which also institutionalize the economic boundaries between the public and private sectors, guarantees for private capital, and the parameters of future socioeconomic reform.

The importance of pacts is that they enable, under certain circumstances, a society to move from a poor equilibrium with transgressions and the lack of fundamental limits on the state to a stable equilibrium of limited government that can support a stable democracy.

How is this accomplished? As the model above suggests, it requires the construction of a focal point with regard to the limits of the state. That requires a compromise among elites and their followers in which each is willing to forgo their ideal form of society in exchange for mutual acceptance of a compromise form that can be sustained. As the above quotes suggest, pacts are a form of elite convergence that allows a previously " 'disunified' elite [to] become 'consensually unified' in regard to the basic procedures and norms by which politics will henceforth be played" (Burton et al. 1992, p. xi). In terms of the model, a pact constructs the new consensus. This is stable when the participants to the pact perceive that they are all better off under the pact than under the status quo. As emphasized above, in order for this to be credible, elites and their followers must be willing to punish those who seek to deviate from these constraints. The importance of the concept of self-enforcement provides an additional set of constraints not always investigated in the literature.

Moreover, the interpretation of pacts as constructing a new, focal equilibrium for the society suggests two predictions. First, pacts cannot be imposed at just any time. In the context of the asymmetric equilibrium, universalistic limits on the state cannot be sustained, for example, because one of the two groups is better off under this equilibrium than under one where limits on the state are explicated and maintained. This suggests that something outside the model must play a role in dislodging the asymmetric equilibrium and hence in allowing a large portion of the elites to participate in a pact. Thus an economic crisis may imply that the old equilibrium cannot be sustained, allowing negotiation of a new agreement that makes all parties to the agreement better off. Consistent with this prediction, Burton et al. (1992, p. 14) suggest that crises and continual conflict often create a situation in which "all factions suffered heavy losses." In terms of the model, it is precisely these situations which bring about the conditions for the construction of a new focal point, the coordination of the disparate political elements in the society, and the implementations of the Pareto optimal equilibrium sustaining limited government and democracy.[24]

---

[24] Nothing in this approach requires that pacts move a society to the Pareto optimal equilibrium, that is, that they necessarily institute a consolidated democracy. For example, as Karl (1990) observes, pacts need not include all major elements of the society and may thus come at the expense of excluded groups.

The second prediction concerns the success of pacts and hence the survival of democratic institutions inaugurated by them. The argument that successful pacts must be self-enforcing implies that, for an appropriately constructed sample of pacts, we should find the following relationship: Those pacts that provide the basis for their own enforcement should be more likely to succeed than those that do not.

Integrating the literature

An important theme throughout this section is that, to be sustained, democracy requires self-enforcing limits. Central to maintaining democracy is that it be in the interests of elected officials to abide by the limits on the state. The emphasis of this section is that students of democracy have given too little attention to the issue of how democracy's limits are enforced. Studies of pacts, for example, should routinely investigate whether a pact creates self-enforcing incentives to maintain the agreement. The same holds for discussions of the consolidation of democracy.

The approach also emphasizes that democratic stability requires the interaction of formal institutions – both representing limits on government action and behavior and specifying a process for policy choice and evolution – and informal attitudes of citizens. Put somewhat differently, these distinctions require that we understand both elite and citizen behavior.

This interaction yields an important insight into how to fit together the disparate approaches in the literature. Students of democracy in the 1960s focused on mass behavior, studying citizen attitudes and the degree and depth of consensus. The more recent literature tends to concentrate on elite behavior, with attention given to pacts, the behavior of elected officials, and political institutions such as voting mechanisms. As Diamond (1994) observes, it is often difficult to see how early and recent contributions to the literature relate to one another.

The approach developed in this paper provides a way to integrate the literature's two components. Both mass behavior and elite behavior are essential to democratic stability. To the extent that focal solutions to the coordination problem occur, it is elites who construct them. And given state institutions, elites make policy choices and choose whether to abide by limits on the state. Elite choices are not independent of mass behavior because the latter provides the incentives that elites face. It is typically too costly for elites to ignore a strong consensus among citizens that the current system should be upheld and defended. When no such consensus exists, elites have fewer incentives to uphold the system and may find it worthwhile to subvert it, especially under conditions of social and economic stress.

4   The Missouri Compromise of 1820 as an elite pact

The Missouri Compromise of 1820 is arguably the most important American constitutional event between 1800 and the Civil War.[25] Although not officially part of the United States Constitution, the compromise was essential to the Constitution's success in the antebellum era. It prevented the breakup of the nation and provided the political basis for sectional harmony for another generation, for the three decades following the agreement. Elite pacts have not typically been associated with the Anglo-American democracies. Nonetheless, elite pacts represent critical steps in consolidation of democracy in both Great Britain and the United States.[26]

The Missouri Compromise illustrates several aspects of the theory: the interaction of informal attitude and norms with formal political institutions, the importance of a consensus about the political institutions, and the central role of constructing a coordinating device for resolving problems concerning the maintenance of political rights and other limits on the state.

Background to the crisis

Although the Federalist party dominated national electoral politics in the late 18th century under the new Constitution, the election of 1800 brought Jefferson and his new party to power. With the new party came new policies and new beliefs about the relationship of the government to society. Hamilton's vision of the national government as an agent of commercial development gave way to Jefferson's vision of agrarian expansionism. Federalists, largely in the commercial Northeast, found their influence waning as many of the Jeffersonian policies deeply hurt their interests. The War of 1812, for example, cut off a major source of their livelihood, the profitable trade with Great Britain. Late in the war, radical Federalist elements met at Hartfold to consider the possibility of secession.

For much of the sixteen years prior to the first statehood bill to admit Missouri in 1819, Northerners enjoyed a one-state advantage over the South. The admission of Alabama as a state and the bill to admit Missouri without any balancing free state raised fears among many Northerners that they would become a permanent minority in the nation. These fears were sufficiently widespread that enough Northerners defected from their coalition with the South and joined disgruntled interests in the Northeast in opposing the admission of Missouri.

The results were two amendments to the Missouri statehood bill in the House of Representatives, where Northerners had a majority owing to their larger

---

[25] This section draws on Weingast (1996c).

[26] The Magna Carta is perhaps the most famous English pact. The Glorious Revolution of 1689 is another (Weingast, 1996b). U.S. history reflects a series of pacts, beginning with the Articles of Confederation and the United States Constitution.

population. The first amendment sought to emancipate slaves living in Missouri; the second, to prohibit the importation of new slaves into the state. Both amendments passed the House on sectional lines, and both failed to pass the Senate. A crisis ensued when neither side would back down from its position.

The central feature of the crisis is that interests in both the North and South felt deeply threatened by a nation dominated by the other section. The sudden defection of their coalition partners combined with the tenacious use of antislavery measures deeply threatened long-term Southern interests. Northerners also felt threatened by a nation dominated by slaveholders. The crisis emphasized the reciprocal nature of sectional vulnerability.

The pact

Political elites resolved the crisis through a pact, known as the Missouri Compromise. The pact accomplished three things. First, it settled the immediate dispute over Missouri statehood by bringing it in as a slave state without the repugnant Northern amendments and by simultaneously admitting Maine as a free state to balance Missouri. Second, it divided the remaining territory of the United States among the two sections so that the slaveholding nature of any state admitted from that region would be clear in advance. Third and most important from our perspective, the Missouri Compromise made explicit the "balance rule," the notion that states would thereafter be admitted in pairs (Weingast, 1996c).

The first component of the pact maintained the then-fragile balance between the sections. The most immediate implication of balance was that each region gained a veto over national policymaking through its equal representation in the Senate. Each section would thus be able to veto any onerous sectionally motivated initiative. The second and third components of the pact ensured that the nation would exhibit balanced growth, that each section's veto over national policy would be maintained for the foreseeable future. In fact, balance was maintained for the next thirty years.

The Missouri Compromise as a self-enforcing agreement

This discussion suggests that the Constitution alone was an insufficient foundation for American political stability. Dominance by one section threatened the other and hence the survival of American democracy.

The solution to this problem rested on two factors. The first was the reciprocal nature of the problem: both sections feared the other, and neither was sufficiently powerful to expect clear dominance.

The second factor concerned the values and preferences held by most American citizens. During this era, most people wanted local political freedom and believed in the market and private property rights (Hartz, 1955; Wood, 1995). Nearly all wanted strong limits on the remote national government in Washington. And yet these limits were not self-enforcing. The fact that most Americans preferred these limits did not imply they were self-implementing (Weingast, 1996c). As the events leading up to the Missouri crisis suggest, citizens disagreed about a host of specific policy issues for which majorities of one section were willing to pursue their own interests to the detriment of the other. Citizen values and preferences alone were insufficient to maintain a limited national government.

To maintain a national government strictly limited in scope, institutions beyond the Constitution had to be constructed that prevented deep incursions into local interests. For the generation following 1820, the balance rule served the needed goal. Balance gave both sections the ability to veto onerous policies. Hence the balance rule provided the basis for a set of long-term durable political coalitions, which emerged during the Jackson presidency, 1828–1836.

All three theoretical elements of the theory were necessary for the success in limiting the national government: citizen consensus on limiting the national government, the interaction of informal values and preferences with formal institutions, and the explicit construction of a set of institutions and new shared beliefs – in this case, balance – that provided for long-term viability of the desired outcome. In terms of the above theory, balance served as a focal solution to the long-term problems of sectional tension that on numerous occasions threatened to disrupt the nation. But balance alone would not have worked had not most citizens, Northern and Southern, valued the ends it provided: limited national government and sectional harmony.

5   Conclusions

This paper, along with Weingast (1996b), develops a unified approach to the political foundations of limited government, democracy, and the rule of law. The unifying theme underlying these problems is the role of widely accepted limits on the state and political officials. The approach rests on the following logic. First, the views, attitudes, and beliefs of citizens about the appropriate limits on the state are critical for understanding the ability to maintain these limits. Second, the model hinges on the observation that the maintenance of boundaries on the state is a massive social coordination problem. Citizens can police the state only if they react to violations of fundamental limits by withdrawing their support from the sovereign or political officials. Unfortunately, natural diversity of interests and experiences implies that individuals are unlikely to have similar views about the role of the state, the appropriate limits on state action, and the rights of citizens. Thus the most natural consequence is coordination failure: Citizens are unlikely to achieve coordination without some form of organization, leadership, or other method of constructing a focal solution to their problem.

The coordination problem has two implications for the maintenance of limits on the state. First, when citizens agree about the appropriate limits on state action, the threat of citizen withdrawal of support puts observation of those limits in the best interests of political actors. Thus citizen agreement implies that limits on the state are self-enforcing. In contrast, when citizens disagree about the appropriate limits on state action, the state can violate what some consider their fundamental rights yet still retain from others the support needed to survive.

The problem of coordination is also exacerbated by politics. Because the positions and interests of citizens differ considerably, violations of the rights of one group often benefit another. For example, the expropriation of wealth can easily focus on specific economic groups or sectors – large landowners, workers, or merchants in international trade. These distributional issues make coordination more difficult as some citizens may form a coalition with the state that benefits them and allows transgressions against others. The absence of a consensus on the boundaries of the state implies that such a coalition is stable once it is formed. Thus the most natural equilibrium of the game is that citizens cannot police limits on the state. This pattern is stable and enduring.

The second implication concerns the resolution of the coordination failure. In the face of the stable equilibrium lacking coordination, establishing limits on the state requires *constructing* a coordination device. An important instance of such a device is the writing of a widely accepted constitution that specifies clear and unambiguous limits on the state. Elite pacts are another instance. And yet, such a device cannot be established at just any time. A state without limits typically transgresses the rights of some citizens while benefiting – and retaining the support of – others. This pattern is stable because the state and its constituents benefit from this circumstance, though those citizens being harmed do not.

Because this pattern is an equilibrium, breaking it is difficult. Doing so requires something exogenous that significantly alters the underlying structure or payoffs of the game. Perhaps the most common example is that some form of crisis occurs in which the status quo cannot be maintained. This forces the state and its citizens to arrive at a new bargain. In some instances this will result in a new asymmetric equilibrium; in others, the resolution of the coordination problem.[27] Another type of exogenous shift that may alter the

---

[27] Scholars have long noted cases of dramatic institutional change following crises. Schumpeter (1918), for example, emphasized the role of financial crises in the evolution of representative systems (see also North, 1981, ch. 11). The fall of communism provides another obvious example.

game concerns changes in the payoffs. If, for example, economic changes imply that the potential gains from establishing rights for the victims increase, a new bargain may exist that allows the other players to cease their transgressions without a significant fall in their own welfare.

This view also emphasizes the complementarity between formal institutions such as constitutions and informal social norms such as consensus among citizens about the appropriate limits on government.[28] In order for the formal institutions of limited government to survive, they must be held in sufficiently high esteem that most citizens are willing to defend them. A central feature of this complementarity concerns those citizens who stand to benefit from potential violations of the limits on government. Maintaining those limits requires that potential beneficiaries do not support such a proposal. Only in this way is the government deterred from making such proposals. When, in contrast, citizens support such proposals, the government can violate the limits on government while retaining sufficient support to survive. In states characterized by limited government, citizens react against violations (as the failure of Roosevelt's court-packing scheme illustrates), whereas in states not characterized by limited government, citizens may support a wide range of violations (as illustrated by a range of constitutional violations and coups in South America).

This paper has focused on the informal mechanisms supporting a constitution, abstracting from the latter's specific features. The claim of the complementarity between formal institutions and informal behavior thus remains nebulous. The focus of this essay is not to suggest that the informal mechanisms are more important, but, instead, to emphasize the importance of informal mechanisms for supporting formal institutions. An illustration may therefore provide sufficient concrete detail to suggest that the two are on equal footing.

The Missouri Compromise illustrated the theory. By creating a balance between the North and South, affording each a veto over national policymaking in the Senate, this agreement helped maintain limits on the national government and thus protected each section from dangerous intrusions by the other. The compromise helped avoid a sectional crisis that could have destroyed the nation. By providing a set of institutions to protect each section's interests, the compromise helped make democracy self-enforcing.

This example illustrates the critical consequences of formal institutions. Yet these institutions could not have survived without the support of the informal mechanisms studied above. The illustrations also reveal a general conclusion

---

[28] This point is made in a variety of contexts. See for example, North (1990, 1993) on economic history and development, Clague (1992) on development, Ellickson (1991) on the law, Ferejohn (1990) on elections in early modern England, Greif (1994) on medieval contracts, Tirole (1994) on corruption, and Weingast (1995) on several settings (18th century England, 19th century United States, and modern China).

about the complementarity of formal institutions and informal mechanisms: The informal mechanisms – the potential reactions of citizens – make the formal restrictions self-enforcing on political actors.

The view developed in this paper has significant implications for a series of problems concerning democracy, the rule of law, and the maintenance of limited government. These are considered in turn.

Stable democracy

The maintenance and consolidation of democracy depends on more than just the formal institutions of democracy such as elections, representation, and legislatures. It also depends upon the appropriate set of citizen attitudes about those institutions. Not only must citizens value the outcomes of democratic decision making, but they must value the institutions themselves. Citizens must be willing to defend those institutions against potential violations by withdrawing their support from a regime that proposes to violate them.

It is this behavior – this citizen duty – that differentiates stable democratic states from unstable ones. It is one thing to impose the formal democratic apparatus on a society and another to develop the appropriate set of citizen attitudes necessary to maintain those institutions. The absence of the appropriate set of citizen attitudes underlies the instability of large numbers of democracies. The most natural equilibrium is the failure of citizens to come to agreement about the appropriate limits on state action.

Perhaps the most important pragmatic implication of this approach is that providing a set of democratic institutions alone is insufficient to ensure democratic stability. The latter requires that a balance be struck among three components: political institutions, of which democracy is a part; citizen attitudes; and public policy. Too many advocates of democracy ignore the fact that it must be lodged in a setting that allows it to survive.

The importance of this point is most easily seen in the context of former Communist regimes that are simultaneously facing problems of transition to democracy and markets. The problem is twofold: proponents of democracy nearly always ignore how political institutions affect economic outcomes (Przeworski, 1991), and proponents of markets ignore the problem of embedding their economic recommendations within a larger political context that can sustain them. Transitions to democracy and to markets are not separable problems that can take place independently; they are dual problems that must be resolved simultaneously.

A final implication of my approach on the question of democratic stability is that it suggests a way to integrate older and newer components of the literature, the former focusing on the behavior and role of citizens and the latter on elites. Both are necessary components of the explanation of democratic stability. It is elites who choose to observe or violate the strictures of democracy; it is also elites who participate in the creation of a new pact. And yet citizens provide an important component of the elite incentive system. To the extent that a consensus exists among citizens that the system ought to be preserved – and that they are willing to punish leaders who propose violations – leaders face substantially higher costs for an attempt to subvert the system. Because citizen reactions constitute an important component of the incentives facing leaders, citizen attitudes and behavior are critical to making the limits of democracy self-enforcing and hence to the success of democratic stability.

Establishing the rule of law

One of the central features of limited government is the *rule of law*, that is, a stable society of laws, the opposite of discretionary political power.[29] An important consequence of the rule of law is the establishment of reliance, that laws have value to citizens because they are predictable. Reliance founded on the rule of law is critical for economic success in large part because of the *fundamental political dilemma of an economic system*: A state strong enough to establish property rights and enforce contracts is also strong enough to confiscate the wealth of all its citizens. The rule of law is a minimal requirement for a state that seeks to avoid the latter.

Scholars typically provide stark contrasts between societies characterized by the rule of law and those characterized by the exercise of political discretion. Dicey, in his classic text on constitutionalism, raised Tocqueville's comparison of the United States and Switzerland in 1848:

> In the United States and in England there seems to be more liberty in the customs than in the laws of the people. In Switzerland there seems to be more liberty in the laws than in the customs ... the Swiss do not show at bottom that respect of justice, that love of law, that dislike of using force without which no free nation can exist, which strikes strangers so forcibly in England. (Dicey, 1914, pp. 108–09)

---

[29] Dicey, Hayek, and Leoni provide three classic statements of rule of law. According to Dicey (1914, pp. 110–15), the rule of law has three characteristics. First, no "individual is punishable or can be lawfully made to suffer in body or goods except for a distinct breach of law established in the ordinary legal manner before the ordinary Courts of the land." Second, no individual is above the law. Third, there must be a guardian and defender of the law and individual rights, typically the courts. Hayek (1960, pp. 170–71) draws on Locke's *Second Treatise on Civil Government* to suggest that: "'Freedom of men under government is to have a standing rule to live by, common to every one of that society, and made by the legislative power erected in it ... and not to be subject to the inconstant, uncertain, arbitrary will of another man.' It is against the 'irregular and uncertain exercise of the power' that the argument is mainly directed ..." Leoni (1961, p. 75) states that it is "'the certainty of the law'... that one requires in order to foresee that the result of legal actions taken today will be free from legal interference tomorrow."

Scholars studying Great Britain constantly emphasize the importance and effect of these attitudes. Rose (1965, pp. 93–94), for example, states "So strongly have libertarian attitudes been internalized by Englishmen that there has not been the need to protect them with the elaborate legal guarantees provided in the United States." The insights of the American Supreme Court Justice, Joseph Bradley, reflect the central insights of the view taken here:

> The privilege and immunities of Englishmen were established and secured by long usage and by various acts of Parliament. But it may be said that the Parliament of England has unlimited authority, and might repeal the laws which have from time to time been enacted. Theoretically this is so, but practically it is not. England has no written constitution, it is true; but it has an unwritten one, resting in the acknowledged, and frequently declared, privileges of Parliament and the people, *to violate which in any material respect would produce a revolution in an hour.*[30]

As our model suggests, it is not merely the laws that provide for a limited government and the rule of law; a societal consensus about the appropriateness of those laws and limits must exist as well.

For the questions studied in this paper, a society characterized by the rule of law is one where the boundaries of the state are respected. Like culture, the rule of law is a societal characteristic. And yet, whether a society is characterized by the rule of law depends upon the attitude and behavior of individuals.

The foregoing discussion shows the importance of tailoring a legal regime to the specific needs and attitudes of citizens. In particular, a legal system designed in the West for implementation in a transition economy is unlikely to be successful unless it is embedded in the larger transition effort in a way that can sustain it. Like the problem of market reform generally, a legal system is of little use if it cannot be sustained.

An important component of the rule of law is the *civil society*, one that allows freedom of association without the need for official sanction of the state. It is clear that freedom of association is necessary for the rule of law. The right to form associations and organizations is central to the ability of citizens to not only enjoy life but to further their own interests and to police the actions of the states. As Schmitter (1986, p. 6) observes in the context of the transition to democracy,

> for an effective and enduring challenge to authoritarian rule to be mounted and for political democracy to become and remain an alternative mode of political domination, a country must possess a civil society in which certain community and group identities exist independently of the state and in which certain types of self-constituted units are capable of acting autonomously in

---

[30] Bradley's dissent in the *Slaughter House Cases*, 1873 (emphasis added).

defense of their own interests and ideals . . . these identities and interests . . . must be organized for coherent collective action.

Our model provides an approach to the microfoundations of the rule of law. Because laws and political limits can be disobeyed or ignored, something beyond them is necessary to police deviations. Our approach argues that the attitudes and reactions of citizens make institutional restriction self-enforcing on political actors.

By way of summary, this essay has provided a unified approach to the problems of limited government, stable democracy, and the rule of law. It emphasizes the complementarity of the formal institutions of society and informal social mechanisms: Maintaining formal institutions – including the rights of citizens and other limits on government – requires a societal consensus about the importance of defending them against potential violations. The approach reveals how the informal mechanisms of citizen reaction can provide for the self-enforcement of limits on government. Because these reactions affect the incentives of political actors, they determine whether the restrictions on government are binding.

References

Almond, G. A., and S. Verba. 1963. *The Civic Culture: Political Attitudes and Democracy in Five Nations.* Sage Publications, Newbury Park, Calif.

Ames, B. 1987. *Political Survival.* University of California Press, Berkeley, Calif.

Anderson, B. 1991. *Imagined Communities: Reflections on the Origins and Spread of Nationalism*, rev. ed., Verso, London.

Baloyra, E. A. 1986. Public opinion and support for the regime: 1973–83, in *Venezuela: The Democratic Experience*, rev. ed., J. D. Martz and D. J. Myers, eds., Praeger, New York.

Barry, B. 1970. *Economists, Sociologists, and Democracy.* Collier–Macmillan, London.

Bates, R. H. 1983. Modernization, ethnic competition, and the rationality of politics in contemporary Africa, in *State Versus Ethnic Claims: African Policy Dilemmas*, D. Rothchild and V. A. Olorunsola, eds., Westview Press, Boulder, Colo.

Burton, M., R. Gunther, and J. Higley. 1992. Introduction: Elite transformations and democratic regimes, in *Elites and Democratic Consolidation in Latin America and Southern Europe.* J. Higley and R. Gunther, eds., Cambridge University Press, Cambridge and New York.

Clague, C. 1992. Rule Obedience, Organizational Loyalty and Economic Development, *Working Paper No. 36*, IRIS Center, University of Maryland.

Converse, P. 1964. The nature of belief systems in mass publics, in *Ideology and Discontent*, D. Apter, ed., The Free Press of Glencoe, New York.

Dahl, R. 1966. *Political Oppositions.* Yale University Press, New Haven, Conn.

  1971. *Polyarchy: Participation and Opposition.* Yale University Press, New Haven, Conn.

Diamond, L. 1994. Introduction: Political culture and democracy, in *Political Culture and Democracy in Developing Countries*, L. Diamond, ed., Lynne Rienner Publishers, Boulder, Colo.

Dicey, A. V. 1914. *The Law of the Constitution* (8th ed., Liberty Classics, Indianapolis, Ind., 1982).

Ellickson, R. C. 1991. *Order Without Law: How Neighbors Settle Disputes*, Harvard University Press, Cambridge.

Ferejohn, J. 1990. Rationality and interpretation: Parliamentary elections in early Stuart England. Hoover Institution, Stanford University, Stanford, Calif.

Friedman, L. 1984. *American Law*. W. W. Norton, New York.

Fudenberg, D., and E. Maskin. 1986. Folk theorems in repeated games with discounting and incomplete information. *Econometrica*, **54**, 553–54.

Gellner, E. 1983. *Nations and Nationalism*, Cornell University Press, Ithaca, New York.

Greif, A. 1994. Cultural beliefs and the organization of society: A historical and theoretical reflection on collectivist and individualist societies. *Journal of Political Economy*, **102**, 912–45.

Hand, L. 1952. *The Spirit of Liberty*, Knopf, New York.

Hardin, R. 1989. Why a constitution? in *The Federalist Papers and the New Institutionalism*, B. Grofmand and D. Wittman, eds., Agathon Press, New York.

Hartz, L. 1955. *The Liberal Tradition in American: An Interpretation of American Political Thought Since the Revolution*, Harcourt, Brace, and Jovanovich, New York.

Hayek, F. 1960. *Constitution of Liberty*, University of Chicago Press, Chicago, Ill.

Horowitz, D. 1985. *Ethnic Groups in Conflict*. University of California Press, Berkeley, Calif.

Karl, T. L. 1986. Petroleum and political pacts: The transition to democracy in Venezuela, in *Transitions from Authoritarian Rule: Latin America*. G. O'Donnell, P. C. Schmitter, and L. Whitehead, eds., Johns Hopkins University Press, Baltimore, Md.

1990. Dilemmas of democratization in Latin America, *Comparative Politics*, **23**, 1–21.

Laitin, D. 1988. Language games, *Comparative Politics*, **20**, 289–302.

1992. *Language Repertoires and State Construction in Africa*, Cambridge University Press, New York.

1994. The tower of Babel as a coordination game: Political linguistics in Ghana, *American Political Science Review*, **88**, 622–34.

Leoni, B. 1961. *Freedom and the Law* (expanded 3d ed., Liberty Press, Indianapolis, Ind., 1991).

Lijphart, A. 1968. *The Politics of Accommodation*. University of California Press, Berkeley, Calif.

1980. The structure of inference, in *The Civil Culture Revisited*, G. A. Almond and S. Verba, eds., Little–Brown, Boston, Mass.

1984, *Democracies: Patterns of Majoritarian and Consensus Government in Twenty-One Countries*, Yale University Press, New Haven, Conn.

Lipset, S. M. 1960. *Political Man*. Anchor Books, Garden City, NY.

1963. *The First New Nation: The United States in Historical and Comparative Perspective*, Basic Books, New York.

North, D. C. 1981. *Structure and Change in Economic History*, Norton, New York.

1990. *Institutions, Institutional Change, and Economic Performance*, Cambridge University Press, New York.

1993. Institutions and credible commitment, *Journal of Institutional and Theoretical Economics*, **149**(1): 11–23.

O'Donnell, G., and P. C. Schmitter. 1986. *Transitions from Authoritarian Rule: Tentative Conclusions about Uncertain Democracies*. Johns Hopkins University Press, Baltimore, Md.

Ordeshook, P. 1992. Constitutional stability, *Constitutional Political Economy*, **13**, 137–75.

Przeworski, A. 1991. *Democracy and the Market*. Cambridge University Press, Cambridge and New York.

Putnam, R. 1993. *Making Democracy Work*. Princeton University Press, Princeton, N.J.

Rabushka, A., and K. A. Shepsle. 1972. *Politics in Plural Societies*. Charles E. Merrill, Columbus, Ohio.

Rose, R. 1965. England: A traditionally modern political culture, in *Political Culture and Political Development*, Lucian W. Pye and S. Verba, eds., Princeton University Press, Princeton, N.J.

Rustow, Dankwart A. 1970. Transition to Democracy, *Comparative Politics*: 337–363.

Schmitter, P. C. 1986. An introduction to southern European transitions, in *Transitions from Authoritarian Rule: Prospects for Democracy*, G. O'Donnell, P. C. Schmitter, L. Whitehead, eds., Johns Hopkins University Press, Baltimore, Md.

Schumpeter, J. A. 1918. The Crisis of the Tax State. Reprinted in *Joseph A. Schumpeter*, Richard Swedberg, ed., Princeton University Press, Princeton, N.J. 1991.

Tirole, J. 1994. The internal organization of government. *Oxford Economic Papers*, **46**, 1–29.

Tsebelis, G. 1990. *Nested Games: Rational Choice in Comparative Politics*, University of California Press, Berkeley, Calif.

Weingast, B. R. 1995. The economic role of political institutions: Federalism, markets, and economic development. *Journal of Law, Economics, and Organization*, **11**, 1–31.

    1996a. Constructing trust: The political and economic roots of ethnic and regional violence, in *Where is the New Institutionalism Now?* V. Haufler, K. Soltan, and E. Uslaner, eds., University of Michigan Press, Ann Arbor, Mich, (in press).

    1996b. The political foundations of democracy and the rule of law, *American Political Science Review* (in press).

    1996c. Institutions and Political Commitment: A New Political Economy of the American Civil War Era. Hoover Institution, Stanford University, Stanford, Calif.

Wood, E. J. 1995. Agrarian Social Relations and Democratization: The Negotiated Resolution of the Civil War in El Salvador, Ph.D. dissertation, Stanford University, Stanford, Calif.

CHAPTER 2

Democracy, competition, and the principle of *Isonomia*: An economic analysis of the political exchange as an incomplete contract

Michele Grillo

1 Introduction

This essay takes an economist's perspective with respect to a long-debated question of political theory, namely, the conflict between democracy and constitutionalism. I intend to show that an economic analysis of the forces that govern competition and contracts in the political arena can shed some light on the tension between the view that constraints on the governing ability of the majority are inconsistent with the very principle of democracy and the opposite view that rule of law and constitutional boundaries are instead necessary conditions for democracy.[1]

By extending some results of the economic theory of incomplete contracts to the analysis of political exchange, I will develop a simple argument in support of the view that the constitutional principle of *isonomia* – that is, the separation of legislature and government, which leads to democratically elected governments being subject to "equal laws" – is a necessary condition for the optimal working of representative democracy.

The essay is organized as follows. Section 1 discusses whether the standard economist's approach to "democracy as competition" justifies the view that democracy can be interpreted per se as an optimal procedure of selection of political leaders. The main argument will be that the democratic procedure may fail in this respect, possibly giving rise to adverse selection, if the conditions of enforcement of the (incomplete) contract that supports the political exchange are not carefully specified. Then, Section 2 reviews some of the main results of the recent economic theory of contracts, especially those concerning the enforcement mechanisms of incomplete contracts. Section 3 focuses on the

---

I am indebted to George Tridimas for comments and to Andrea Boitani, Giacomo Costa, Michele Polo, and Lorenzo Sacconi for helpful discussions.
[1] For a recent assessment of this debate, see the volume edited by Elster and Slagstad (1988).

incomplete contract that supports the political exchange. By extending some results obtained by Aghion and Tirole (1997) on the optimal allocation of formal and real authority in organizations, I will argue that the constitutional principle of *isonomia* achieves the important result of maximizing congruence between the objectives of the citizens and those of the elected leader, which in turn leads to the optimal solution of the principal-agent problem involved in the political exchange. The constitutional agreement on the principle of *isonomia* satisfies the property of being both efficient and self-enforcing.

2   Democracy as competition

The economist's approach to democracy usually stems from what can be labeled the "Schumpeterian perspective." According to this perspective, democracy is defined as "an institutional arrangement for arriving at political decisions in which individuals endeavor to acquire political office through a competitive struggle for the votes of a broadly based electorate."[2]

The Schumpeterian perspective focuses on "vertical democracy," that is, democracy as a system of (selecting a) government. The essence of democracy resides in competitive electoral contests for the election of leaders who, for a period following an election, have the responsibility of government. Although Schumpeter's (1976) views in *Capitalism, Socialism and Democracy* were mainly suggested by him as a positive description of the working of democracy in contemporary democratic societies, economists' present-day acceptance of his perspective can hardly be disconnected from the "value" that can be attributed to such a procedure of selection, that is, from whether it is possible to extend to political competition the widespread assessment of economic competition as an impersonal social mechanism able to induce the "optimal" division of labor in society.[3]

Once the social relation between voters and representatives is understood as an act of (political) exchange, then, as is true of any act of exchange in the market for goods and services, it is natural to see it as reflecting the underlying arrangement of social division of labor. Accordingly, in a normative perspective, the "economic theory of democracy" becomes an inquiry into whether the Schumpeterian description of "democracy as competition" justifies democracy

---

[2] From Becker (1958), p. 106.

[3] I do not intend to say that Schumpeter himself was inattentive to the efficient properties of the results that can be expected when the political leaders are selected by democratic procedures. Schumpeter's views on these issues are plausibly descended from Max Weber's, whose disenchanted support to parliamentary democracy could, according to Raymond Aron (1967, p. 247), be explained as arising more from seeing it "as a way of improving the recruitment of leaders rather than as a matter of principle." However it is only with modern public choice that the *presumption* of competition was turned into an *analysis* of the efficient results of democracy.

as a mechanism capable of giving rise to the optimal division of labor in the political arena. In other words, we ask whether a theoretical presumption can be given to the conclusion that the leader selected through a competitive electoral contest will be the agent in society capable of providing the most desirable solution – from the society's standpoint – to the collective choice problems that he has been appointed to solve, that is, the person whose electoral platform has resisted a competitive struggle for being very sensitive to the values of the electorate and capable of running the political sector efficiently.

If reasons can be found to be confident that, at least under ideal conditions, democracy as competition produces optimal results in the political arena, then it becomes difficult to resist the conclusion that the presence of constitutional constraints on the governing ability of the majority ought to be viewed as unjustified, inconsistent with the very reasons of democracy, and ultimately even harmful.

It might be objected that, even if one concedes that "ideal" democracy parallels "ideal" competition,[4] outside the ideal world things are not so simple and clear-cut. A political exchange always shows two crucial features: (i) it has an intertemporal dimension; (ii) it is a typical instance of a social relation supported by an "incomplete" contract. Even if one accepts that competition is an adequate procedure for selecting the optimal electoral platform, what voters vote for is only a "promise", moreover stated in vague terms: the selected platform will be implemented only _after_ the elections, and its implementation will deal with contingencies that are not, and normally cannot be, precisely specified during the electoral campaign.

Modern economic literature (as well as classical political literature) is full of opportunism and cheating that may plague intertemporal exchanges. Putting the problem of contractual incompleteness aside for a moment, reputation mechanisms, arising from long-term relationships, have been easily called upon to solve intertemporal opportunism and have been extended from economic markets to political markets: In its simplest terms, the argument says that the opportunist party that cheats – when actually implementing its electoral program – will be punished by not being reelected in the next _competitive_ electoral contest. Thus the first distinguishing feature of democracy is its artificial structuring of the political game as a repeated game: Electoral contests take place at fixed intervals.

Per se, the reputational effects reinforce the conclusion that competition can be seen as the ultimate mechanism to produce 'optimal' results. Thus, provided that the harshness arising from the intertemporal nature of the political exchange is smoothed away by long-term reputational effects in a competitive environment, it would seem again that no theoretical justification can be found for the presence of constraints on the governing ability of the (leader competitively

---

[4] As argued by, for instance, Becker (1958).

selected by the) majority. Again, such constraints ought to be viewed as inconsistent with the essence of the democratic procedure and possibly harmful.

A quite broad perspective on these issues has been taken by Donald Wittman (1989) in a recent important paper where he argues that "democracies produce efficient results" (title of his paper) or, as is more precisely the author's contention in the text, that "democratic markets work as well as economic markets" (p. 1395). Wittman develops a theory of institutional response, by which he shows "how various political institutions, such as political parties, candidate reputation, and government structure arise in order to mitigate the potential for principal-agent problems in democratic systems" (p. 1396). Wittman's contribution raises a lot of insightful points – as a relevant instance, see his argument that the provision of a public good is always efficient when the tax structure is designed jointly with the amount of the public good. However, Wittman needs to assume that the democratically selected leader acquires no power to alter the rules that govern the mechanisms and the institutions described above. Here – it seems to me – lies the crucial argument *against* the sufficiency of the democratic procedure alone as an optimal mechanism for selecting a leader: Whether the leader is given such power is itself a collective decision that cannot be enforced by competition alone except through a circular argument.

The argument put forward in the previous paragraph focuses on the conditions of enforcement of the contract that supports the political exchange and, as will be made clear in the following sections, crucially hinges upon this contract's incompleteness. It is important to point out that this argument by no means represents a breaking point in the parallel between political competition and economic competition. Recently, as a consequence of the deeper understanding of the nature of contracts governing the relationship between agents who specialize in the social division of labor, economists have started to feel uncomfortable with the presumption of competition as the mechanism that guarantees the 'optimal' division of labor in society.[5] Broadly speaking, the basic idea is that competition gives the right incentives for people to act in accordance with the optimal division of labor, provided that the contracts that people enter into in order to regulate their exchanges are structured in such a way as to be enforceable. Otherwise, competition may give rise to adverse selection.

To clarify this view and to extend it to the analysis of the political exchange, in the next section I will briefly review some of the main results of the recent economic theory of contracts, focusing on enforcement mechanisms of incomplete contracts. Then I will turn to the incomplete contract that supports the political exchange in order to provide an economic interpretation of the classical constitutional principle of *isonomia* as a prerequisite for democracy to act as a selection mechanism of 'optimal' political leaders.

---

[5] This gives a major explanation for the switch from the analysis of competition to the analysis of contracts in modern microeconomics.

3   Incompleteness of contracts and the problem of enforcement

The problem of enforcement of contracts is linked with the distinction between complete and incomplete contracts. Before expanding on this point, let me briefly recall the main definitions and concepts of the economic theory of contracts. We say a contract is *complete* when the parties to the contract explicitly or implicitly specify a profile of actions that they agree to perform, possibly conditional upon the states of the world or the actions of the other parties. A contract is said to be *incomplete* when some contingencies are left out of the parties' agreement.

The economic theory of contracts (mechanism design theory) has by now made clear that parties can always design a mechanism that leads, for each state of the world, to an outcome analogous to the outcome of a completely contingent contract.[6] However, the cost of writing a complete contract or designing the adequate mechanism may in many circumstances outweigh the expected benefits, owing to the very complex machinery that may be involved in specifying precise provisions for every conceivable future event in such a way as to make the relevant actions verifiable, and hence enforceable by a third party (such as a court).[7] Thus when the contracting costs are high, the parties may prefer to economize on some of these costs by leaving some contingencies out in the initial contract.

Under contract incompleteness, however, the character of the initial contract changes radically. Indeed, as soon as some contingencies are left out, parties cannot avoid the question of what happens if they find themselves in a state of the world that was left unspecified. Under these circumstances, the initial contract must either explicitly or implicitly specify which party has the right to choose what actions will be performed by each party. Thus, unlike a complete contract where each party retains full command over its own set of actions all along the relationship, an incomplete contract is an agreement whereby the parties implicitly or explicitly specify that some command over the choice set of some individual i is handed over to some other individual j. Because the content of such an agreement specifies when and under what conditions individual j will be permitted to choose the action that individual i will have to perform, the concept of "authority" is introduced in the economic analysis.

The problem of enforcement of contracts is linked to the distinction between complete and incomplete contracts in the sense that a complete contract is, by definition, a completely enforceable agreement. In an abstract perspective, the

---

[6] Moore (1992).

[7] That the relevant actions be "verifiable" to a third party may not be a necessary condition for the enforcement of the terms of the contract, provided that the parties are involved in an indefinitely repeated relationship. Under these circumstances the parties are said to enter a *self-enforcing* contract. For a contract that regulates a repeated relationship to be self-enforcing, it is sufficient that compliance by each party with the terms of the contract can be observed or even statistically inferred.

exact specification of the set of actions that each part has to perform, conditional upon the states of the world and the actions of the other party, reduces what might otherwise appear to be a very complex social relationship to a simple "simultaneous" act of exchange. The very point of simultaneity is that it lays the foundations of the enforcement of the contract: party A's right hand can be confident in giving because it knows that the left hand is simultaneously taking, and the same is simultaneously true for party B. The two actions involved in a simultaneous act of exchange enforce each other. In particular, it may be interesting to see how the "simultaneity" property is satisfied by self-enforcing contracts, that is, contracts that are enforced by indefinite repetition of the relationship: As the game-theoretical analysis of the relationship points out, the relevant actions are completely spelled out in the equilibrium strategy profile of the supergame, and the players have to compute the equilibrium once and for all at the starting point of the game.

Things are different in the case of incomplete contracts because here enforcement is a genuine problem. We might first consider that, even in the case of an incomplete contract, there can exist a simple arrangement with the analogous function of reducing the, however complex, relationship to a single simultaneous act of exchange. This is the way the problem is dealt with in the seminal model analyzed by Grossman and Hart (1986) and Hart and Moore (1990). Let the content of the incomplete contract be the assignment to party A of the command over the choice set of party B. Given that party B loses command over his choice set, it is intuitive that the surplus that accrues *ex post* to him will be lower than the surplus that he would guarantee himself in the absence of a contract. However, party B will be willing to sign the incomplete contract if party A can adequately compensate him *ex ante* for the loss in the participation in the social surplus. In their model Grossman and Hart (1986) and Hart and Moore (1990) explicitly make the crucial assumption that all individual agents are sufficiently wealthy to guarantee adequate compensation *ex ante*.

In the model analyzed by Grossman and Hart and Hart and Moore, control and authority, that is, command over B's choice set, is conferred by the ownership of an asset, which gives the owner the right to take decisions concerning the use of this asset. Under these circumstances, *ex ante* full compensation is guaranteed, provided that all individual agents are sufficiently wealthy to purchase *in a market transaction* any assets they ought to. Under more general circumstances, when authority results from an explicit or implicit contract allocating the right to decide to a member of an organization, *ex ante* full compensation cannot be mediated by the impersonal working of the market but must explicitly be inserted in the provisions of the contract for the incomplete contract to be reduced to a simultaneous act of exchange.

If we relax the assumption that *ex ante* full compensation is always possible and suppose instead that a wealth constraint is binding for the agent to whom the authority should be assigned, there seems to be no way of reducing the relationship to a simultaneous, mutually enforcing, act of exchange. The only way agent A can acquire command over the choice set of agent B is by making B willing to accept a promise for a "future" compensating payment.

One might still argue that, even if full compensation is not possible *ex ante*, an incomplete contract can, in an abstract perspective, be made analogous to a simultaneous act of exchange when the party to whom authority is to be allocated is involved in repeated interaction. This is the ultimate meaning of David Kreps' (1990) theory of "corporate culture." In his paper, Kreps shows how the reputation mechanism can be extended from (self-enforcing) complete contracts to (self-enforcing) incomplete contracts. Although an incomplete contract cannot specify *ex ante* how the unforeseen contingencies will be met, parties always "have *ex ante* some idea of the meaning of appropriate or equitable fulfillment of the contract," (p. 93) which includes adequate compensation *ex post* when compensation *ex ante* is not possible. As Kreps put it, "unforeseen contingencies follow patterns" (p. 117): The party to whom authority is assigned in repeated interaction can build a reputation of guaranteeing adequate compensation *ex post* by applying "some sort of principle or rule that has wide applicability and is simple enough to be interpreted by all concerned" (p. 93). Thus the quality of the principle, and the level of commitment that the party shows to the principle, will determine whether and to what extent this agent will be "credited" with authority, *in competition with other agents.*

The last sentence helps clarify a crucial point: In cases of repeated interaction, the building of reputation can allow a wealth-constrained agent to have authority conferred to him upon the promise of a future compensating payment. The enforcement of the terms of the incomplete contract, however, depends upon the condition that the authority conferred is not authority to alter the competitive conditions under which the "market" for the allocation of authority operates. This is the crucial element that one faces when trying to extend Kreps' analysis of corporate culture to a political context, although the essential point that Kreps makes – that is, the importance of an organizational reputation in solving problems of unforeseeable contingencies – is similar to the ideological reputation of parties: The nature of competition in political systems is in fact in this respect quite different from that in economics.[8]

I will explicitly deal with the political context in Section 4. But now let me conclude this outline of the economic theory of contracts by elaborating further on what seems to me to be the essential point: that is, when there is no way of reducing an incomplete contract to a simultaneous act of exchange, then (at least some) parties become involved in a "financial" relationship. To clarify this point, let us recall the seminal model analyzed by Grossman and Hart (1986) and

---

[8] This point has been raised by Hinich and Munger (1993).

Hart and Moore (1990) and consider again, within that framework, the case of a wealth-constrained entrepreneur who cannot purchase, and thus acquire control of, the assets he needs to set up a firm. If he has reasons to be confident that the assignment of the rights of control to himself is a wealth-maximizing allocation, he will look for outside finance, that is, for a *lender* that will credit him with the amount of money that he needs for the purchase, upon the promise of a future payment out of the greater surplus he will be able to produce. If we leave the Grossman, Hart, and Moore framework, "credit" need not be interpreted in a material sense: When authority results from an implicit or explicit contract that allocates the right to make decisions to a specific member of an organization, then this agent is "credited" by his partners in the sense that they agree to act upon his authority *before* the large collective benefits that are expected from the organization accrue.

As has been pointed out by Hellwig (1989) and by Aghion and Bolton (1989, 1992), the financial structure of the firm can be viewed as a *governance structure* à la McNeil–Williamson that parties design to deal "optimally" with unforeseen or unspecified contingencies. It consists of a careful assignment of rights of control and authority among the parties, whereby they specify whether and under what conditions, during the relationship, control is allocated to the "borrower" or to the "lender." The important implication of this perspective is that the – possibly conditional – allocation of rights of control and authority among the parties has, in many circumstances, to serve also as a way of endogenously providing enforcement to the incomplete contract that governs the social relationship concerned. In fact, the assignment of rights of control and authority in an incomplete contract has to be "careful" in two respects. First, it must give the parties the right incentive to act in accordance with society's efficiency. Second, it must be structured in such a way as to guarantee enforcement.

This latter aspect is often neglected in most literature on incomplete contracts, as far as this literature assumes the exogenous existence of a judiciary with the power of enforcing the agreements concerned – to be more specific, the standard assumption is that courts (exogenously) exist that, although not able to enforce (nonverifiable) actions contracted upon by the parties, are able to enforce an agreement on the (verifiable) allocation of a given bundle of "rights." For the reasons discussed in Section 2, when trying to extend the theory of incomplete contracts to the analysis of the political exchange, one cannot easily depend on an external mechanism to tackle the enforcement problem. However, provided that the conditional allocation of control and authority is designed with due care, self-enforcing mechanisms can be relied upon. The simple intuition behind this conclusion is that, as long as the content of an agreement among a set of agents in society is the assignment of certain bundles of (mutually compatible) rights, then the ensuing social relationship lends itself to being easily interpreted as a repeated game in continuous time: At each instant in time, agents decide whether to act in accordance with the agreed-upon allocation of rights or to disregard it. As is well-known from the Folk Theorem of noncooperative games, almost everything from such a structure can be singled out as a noncooperative, that is, *self-enforcing*, equilibrium.

Having argued that a properly specified allocation of a certain bundle of rights can be supported by a self-enforcing agreement, I will now try to give more substance to the content of such an agreement by focusing on an important aspect connected with the optimal design of the, possibly conditional, assignment of rights of control and authority in an incomplete contract: The separation between *formal* authority (that is, the formal right to decide) and *real* authority (the effective control over decisions). This issue has been analyzed in a recent contribution by Aghion and Tirole (1997), and their results will be summarized in the rest of this section. [The reasons for concentrating on this contribution will be clear in Section 4, in which I apply the analysis of the separation between formal and real authority to compare, in the context of political exchange, *direct democracy* (where formal authority resides in the assembly of all members of society, although real authority can be held by some society's agent) and *representative democracy* (where formal authority is, upon specified conditions, shifted to some delegated representative)].

Aghion and Tirole analyze a generic principal-agent relationship to endogenously determine the amount of real authority conferred to an agent from that person or those persons who retain the formal authority. They show that the way real authority is endogenously allocated for every assignment of formal authority has a bearing on the optimal structure of the initial incomplete contract, that is, on the assignment of formal authority among the parties. Aghion and Tirole call the situation in which the principal retains formal authority over the agent "integration," that is, the right of reversing the agent's decision; they call the situation in which formal authority is handed over to the agent "nonintegration." Their contribution proceeds in two steps.

They first show that under integration, whenever some real authority can be handed over to the agent, a fundamental trade-off is always faced between the agent's initiative and the principal's cost of losing control over the relevant choice: The greater the amount of resources that the principal devotes to control, the less the initiative taken (hence the amount of resources spent) by the agent. This basic trade-off between resources spent on control by the principal and on initiative by the agent then determines the optimal allocation of real authority within an organization when formal authority is allocated to the principal: Intuitively, the higher the cost of control by the principal who has formal authority, the higher will *ceteris paribus* be the amount of real authority conferred to the agent.

The second step of Aghion and Tirole's analysis is the derivation of a theory of optimal allocation of formal authority. Here the key variable is a parameter of "congruence" that is defined as the *ex ante* probability that, when a decision needs to be made, the principal and the agent will share the same preferences as to the best alternative to choose. Aghion and Tirole show that the "optimal allocation of formal authority" involves integration, that is, allocation of formal authority to the principal, when congruence is low; whereas nonintegration – that is, formal authority conferred to the agent – dominates when congruence is high. Indeed, a monotonic relation is obtained: There exists a cutoff value of the congruence parameter a^*, such that integration is optimal *if and only if* $a < a^*$.

The results obtained are very simple and the intuition behind them clear-cut: When congruence is low, the principal prefers to retain control – that is, formal authority – and then to decide, upon the evaluation of the trade-off between initiative and cost of control, the allocation of formal and real authority.[9]

4   Political exchange, competition, and incomplete contracts

How can the economic analysis of incomplete contracts help us to understand the nature of the political exchange between the voters and the leader selected through a democratic, that is, competitive, electoral contest? My argument in this section is twofold. First, I argue that, even in democratic, that is, competitive, conditions, political exchange is a typical instance of a social relation supported by an incomplete contract for which enforcement is a genuine problem. Under these circumstances, competition may operate as an adverse selection mechanism. Second, I show that useful implications for the subject of democracy and constitutionalism can be derived from analyzing the political exchange with a view toward the mechanisms of allocation of control that are designed under incomplete contracting conditions.

4.1   *Political exchange and competition*

The political exchange is indeed typically supported by a fundamental incomplete contract that by no means can be reduced to a simultaneous, hence self-enforcing, act of exchange. In stylized terms it stipulates that some command over the choice set of individual i – the right to choose in collective decision problems – is entrusted to some other individual j, the political leader. This description applies to *every* kind of political régime, be it authoritarian, democratic, or whatever. What is specific to democracy is that the command over the choice set of individual i is handed over to individual j within the limits that individual j has himself set in his electoral platform. And, because this platform is designed with the purpose of winning a competitive electoral contest, these limits are sanctioned by majoritarian consent and endogenously determined by competitive pressure. However, this is not the end of the story: Because an

---

[9] A parallel result is that, for the same reasons, the agent prefers nonintegration under the same circumstances.

electoral platform is only a "promise," when voters agree to select their leaders through a competitive electoral contest they wish these limits to be actually at work when the electoral platform is implemented. What is the force that puts these limits to work? Can the answer be the risk of losing the next competitive election, when after a given, institutionally fixed, period of time the candidates will compete anew for the incomplete contract, that is, for a new assignment of the right to choose in collective decision problems? It cannot lest the argument become circular. The competitive mechanism cannot enforce itself, because it cannot guarantee that when the command over the choice set of some individuals is handed over to some other individual, a possible effect of this command will not be to alter the ideal conditions under which competition in the "market" for leadership operates. In the abstract context of a repeated game, the crucial point is that the punishment strategies can be made no more available to some players as a direct result of the incomplete contract.[10] In other words, the democratic procedure cannot prevent democratically conferred power from becoming arbitrary, that is developing an "effective capacity to prevent political outcomes that would be highly adverse to [its] interests."[11]

The classical argument for constitutionalism lies, of course, in this (which was Locke's) concern over how power, whoever exercises it, can be prevented from becoming arbitrary. Simply, what I intend to point out here is that the constitutionalist argument consistently follows in an economist's perspective from an analysis of "democracy as competition" and of the nature of the incomplete contract that supports the political exchange in democratic societies. The belief that "when all power [is] made subject to democratic control, all the other constraints on governmental power could be dispensed with"[12] ignores that if democracy was only rooted to the competitive electoral contests in which it consists, then "democracy as competition" would in fact operate as an adverse selection mechanism: In stylized terms, the only electoral platform (a "promise") deserving to be "credited" would be the one that does not conceal the candidate's intention of using the majoritarian support in order to change the rules of the competitive political game, that is, to alter in his favor the conditions under which competition in the market for leadership operates.

Thus for democracy to act as an "optimal" selection procedure of the leader it is a necessary prerequisite that the incomplete contract that supports the political

---

[10] On this point, see the discussion by Adam Przeworski (1991, p. 23ff).

[11] This is the definition that Przeworski (1988) gives to "authoritarian regimes." It highlights the possibility that authoritarian regimes may coexist with *formal* democratic institutions in at least two respects: (i) a competitive regime in which the power apparatus retains the capacity to intervene (*ex post*) to correct undesirable outcomes; (ii) a competitive regime in which the democratically elected leader retains the power to (*ex ante*) condition (through, for instance, the control of the media) the process of formation of public opinion.

[12] Hayek (1982), vol. III, p. 138 (he strongly opposed this belief, of course).

exchange carefully specifies the allocation of control between the voters and the elected leader and that the rules that govern this allocation lie outside the control of the democratically elected leader.

The preceding analysis strongly supports the conclusion of the constitutional tradition of the eighteenth century: that the sovereignty of the people must be taken care of not by democracy but by some sort of contract.[13] My main argument in what follows will be that the economic analysis of contracts can offer guidance in addressing the question of how to design the constitutional "contract" in order that: (i) the rights of control and authority be carefully assigned to the parties in the political exchange; (ii) the framework of promises and agreements of which the constitutional contract consists fulfill the self-enforcing, that is, noncooperative equilibrium, property.

Although the two points are intertwined, it is convenient to grasp each of them separately. The first point is specifically concerned with which particular class of "constitutional" rules are to be invoked as an important prerequisite for "democracy as competition" to act as the optimal procedure of selection of the political leader. The second point is concerned with the condition that, to avoid infinite regress, constitutions must be in a repeated-game equilibrium, that is, with the self-enforcing property of an agreement whereby agents in society choose to adhere to that particular class of constitutional rules. I will expand on the former point in Section 4.2, where I argue that *isonomia* is such a rule. As far as the latter is concerned, I simply make the point that a constitutional rule is a set of mutually agreed boundaries within which agents accept to act, that is, an allocation among society's members of – mutually compatible – bundles of rights. Thus the game that supports the emergence of a specific class of constitutional rules lends itself to being interpreted as a repeated game in continuous time. It is a straightforward application of the so-called Folk Theorem of noncooperative games that from such a structure almost everything can be selected as a self-enforcing equilibrium.[14] The crucial element that connects the two points is the condition that the agreed-upon constitutional boundaries be set in such a way as to always preserve symmetry in the availability of reciprocal punishment strategies for all players concerned.

4.2   *Political exchange and incomplete contracts*

In this final section I intend to offer a simple argument, based on the economic analysis of incomplete contracts, to support the view that a main pillar of constitutionalism, namely, the classical principle of *isonomia*, or rule of law, is a condition that, by embedding in a self-enforcing, efficient, structure the

---

[13] On this point, see the discussion by Francis Sejersted (1988, p. 132).

[14] Barry Weingast (1997) provides an explicit analysis of how the Rule of Law can emerge as a self-enforcing equilibrium of an appropriately specified game.

incomplete contract that supports the political exchange, allows the democratic procedure of selection of the leader to work "optimally." Though set in a different perspective, the argument that will be developed will come very close to the one that underlies the classical analysis of Hayek (1982).

The relevant question can be formulated in the following terms: With a view to the careful design of the incomplete contract that supports the political exchange, what is the amount of formal authority – that is, the right to make decisions on specified matters – that is to be conferred to a democratically elected leader? In what follows I will substantially borrow from the theory of optimal allocation of control in organizations, introduced in Section 3, and extend some of these results to the political realm.

I will assume as the starting point the "ideal" condition of direct democracy, which is, according to Sartori (1993), "democracy without representatives." In a direct democracy, formal authority, that is, the right to make collective decisions, resides in the assembly of all the members of the *polis*, or the communal village. Dahl (1982) suggests that direct democracy should be contrasted to representative democracy only up to a point. In a direct democracy, in fact, although no one is formally entitled to *decide* on behalf of the people, there will always be "agents" appointed to *act* on behalf of the assembly, delegated to implement the collective decisions taken. Moreover, under prevailing conditions, the principal-agent relationship between the assembly and the delegated person or persons will be characterized by contractual incompleteness: Those appointed to particular tasks by the assembly will find that they have some real authority in their hands. This implies that formal authority need not confer *real* authority. On the contrary, though without formal conferment, a delegate will find that he will be left with the authority to make decisions in a number of circumstances in which actual control by the assembly would involve an inefficient waste of resources.

On the other hand, in representative democracy, some formal authority is conferred to the elected leader. The content of the incomplete contract that supports the political exchange can be deemed to be the precise specification of this *formal* authority. This makes the contrast of direct to representative democracy a specific instance of the theoretical problem analyzed by Aghion and Tirole (1994), although these authors do not directly address the political problem that I investigate here. Their case of "integration" (i.e., the situation in which the principal retains formal authority over the agent) parallels, in our context, *direct democracy* whereas "nonintegration" (formal authority handed over to the agent) may correspond, though in different degrees, to the actual working of most democracies, where a given set of rights of decision, that is, a given amount of formal authority, is conferred to the democratically elected government.

The work by Aghion and Tirole reviewed in Section 3 offers a number of valuable insights. According to their first result, the basic trade-off between resources spent on control by the principal and on initiative by the agent determines the optimal allocation of real authority within an organization: the higher the cost of control by the principal, the higher *ceteris paribus* (i.e., given the amount of formal authority allocated to the principal) will be the amount of real authority conferred to the agent. This fits well with the classical explanation (both historically and theoretically) of the evolution from ideal direct democracy to systems in which authority is increasingly conferred to some delegated agent as the result of the enlarging of the society. On the one hand, the immediate effect of the enlarging of the society is the rise in the cost of the principal's control in a multiprincipal context. On the other hand, when population increases, the benefits from specialization – social division of labor – increase as well (Stigler, 1951). Thus the cost that the agent will bear for any given amount of effort expended in exerting initiative decreases with the increase in population. In conclusion, both effects work in the same direction: As population increases, the basic trade-off is solved for larger amounts of real authority conferred to the agent. The second result obtained by Aghion and Tirole is the derivation of the optimal allocation of formal authority, which depends on the value of the "congruence" parameter: When congruence is low, the principal prefers to retain control, that is, formal authority, and then to decide, upon the evaluation of the trade-off between initiative and cost of control, the allocation of formal and real authority.

To extend these results to the context of political exchange, we have to combine three crucial elements. First, the trade-off between initiative and cost of control implies that integration, that is, direct democracy, always has a cost in terms of social division of labor. Second, as the discussion above shows, the opportunity cost of direct democracy increases with the increase in population. Third, the assumption that congruence is low seems, in the absence of further specification, appropriate to the issue at stake, that is, the allocation of political power.[15] This implies that when population is large and congruence is low we are confronted with a poor alternative: either to bear the high opportunity cost of integration implied by direct democracy[16] or to accept that delegation of

[15] "In contriving any system of government, and fixing the several checks and controls of the constitution, every man ought to be supposed to be a knave, and to have no other end, in all his action, than private interest" (David Hume, 1963, p. 40).

[16] To emphasize the high opportunity cost of direct democracy when population is large is not to ignore that there exist instances of direct democracy that should always be preserved in the optimal design of political institutions. Mueller (1996) stresses that constitutional design must be sensitive to the consideration that the collective decision rule has to be more restrictive, when the issue to be decided upon is itself more important. At a less abstract level, Bruno Frey (1994) focuses on the Swiss experience of popular initiatives and referenda to highlight the efficiency properties of direct democratic institutions in at least two respects: (i) to help the political process develop as an ongoing process of deliberation by stimulating discussion among citizens and between politicians and voters; (ii) to enable voters to break the coalition of all established politicians and parties directed against them as taxpayers. However, the frequency of ballots and other popular initiatives has to be low enough to give voters the right incentive and opportunity to become adequately informed to participate actively in the decision.

formal authority to the elected leader will lead to decisions that will benefit the agent against the principal.

Aghion and Tirole treat congruence as exogenous in their analysis but discuss at length the possible ways of endogenizing it (see endnote 11). It is intuitive that to endogenize the congruence parameter is a possible way of escaping the poor alternative described above. This can be done by carefully designing the agent's bundle of rights, which determines the boundaries of his set of possible actions, in such a way that, although congruence *ex ante* is low, congruence *ex post* – that is, the probability that the alternative preferred by the principal will also be the one preferred by the agent given the restriction of the agent's set of possible actions – rises substantially. I argue that, in the political setting, *isonomia* can be interpreted as an abstract principle, the purpose of which is to make the value of the congruence parameter adequately high. The principle of *isonomia* in fact implies that every government is government under the law, within the boundaries of the law, and not a law-making government, that is, a government that can evade those boundaries through freely displacing them. In other words, *isonomia* guarantees congruence in that it "ensures that the perspective of the ordinary citizen, subject to the law, is represented within the law-making process."[17]

Let me substantiate my argument by offering two comments to clarify the property of the constitutional principle of *isonomia* of being efficient and self-enforcing, respectively. First, *isonomia* allows democracy to act as an optimal mechanism of selection of political leaders because it guarantees that the authority conferred through a democratic procedure cannot be used by the incumbent leader to alter in his favor the competitive conditions under which the market for leadership operates. No "equal law" can in fact lead to an alteration in the conditions of symmetry that govern a truly democratic contest. Second, the comparative static analysis of Aghion and Tirole's model associates Pareto-superior equilibria to higher values of the congruence parameter. This suggests that, at the constitutional level, that is, *before* formal and real authority is allocated, all

---

[17] From Holmes (1988, p. 230). In the paper from which the quotation is taken, Holmes suggests that the widely shared view of "constitutional democracy" as an oxymoron hinges upon the common description of constitutionalism in purely negative terms as a device for limiting the power of government. He also particularly blames Hayek (1960) for insisting on this reductionist approach. Holmes claims that the tension between democracy and constitutionalism disappears as soon as the positive purpose of constitutional design as "possibility-generating restraints" is clarified and he carefully analyzes a number of positive enabling functions of constitutional rules, such as the separation of powers. The economic analysis of incomplete contracts shows that the view that constitutional constraints accomplish positive functions is in a sense a "natural" one: By allowing more efficient contracts – that is, contracts that allocate authority more efficiently – to be explicitly or implicitly signed, they help both to reduce transaction costs and to enjoy the benefits of a deeper social division of labor.

agents in society always have an incentive to reach an *ex ante* self-enforcing agreement concerning the allocation of mutually compatible bundles of rights, the purpose of which is to increase the value of the congruence parameter. I stress the point that the conditions for such a constitutional agreement to be self-enforcing are greatly enhanced by its being specifically structured in such a way as to preserve symmetry. Thus it can be concluded that *isonomia* should be seen as the Pareto-superior equilibrium in the set of equilibria of the constitutional game that allocates formal political authority.

5   Conclusions

It was the aim of Hayek's (1960, 1982) contribution to political theory and philosophy of law to assert the value of *isonomia* as the founding constitutional principle of a free society. According to Hayek (1982, ch. III, p. 124), it is "the basic principle of a free society, that the coercive powers of government are restricted to the enforcement of *universal rules of just conduct*," that is, rules that equally bind the government itself and its citizens (italics added).

As Hayek made clear in his contribution, no political society, historically or presently, has ever thoroughly satisfied the condition that its elected leaders always act under the constraint of being subject to "equal laws." In Volume 3, Chapter 17, of *Law, Legislation and Liberty*, Hayek set himself to the formidable task of designing a "model constitution" that fulfills this condition. Hayek's contribution has not yet received the attention and the discussion that it deserves. In this paper, I have endeavored to provide a small step in this direction by showing how a conclusion with such a Hayekian flavor can, perhaps unexpectedly, also be drawn from the economic analysis of contracts.

References

Aghion, P., and P. Bolton. 1989. The financial structure of the firm and the problem of control, *European Economic Review*, **33**(2–3), 286–293.
    1992. An incomplete contracts approach to financial contracting, *Review of Economic Studies*, **59**(3), 473–494.
Aghion, P., and J. Tirole. 1997. Formal and real authority in organizations, *Journal of Political Economy*, **105**(1).
Aron, R. 1967. *Main Currents in Sociological Thought 2: Pareto, Weber, Durkheim*, Penguin Books. Harmondsworth, Mddx., U.K.
Becker, G. 1958. Competition and democracy, *Journal of Law and Economics*, **1**, 105–109.
Dahl, R. 1982. *Dilemmas of Pluralist Democracy*, Yale University Press, New Haven, Conn.
Elster, J., and R. Slagstad. 1988. *Constitutionalism and Democracy*, Cambridge University Press, Cambridge and New York.
Frey, B. S. 1994. Direct democracy: Politico-economic lessons from Swiss experience, *American Economic Review, Papers and Proceedings*, **84**(2), 338–342.

Grossman, S., and O. Hart. 1986. The costs and benefits of ownership: A theory of vertical and lateral integration, *Journal of Political Economy*, **94**(4), 691–719.

Hart, O., and J. Moore. 1990. Property rights and the nature of the firm, *Journal of Political Economy*, **98**(6), 1119–1158.

Hayek, F. von. 1960. *The Constitution of Liberty*, Routledge and Kegan Paul, London.

1982. *Law, Legislation and Liberty*, Routledge and Kegan Paul, London.

Hellwig, M. 1989. Asymmetric information, financial markets, and financial institutions, *European Economic Review*, **33**(2–3), 277–285.

Hinich, M., and M. Munger. 1993. Political ideology, communication and community, in *Political Economy: Institutions, Competition, and Representation*, W. Barnett, M. Hinich and N. Schofield, eds., pp. 25–50, Cambridge University Press, Cambridge and New York.

Holmes, S. 1988. Precommitment and the paradox of democracy, in *Constitutionalism and Democracy*, J. Elster and R. Slagstad, eds., pp. 195–240, Cambridge University Press, Cambridge and New York.

Hume, D. 1963. *Essays: Moral, Political and Literary*, Oxford University Press, Oxford and New York.

Kreps, D. 1990. Corporate culture and economic theory, in *Perspectives on Political Economy*, J. E. Alt and K. A. Shepsle, eds., pp. 90–143, Cambridge University Press, Cambridge and New York.

Moore, J. 1992. Implementation, contracts, and renegotiation in environments with complete information, in *Advances in Economic Theory: Sixth World Congress*, J. J. Laffont, ed., Vol. I, pp. 182–282, Cambridge University Press, Cambridge and New York.

Mueller, D. C. 1996. *Constitutional Democracy*, Oxford University Press, Oxford and New York.

Przeworski, A. 1988. Democracy as a contingent outcome of conflicts, in *Constitutionalism and Democracy*, J. Elster and R. Slagstad, eds., pp. 59–80, Cambridge University Press, Cambridge and New York.

1991. *Democracy and the Market*, Cambridge University Press, Cambridge and New York.

Sartori, G. 1993. *Democrazia. Cos'è*, Rizzoli. Milano.

Schumpeter, J. 1976. *Capitalism, Socialism and Democracy*, Allen and Unwin, London.

Sejersted, F. 1988. Democracy and the rule of law; Some historical experiences of contradictions in striving for good government, in *Constitutionalism and Democracy*, J. Elster and R. Slagstad, eds., pp. 131–152, Cambridge University Press, Cambridge and New York.

Stigler, G. 1951. The division of labor is limited by the extent of the market, *Journal of Political Economy*, **59**(3), 185–193.

Weingast, B. 1997. The political foundations of democracy and the rule of law. *American Political Science Review* (in press).

Wittman, D. 1989. Why democracies produce efficient results, *Journal of Political Economy*, **97**(6), 1395–1423.

CHAPTER 3

Constitutional democracy: An interpretation

Dennis C. Mueller

1   Definitional issues

One might define democracy as a system of government in which the citizens choose either the persons to govern them, or the policies of the government, or both. If we define a constitution as a set of rules by which the above choices are made and the set of constraints upon the citizens and those in government, then all democracies have constitutions; for all democracies have rules for electing representatives, for deciding referenda, and for running town meetings. All democracies have rules, implicit or explicit, constraining those in and out of government.

Although all democracies have constitutions that define their institutions of government, all do not have *written* constitutions. The best known example of a country without a written constitution is, of course, Great Britain. Its governmental institutions are the result of an evolutionary process spanning seven centuries. So venerable are the institutions of government in Great Britain that scholars and laymen alike commonly speak of "The British Constitution" as if it was a document like the U.S. Constitution that could be read and whose language could be interpreted, a document that could in its entirety be discarded or rewritten. Most importantly, because the British Constitution is unwritten, it is difficult to interpret it and say when it is violated. Thus in Britain no Supreme or Constitutional Court exists that has the authority to declare acts of Parliament in violation of the constitution and thereby null and void. Should Parliament decide not to follow one of the customary rules that are thought to be part of the British Constitution, it can. Perhaps no rule is more fundamental to the preservation of democracy in Great Britain than the rule that governments stand for reelection periodically and step down when defeated. But when in 1716 the Parliament deemed it expedient to delay the election, and thus change the maximum interval from 3 to 7 years, it did so.[1] In principle, Parliament could do the same anytime it wishes.[2] An essential feature of constitutional democracy as we shall define it is that it has a written constitution.

There are many ways to measure the success of a constitutional democracy. Many consider longevity one of them, and by this yardstick, Great Britain must certainly be judged a success. We shall, however, measure the success of a democracy by how well it is likely to advance the welfare of its citizens. Presumably, a set of institutions that advances the interests of a polity's citizens is one that the citizens would wish to retain and protect. Therefore such a system should also exhibit considerable longevity.

Now that we have decided to limit our attention to written constitutions, the next obvious question to address is, who writes the constitution? If the constitution is to define a set of institutions that advances the welfare of the citizens, then the obvious choice to write the constitution is the citizens themselves. This proposition is so obvious that it does not require elaboration. Yet no country's constitution in operation today has literally been written by its citizens, and in only a few cases have the citizens played much of a role at all. That many constitutions do not serve as positive forces advancing citizen interests is thus not surprising. In this essay, I shall explore some of the issues that arise when one conceives of a constitutional democracy as being formed by a constitution written and ratified by the citizens. We begin by discussing the purpose of government.

2   The purpose of government

The constitutional perspective on democracy is well captured by Abraham Lincoln's description of American government as being *of* the people, *by* the people, and *for* the people. A government formed by rational people to advance their individual interests, however noble or narrow these may be, will be a government for the people. If all people participate in and agree to the institutions of government, then these institutions will serve the interests of all of the people. The normative foundation of constitutional democracy rests on the unanimous agreement of the community with the constitutional contract that creates government, a unanimous agreement that arises because the institutions defined in the constitutional contract are designed to advance the interests of all citizens.

Numerous other normative objectives have been proposed. Whatever their intrinsic merits, if the objectives cannot secure the unanimous support of the community, they effectively impose the opinion of some person or group over

---

[1] For a discussion of the constitutional significance of this step, see Dicey (1915, pp. 4–11).

[2] Indeed, it did again in 1939. Why democratic procedure should be set aside in time of war is not clear.

the opinions of other members of the community. Any normative defense of such objectives must be based on an elitist line of argument. The ethical observer, those born with divine rights, or the chosen few are to select goals for the community, design the institutions for achieving these goals, and presumably run the institutions once they are in place. In rejecting this elitist position, we are forced to confine ourselves to the investigation of those goals and institutions that are, in principle, capable of unanimous support.

Fortunately, the set of institutions meeting this criterion is rich and varied. Social life presents many situations in which the welfare of all can increase through agreements that place certain constraints on future behavior and that commit all to contribute time or money for the provision of public goods. The common risks a society faces and the common affection people have for one another can induce them to establish institutions for transferring income from those who are more fortunate to those who are less so. Both improvements in allocative efficiency and certain forms of redistribution can in principle win the unanimous support of the citizens. These activities are the raison d'etre of government.[3]

3   The sorcerer's apprentice problem

The specter of a government that, once created, turns upon its creators has haunted most students of government. This danger is most conspicuous in Hobbes' alternative to anarchy – transfer all authority to an absolute monarch – but is present in all solutions that rely on a government if those in government are even partly motivated by self-interest. In creating a constitutional government, the citizens face a fundamental "principal–agent" problem. Ideally, they would make all decisions collectively and unanimously, including the choice of a constitution, but such a collective decision rule is impractical. While decision making costs are economized by choosing agents to make decisions for the citizens, opportunistic behavior by the agents may lead to outcomes that do not advance citizen interests to the maximum degree possible. In extreme cases the agents may claim most or all of the gains from social cooperation.

The Founding Fathers of the United States were well aware of this principal–agent problem and sought to mitigate it through the "checks and balances" built into the Constitution. But these checks and balances have not prevented the government from becoming a Leviathan and now often produce deadlocks between the branches of government that hinder it from efficiently providing those goods and services that everyone expects from it.

---

[3] For further discussion of the properties of collective decisions capable of generating unanimous support see Buchanan and Tullock (1962), Mueller (1989, chs. 2 and 23) and Chapters 4 and 16 of my *Constitutional Democracy* (Mueller, 1996). All future references to this book will be denoted *CD* followed by chapter numbers.

Any society that creates a set of democratic institutions must confront the sorcerer's apprentice problem. How can government be given sufficient authority to act effectively on the citizens' behalf to advance their interests, and at the same time be kept from allowing those in government or with influence over it to use this freedom and authority to advance their interests at the rest of the citizenry's expense? A complete answer to this question cannot be given in this paper, but I shall attempt to outline what such an answer would look like.[4]

4   The legislative branch

The purpose of government is to provide those goods and services that individuals cannot efficiently provide for themselves, or that the market does not efficiently provide, to advance the welfare of all citizens. To achieve this goal, the preferences of all citizens must be recorded as inputs to the decision of what goods and services in what quantities should be supplied. Although two-party representative government can accomplish this goal under certain assumptions, I do not take up this possibility here. Instead, I assume an ideal form of proportional representation in which the preferences of all citizens are represented in the parliament in proportion to their number in the population.[5]

If the parliament made its decisions using the unanimity rule, it would ensure that all were made better off by each government action. The standard objection to its use is that it raises decision making costs to such an extreme as to make government ineffective. To avoid this possibility, some less-than-unanimity rule is required. As the majority required to pass an issue falls, the likelihood that the government will undertake actions that harm some citizens rises. In a now classic discussion, Buchanan and Tullock (1962, pp. 63–91) determined the optimal majority for a parliamentary voting rule by balancing the increase in decision making costs, which accompany higher required majorities, against the expected increase in costs borne by those who lose under a lower required majority.

The concern is often raised that representative bodies sometimes pass measures in the heat of the moment that are later thought to harm a substantial fraction of the population. To avoid this danger, parliamentary rules often require that a measure be read before the parliament more than once before it can take effect and stipulate intervals between each reading. One justification for a second chamber in the parliament is that the need to pass through two assemblies slows a bill up, allowing its advantages and disadvantages to be more thoroughly understood (*The Federalist*, 1937, pp. 409–10).

---

[4] For a more complete discussion, see *CD*.

[5] For a discussion of how such an ideal system of representation can be achieved, see Tullock (1967, ch. 10), Mueller, Tollison, and Willett (1975), and *CD*, 8 and 10.

If these arguments have merit, then decision making costs, that is, the time spent debating and reformulating an issue to achieve a particular majority, may not be costs at all, or at least are not costs until one reaches very high qualified majorities. Stated alternatively, the same objective as requiring a bicameral parliament, or second and third readings of bills, can be accomplished, more or less, simply by requiring a large majority of the votes of the single chamber of the parliament to pass any bill. (A second reason given for requiring a second chamber of parliament is that it raises the effective majority required to pass an issue (Buchanan and Tullock, 1962, ch. 16). Quite obviously and trivially this objective can be accomplished by requiring a higher majority in a unicameral parliament.)

Other justifications for a second chamber of parliament have been put forward, but we shall not take the space to discuss them here (see, however, *CD*, 13). To adequately represent individual preferences on national allocative efficiency and redistribution issues, one needs but one house in the parliament with individuals with a particular set of preferences represented in proportion to their number in the population. The competition for votes among the existing parties and the entry of new parties can be relied upon to ensure that those proposals that can potentially improve the welfare of all citizens get made.

Thus a properly constituted parliament should be capable of undertaking the positive activities of government, of seeing that those goods and services that benefit all get provided. To help ensure that only those goods that benefit all get provided, a high qualified majority can be employed. A high qualified majority would be the primary constraint against those in the legislative branch undertaking actions that harm the population. Other constraints might include prohibitions against certain actions being proposed, or still higher majorities required to pass those types of issues that are least likely to benefit all citizens.[6]

5   The executive branch

There exist two fundamentally different views regarding the function of the executive in a republican form of government.[7] One sees the executive as an agent of the legislature, that is, a set of administrators who expeditiously carry out the policies enacted by the legislature. The other sees the executive as a balance to the legislature, a separate location of legitimate authority that acts as a check on the legislature. In their extreme form these two views of the

---

[6] For a discussion of some of these, see *CD*, 15.

[7] Gwyn (1986) lists *five* different theses justifying a separation of powers of which these are two. The other three are compatible with one or both of the two theses discussed in the text. One also encompasses a separate judiciary, which we take up briefly below.

proper role of the executive are diametrically opposed. The U.S. Constitution is generally cited as the embodiment of the checks and balance view, although a good argument can be made that the original intent of the Founding Fathers in defining the executive branch was to promote the efficient execution of the work of the Congress (Fisher, 1972, pp. 15–16, 26). We shall briefly discuss both of these views of the executive branch's role.

5.1   *The chief executive as agent of the legislature*

In a multiparty system each voter is represented by a party that takes a position reasonably close to that favored by the voter. The parliamentary voting rule selects the best outcome given this mode of representation. Additional input into *what* should be done is not required. The role of the executive branch is to see that what was voted to be done gets done. The chief executive monitors bureaus in the executive branch to ensure that they carry out their tasks efficiently and do not place their own objectives over those of the parliament. Under this interpretation, the chief executive is an agent of parliament and logically should be chosen by it.

There are any number of ways in which the chief executive could be elected. I describe but two. Because the chief executive provides a sort of public good for the parliament – good management of the executive branch – it is logical that the parliament chooses the person to fill this position. The president is elected by the parliament in several countries today (e.g., Italy), and a proposal to have the House of Representatives elect the President of the United States was almost adopted at the Philadelphia Convention (Sundquist, 1986, p. 25). Given the public-good nature of the president's administrative role, if a supramajority of two-thirds or three-quarters of the parliament is required to pass public-goods issues, then the same majority should be required to elect the president. Such a rule would require the agreement of two or more parties in most instances and thus favor the election of nonpartisan candidates, or at least individuals known to be fair and evenhanded. The chief executive under this alternative would be selected on the basis of her administrative competence, not her politics.

Under this first procedure it could arise that no candidate can achieve the required majority. The chief executive's office remains open with parliament locked in a struggle to find a consensus candidate. This possibility can be avoided by requiring only a simple majority of votes in parliament for election and a runoff if no candidate receives an absolute majority on a first ballot. Each party might be allowed to nominate a candidate and a runoff held between the top two vote-getters should no candidate receive an absolute majority on the first ballot. If one party has a majority of seats, it could, under this alternative, choose one of its own members to be president. As always, the simple majority rule enhances the danger of redistribution in some form to the party or coalition of parties in the majority, while reducing decision making costs. A majority party in parliament could strengthen its ability to achieve its goals by choosing a chief executive to supervise the implementation of the parliament's decisions who shares the majority party's objectives.

5.2   *The executive branch as a check on the legislative branch*

The separation of the powers of government into three branches is often viewed as the distinguishing feature of the United States Constitution. But a more accurate characterization is that each branch jointly exercises the powers of government. Together they *share* these powers (Neustadt, 1960; Huntington, 1968, pp. 109–21). The President and both Houses of Congress are now popularly elected. Each can claim with some legitimacy to represent "the will of the people." When running for office, Presidential candidates promise policies that they intend to implement if elected, as if they could function as a legislative branch. The President proposes legislation and exercises some of the power of an agenda setter. By exercising his veto authority, the President often forces modifications of a bill or its defeat. Thus the President of the United States does not merely execute the policies mandated by the legislature, but rather shares in their development and enactment.

Government as a system of checks and balances evolved during the fourteenth through the sixteenth centuries in Europe. The monarch was the representative of *all* of the people in Tudor England, and a Member of Parliament represented purely local or corporate interests (Huntington, 1968, ch. 2). Although by the end of the eighteenth century, Europeans were well on their way to replacing this system with one in which governmental authority was vested in a single body, for instance, the parliament, it was the Tudorial system of divided authority that the Founding Fathers of the United States chose to enshrine in the Constitution. The checks and balances built into the Constitution reflect deep-seated fears of the potential excesses of a democratically elected legislature[8] and of a powerful chief executive who might assume the arbitrary authority of a king. Ironically and illogically, as the system has evolved it has worked admirably to prevent the legislative assembly from acting rashly, while at the same time granting the President ample authority for unilateral action in the areas of foreign affairs and war-making powers.[9]

Whereas the President has considerable latitude when it comes to committing the nation to war, he can implement his domestic program only with the concurrence of both Houses of Congress. Those bills that do become law are

[8] This same fear originally led to the Senate's not being popularly elected.
[9] See Schlesinger (1989).

a compromise between the broad national interests represented by the President and the more narrow geographic interests represented in the two Houses of Congress. There is no theoretical reason to presume that these compromises are the best outcomes a political system could produce. The record of the United States in recent years on crime, education, health care, the budget deficit, and other important domestic issues suggests that the richest country in the world has not achieved its potential. The U.S. system of checks and balances has produced frequent stalemates, preventing either branch from implementing a coherent program.

Although an ambiguous division of authority in the United States has produced deadlocks and frustration, in other countries the outcomes have been much worse. The collapse of the Weimar Republic was arguably due to the ambiguous division of authority in the Weimar Constitution among the President, the Chancellor, and the Parliament.[10] Most Latin American democracies have modeled their constitutions after that of the United States and established strong presidencies. They have not, however, chosen electoral rules to ensure that the president's party has a majority in the parliament. Thus, as in the United States, often neither the president nor the parties in parliament can deliver the programs they promise during election campaigns. The ineffectiveness of presidential government in Latin America has often led to fiscal irresponsibility, inflation, and eventually to dictatorship.[11]

Instead of turning the executive branch into the opposition of the legislature rather than its agent, the constitution can place two alternative checks on the legislature. The first is simply defeat in the next election. This check is the main constraint on government in a two-party system, but even in a multiparty system, the threat of a loss of seats is always there. The more fearful the constitutional convention is of an elected parliament's actions, the shorter the interval between elections it will wish to stipulate.[12] James Madison, often cited as a champion of checks and balances, regarded frequent popular elections as "no doubt the primary constraint on the government."[13]

The second constraint on the parliament is the requirement that legislation receive a supramajority vote. An alternative to a separate branch of government that can veto actions of the legislative assembly is to require substantial consensus in the parliament to pass legislation.[14]

---

[10] See Eyck (1962, ch. 3), Lepsius (1978, pp. 47–50), Carstairs (1980, pp. 165–6), and *CD*, 3.

[11] See Sigmund (1990, pp. 208–10), Valenzuela (1990, p. 66), Lamounier (1990, p. 129), and *CD*, 2, 18.

[12] The fear of democracy at the end of the eighteenth century is also apparent in state constitutions that sometimes required that governors be elected biannually if not annually.

[13] As quoted in Gwyn (1986, p. 71).

[14] Public choice has developed several novel voting procedures with arguably more attractive properties than a supramajority rule (see *CD*, 11).

6   Rights

The higher the majority required to pass an issue in the parliament, the more protection an individual has against the parliament's passing legislation that adversely affects her. There are some issues for which the harm done to the losers, relative to the gains to the winners, are expected to be so large that the constitution framers may deem the unanimity rule to be optimal.[15] An example might be a bill to arrest and detain indefinitely members of a particular ethnic, religious, or political group, even though they were accused of no specific crime. At a time when the targeted group was thought to be a potential source of violent actions against other members of society or the state, such a measure might reduce the anxiety of the vast majority of the citizens. But the costs imposed on innocent members of the targeted group could be enormous, obviously. At a constitutional convention, individuals who are uncertain about whether they or their descendants might someday be members of a targeted group will want to protect themselves against the possibility of such legislation passing. One way to accomplish this would be to require a still higher fraction of the parliament to agree for this legislation to pass than is necessary for passage of ordinary legislation. The greatest protection would be provided by the unanimity rule, because it would allow a threatened minority to veto all such legislation.

Because the unanimity rule would be specified for use only for those classes of decisions in which minorities stand to suffer great losses, these minorities can be expected in most instances to exercise the veto that the unanimity rule gives them by voting against such proposals.[16] The transaction costs of collective decision making can be reduced if issues of this type are not voted upon using the unanimity rule, but rather are dealt with by granting all individuals unconditional rights, for example, to a specific indictment if arrested, a fair and speedy trial, and a right to free speech. Because individuals need not exercise their rights, as when offered a sufficiently large bribe, the same outcomes can be expected when rights are assigned as when a unanimity rule would be required but at lower transaction costs.

Thus the delineation of rights is an important protection against the sorcerer's apprentice problem as it manifests itself through actions of government.

7   Federalism

Federalism can both facilitate the revelation of individual preferences, thereby making government more efficient, and constrain the government's ability to

---

[15] For a demonstration of this proposition and further discussion, see Mueller (1991) or *CD*, 14.

[16] In most instances but not all. Free speech is an issue that has the characteristics for which unanimity is likely to be the optimal voting rule. The publishers of pornography might be willing to vote for a ban on certain forms of pornography, however, if offered a high enough bribe by the rest of the community.

harm the individual. We begin by discussing one of federalism's roles in revealing individual preferences.

7.1   *Voice voting in a federalist system*

Public goods generally have a geographic component to them.[17] The Golden Gate Bridge is used by residents of the bay area of San Francisco, not by those of Chicago. The same can be said of most externalities. If a student sets off fireworks on the Berkeley campus it disturbs, or perhaps benefits, other Berkeley students, but probably not people in San Francisco and certainly not those in Chicago.

In a world of zero-transaction (decision-making) costs and in which the unanimity rule is used in the national (highest) legislative level, no other level of government would be necessary. All collective decisions for all citizens could be made in a single legislative body formed of representatives from across the entire country.

But the zero-transaction costs assumption is untenable. San Francisco wants a bridge, Chicago more police protection, Berkeley a second, weekly trash pickup. The agenda of a single, national legislature would be too crowded to ever discover all the combinations of expenditures and revenue sources that both promise net benefits to the individuals affected and could win unanimous support. Moreover, the number of representatives needed in the national legislature to convey the required information concerning the nature of the local, regional, and national public goods and externalities would be so large that it would be unable to function. A breakdown of the decision-making process into smaller political units is required to economize on its costs.

At the other extreme, one can imagine a separate polity for each collective decision – one to decide whether to build the bridge, another for national defense, a third for trash pickups. Where the decision had only local impact, citizen participation could be direct. Even on national issues like defense, it would be more likely that a citizen's views were effectively represented if the person or party she voted for represented her views on only one issue. But, under this arrangement, the citizen, or her representatives, could literally be member to hundreds of assemblies. Although every voter's preferences would be represented more effectively, and each assembly could make decisions more efficiently, the time required for the citizen to participate directly and to select representatives, coupled with the costs of running each assembly, make this option infeasible. A tradeoff is required between the costs of combining different collective decisions in a single assembly and the costs of establishing different assemblies.[18]

---

[17]   See Oates (1972, chs. 1 and 2) and Starrett (1988, ch. 4).

[18]   See Dahl (1967), Tullock (1969), Oates (1972, pp. 38–49), Breton and Scott (1978, pp. 4–9, 34–47), Tullock (1991, ch. 3), and Inman and Rubinfeld (1996).

7.2   The problem of overcentralization

Alexis de Tocqueville (1945, pp. 165–71) thought that the United States had preserved the political liberty of a small country, despite its size, because of its federalist structure. The Founding Fathers did place language in the United States Constitution to constrain the federal government to specific activities. But the Constitution's general language and broad interpretations by the Supreme Court have allowed a tremendous centralization of governmental activity at the federal level.[19] The lesson from the experience of the United States is that special effort must be made to safeguard a nation against these eventualities.[20] We briefly discuss five constitutional provisions that help maintain the integrity of a federalist system.[21]

7.2.1   A constitutionally defined division of authority: The constitution of the nation state can explicitly delimit the issues that the national legislature can and cannot consider. Defense budgets are a legitimate national issue, elementary school budgets are not. In addition, the constitution could define the conditions necessary to place an issue on the national legislature's agenda. Any issue that concerns *only* the citizens in a lower political unit should not be decided at the national level. If the citizens in only two lower political units are affected, the issue can probably be efficiently resolved through bilateral negotiation. Government action at the national level may save on interjurisdictional bargaining costs, however, when an issue affects several lower level governmental units. To provide for these cases, the constitution could stipulate that an issue having a substantial impact on the citizens of more than X regional governments can be included on the national agenda, where X might be one-half of the regional jurisdictions.[22] The determination of whether an issue satisfied these criteria would be subject to some form of judicial review.

7.2.2   The choice of voting rule: No overcentralization problem would exist if the national legislature made decisions under the unanimity rule. Assuming effective representation of all citizens, only issues or packages of issues that

---

[19] See Friedrich (1968, pp. 17–24), Niskanen (1992), and Weingast (1992).

[20] Whereas in most federalisms the greatest danger to the appropriate assignment of functions appears to be overcentralization, the reverse can happen if the authority of the central government is not clearly defined and protected. Quebec's resistance to the central government's efforts to raise an army with the draft in World Wars I and II is an example. The constitution must protect each level of government from encroachments by other levels.

[21] For a more detailed discussion see *CD*, 6.

[22] By regional governments I mean states in the United States, provinces in Canada, and Länder in Germany. To avoid logrolling packages of issues in which the required X was obtained by putting together X separate issues, each of concern to only one region, the constitution could further prohibit the bundling of unrelated issues into a single bill.

promised net benefits to all citizens in the nation would pass. San Francisco would get its bridge only if it paid its entire costs. Knowing this, San Francisco citizens would not bother trying to get the issue on the national agenda, because the transaction costs of getting it to pass at the urban or regional level would be lower. But under the simple majority rule San Francisco might join forces with Chicago and other cities and get a majority of the national legislature to favor a package of local public goods for the coalition of city interests, unless such bundling of separate issues was effectively prohibited by the constitution. The higher the effective majority required to pass an issue in the national legislature, the less likely overcentralization is.

7.2.3   The method of representation: The danger of local issues gravitating upward in a federalist system is greater if representatives are selected on a geographic basis than if they are selected at large at the national level. If the citizens of San Francisco select one or more individuals to the national legislature to represent their interests, it is quite likely that they will try to get the rest of the country to finance their bridge, if it is at all possible. But if the United States were a single electoral district from which citizens from San Francisco and all other parts of the country chose representatives or parties, it is unlikely that any person or party would think it could win enough votes to be elected by promising a bridge to San Francisco. Competition for votes across the nation would drive candidates to focus more on national issues. Candidates would have to choose issues to win votes in both San Francisco and Chicago. This is not to say that no local issues would find their way into candidates' platforms. A pork-barrel party might package many local issues together. A Western party might represent the interests of a particular region, and so on. But the tendency for centralization should be weaker when representation in the national parliament is not geographically based.

7.2.4   A second house of parliament: Another way to protect a federalist structure is to represent the individual regional governments directly in a second chamber. There are different ways to do this, but the simplest would have a delegation from each regional state, with the membership of the delegation roughly proportional to the distribution of party representation in the region's parliament. The constitution could require either that all legislation must pass in both chambers, or, more narrowly, that any legislation that might possibly affect the several regions differentially pass both houses.

Both the Swiss Council of States and the Bundesrat (Germany's second house) have functioned in this manner. In Germany, however, both the federal and regional (Länder) governments share overlapping authority in most governmental areas, and the post-war period has seen a gradual shifting of power to the central government, as has occurred in the United States (Goldman, 1973, pp. 528–36; G. Smith, 1989, pp. 266–77; Wilson, 1990, pp. 282–3).

7.2.5   Referenda: The fifth possible protection of a federalist structure is to allow citizens to demand a referendum to approve any legislation passed by the federal parliament. This option exists in Switzerland and it is one reason why government in Switzerland has remained smaller and more decentralized than in its European neighbors.

The possibility of calling a referendum acts as a check against all legislation that the central government might enact that the citizens did not approve. As a particular check against centralization and interregional redistribution, the constitution could require that any federal legislation that is likely to have a differential impact across the regions must also be approved by referendum in the individual regions by at least X fraction of the regions, where X might be one-half, two-thirds, or more. Constitutional amendments in Switzerland must be approved by a majority of the cantons in referenda.

7.3   *Voting via exit or voice*[23]

Below the nation-state level, and increasingly even at the nation-state level, individuals can reveal their preferences for government policies by exiting to a different polity if the voice option is ineffective.

The potential of this option is indeed considerable. Difficulties arise in the provision of public goods because all individuals must consume the same public good in the same quantity, yet all individuals do not have the same "tastes" for every public good. If people can vote-with-their-feet, they can sort themselves into groups of homogeneous tastes for public goods. No conflicts need remain and voice voting, if it takes place, can use the unanimity rule. Each citizen chooses that polity that allows him to consume exactly the bundle of public goods and services he desires at a tax price he is willing to pay.

The cost of voting with one's feet instead of one's lungs is sufficiently great that one expects individuals to resort to this option only when they are extremely dissatisfied with the public goods provided by the government. In general, it is the wealthiest citizens in a community who are most mobile, and their departure is the costliest to the government. The collapse of the communist countries of East Europe was in large part a result of their inability to stem the departure of their most valuable citizens. Thus exit within a federalist system is a possibly powerful constraint on governmental failure and can even impose some discipline on the national government.

---

[23] For a recent discussion of the exit/voice alternative in a federalist system, written from a constitutional perspective, see Marlow (1992).

8   The judiciary

8.1   *The selection of judges*

Central to the concept of constitutional democracy is the distinction between the constitution as the *fundamental law*, to use Hamilton's term (*Federalist*, 1937, no. 78), and the normal laws and actions of government. We think of the constitution as a contract joined by all of the citizens of the political community. The drafters of the contract must take into account the potential opportunistic behavior of all parties covered by it and the potential for conflict among these parties. An arbitrator is required, or more accurately, an institution for arbitration. Call this institution the judiciary.

In private contracting the impartiality of the judge can be secured by *all* parties agreeing to the contract's terms, including the identity of the arbitrator, before the contract is signed. To secure an impartial judiciary, ideally *all* citizens would concur in the selection of judges. As a practical matter, this solution is impossible. All citizens, even by referendum, will not agree on which persons should be judges.

The most obvious alternative to citizens selecting judges is for their representatives, that is, the parliament to do it. To ensure impartiality, the optimal voting rule in the selection of judges by the parliament would be the unanimity rule. When less than unanimous agreement suffices to pass ordinary legislation, a dissenting minority can be tyrannized to a degree by the majority. If the same majority has the authority to choose those who will judge the merits of appeals by the minority to the courts, the possibility of the minority's tyrannization increases. The requirement that a minority concur in the selection of judges is a safeguard against its inevitable defeat in both the parliament and the courts.

The higher the majority required to appoint a judge, however, the greater the likelihood that parliament will be unable to agree on any person and that judgeships will remain vacant, to the entire community's loss. This danger, although a possibility, should not be exaggerated. At issue is the impartiality and intelligence of a candidate for a judgeship. Although individuals and their representatives may disagree on substantive issues, this does not necessarily prevent them from agreeing that a particular person can be expected to interpret the law fairly. The lawyers representing a plaintiff and a defendant may disagree on the merits of a case, but this does not prevent them from agreeing on the identities of the members of a jury.

Nevertheless, in some communities the danger of deadlock on the appointment of judges may be sufficiently grave as to warrant an institutional safeguard to avoid it. One way to accomplish this is to invest some person or group with the authority to nominate candidates for judgeships and stipulate that the nominees assume their posts after a specified interval of time, say six months, *unless* parliament agrees by the required supramajority to substitute another identified person in the nominee's place. This procedure would ensure that judgeships do not remain vacant should the parliament not be able to agree on any individual to fill a judgeship but allows the people's representatives to substitute a person they deem to be better suited to be a judge than the one nominated when they do agree on a substitute.

Should the nominators under this procedure be in the legislative, the executive, or the judicial branches? Rather obviously they cannot be in the legislative branch, say, as a judiciary appointments committee in the parliament. To ensure impartiality, this committee would have to contain representatives from all parties so that all citizens were represented and use the same supramajority rule as the whole parliament uses to approve judicial appointments. But then this committee would be vulnerable to the same danger of deadlock as the parliament as a whole.

If the chief executive is elected by a supramajority vote of the parliament, and one of the chief executive's assigned tasks is to nominate persons for the judiciary, then the impartiality of a person would be one of the factors members of parliament would consider when electing a chief executive. The use of a supramajority rule to elect the chief executive would help guarantee this person's impartiality in the same way that the use of a supramajority rule to appoint judges helps guarantee their impartiality. Thus the impartiality of the judiciary could be ensured and the possibility of deadlock avoided by authorizing the chief executive to nominate candidates for judgeships when the chief executive is elected by a supramajority vote of the parliament. The supramajority requirement in the election of the chief executive would help to ensure her impartiality, and the supramajority requirement would induce an impartial selection of any person whom the parliament chose to substitute for the chief executive's nominee.

When the chief executive is elected by plurality or majority vote, she is almost certainly a member and quite likely the leader of one of the parties. She is likely to nominate candidates with ideological positions supportive or sympathetic to that party's ideology, and if a supramajority of the parliament is required to replace her nominee with another person, the chief executive will be nearly free to appoint all members of the judiciary. Impartiality is lost.

One of the complaints lodged against England in the Declaration of Independence concerned the impartiality of judges in the colonies who were appointed by the king. The early constitutions of the individual states often authorized the governor to appoint judges and were accused of having produced a "spoils system" by reformers in the Jacksonian era (Dubois, 1980, p. 3). The nomination of federal judges, including Supreme Court judges, by a popularly elected President coupled with the requirement that only a simple majority in the Senate approve a nomination has had the predictable result that the selection of "judges in America is a political process with a political result" (Corsi, 1984, p. 153, see also pp. 117–32; Murphy and Pritchett, 1979, pp. 122–61). If the constitution is to ensure the impartiality of the judiciary, it cannot entrust the nomination or appointment of judges to a popularly elected chief executive.

The third possible location of a nominator of judicial candidates is in the judiciary itself. Suppose that the usual type of hierarchical judiciary exists. Cases are tried at the lowest level of courts, appealed to one or more intermediate levels, and often tried again at a superior court of last appeal at the top. The career pattern for a typical judge is an appointment from private practice to a judgeship at the lowest level of courts and perhaps from there to a nomination to a judgeship at a higher level. Those in the best position to observe which trial lawyers have the potential to be good judges are the judges at the lowest court level, that is, those hearing the cases prepared by the trial lawyers. Similarly, the people in the best position to appraise the talents of a lower court judge are the judges at the next higher level, who must review the opinions of the lower court judges on appeal. These considerations suggest that the best place to locate the nominators of judges is in the judiciary itself.[24] Vacancies at a particular level of the judiciary could be filled by nominees of the judges in office at that level at the time the vacancies occur, *unless* the parliament voted by the constitutionally required supramajority to substitute some other person.[25]

Such a system would appear to present the danger that the judiciary becomes a self-selecting and self-perpetuating institution. If it ever became populated by individuals who were incompetent or corrupt, it might prove difficult to displace them and reform the system. Two observations can be made in this regard.

First, there are incentives built into the system to encourage competency. The work at any level of the judicial hierarchy is likely to be lighter and more enjoyable for a given judge if his colleagues at that level are industrious and intelligent rather than slothful and dull. Thus the judges at each level have a selfish interest in seeing the most competent of the possible candidates join them as well as a social responsibility to nominate those persons who will best serve the interests of the community. An individual ambitious to move to higher levels in the judicial hierarchy will carry out his judicial responsibilities to the best of his ability so as to impress his superiors.

---

[24] One of the reforms tried in several of the states in the United States has been to vest judicial nominations in a commission composed of lawyers selected by the State Bar Association. This system, often called merit selection, is in the same spirit as the proposal in the text. In practice, however, it has not generally succeeded in removing partisan politics from the judicial selection process (Watson and Downing, 1969; Dubois, 1980, pp. 4–20). Also see Marshall, in Murphy and Pritchett (1979, pp. 155–9).

[25] Article II of the U.S. Constitution provides that the President nominate candidates for the Supreme Court. However, it further stipulates that "Congress may by Law vest the Appointment of such inferior Officers as they think proper, in the President alone, in the Courts of Law, or in the Heads of Departments". Should judges beneath the Supreme Court be deemed to be "inferior Officers," then the U.S. Constitution would allow a procedure like that described in the text at all judicial levels other than that of the Supreme Court.

The second line of defense is the authority the parliament would possess to substitute its own nominees for those of the judiciary. If an incompetent or corrupt judiciary were to devolve under such a system, the parliament would possess the authority to reform the judiciary by substituting its own preferred candidates over those nominated by the judiciary. If the judiciary came into need of reform, the citizens through their elected representatives could replace the existing cadre of judges.[26]

The system just described resembles in many respects those used in Europe to select judges. In some countries like Germany, judges pursue separate courses of study and effectively serve as apprentices in lower courts as they work their way up to higher levels. The selection of judges at all levels except the very highest, where appointment is by a supramajority vote of the parliament, is from within the judiciary.[27] Some of the best judges to have served on the highest courts in the United States have come from outside the system, however (Frankfurter, 1957). A purely technocratic judiciary would deny the highest level courts the opportunity to appoint distinguished members who had not served on lower courts. Thus, although one would expect many nominees to come from within the judiciary, there would be no need to limit them to this group.

8.2   *The control of the judiciary*

In establishing government, the constitutional convention confronts a classic example of the principal-agent problem. It must design institutions – executive, legislature, judiciary – so that their future members have incentives to act not in their own narrow self-interest, but in that of the citizenry at large. The most important check on the legislative branch is, of course, the necessity for its members to be elected. The chief executive must also win the votes of either the parliament or the populace at large. Additional protection against the injurious actions of the citizenry's agents in the executive and legislative branches is provided through the constitutional authority granted the judiciary to overturn actions by either of the other two branches if they violate the provisions of the constitutional contract. But judges are also agents with interests and ideologies that may run counter to those of the citizens. What incentives will force them to act on the citizens' behalf? What institutional device checks the avaricious appetites of judges?

---

[26] The requirement that a supramajority (say three-fourths) of parliament agree on a substitute for a nominee of the judiciary would allow an organization like the Mafia to sustain a corrupt judiciary by "buying" the votes of only one-fourth of the parliament. To curb corruption at this level, the citizens would have to be sufficiently mobilized to defeat members of parliament who had been bought and thereby force the parliament to reform the judiciary.

[27] For an account of the German system, see Langbein (1985).

These are among the most difficult questions a constitutional democracy must face. It puzzled the founders of the United States and has troubled thoughtful observers ever since. Abraham Lincoln posed the question most poignantly: "If the policy of the government, upon the vital questions affecting the whole people, is to be irrevocably fixed by the decisions of the Supreme Court the moment they are made, as in ordinary cases between parties in personal actions, the people will have ceased to be their own masters, having to that extent resigned their government into the hands of that eminent tribunal."[28]

The solution the founders of the U.S. republic decided upon was (1) to have judges nominated by the President and approved by the Senate, (2) to have the appointments last for life, subject to good behavior, and (3) to deny both branches the power to reduce a judge's salary. The first solution has failed to keep the nomination and approval process from becoming politicized, but the second two have arguably freed judges to act independently regardless of any political obligations they have accumulated on their way to office.

Although lifetime appointments and financial security[29] allow members of the judiciary to act in the citizenry's behalf even when that requires blocking actions by the legislative or the executive branches, these provisions do not ensure that the judiciary always acts in the interests of the citizens. Impeachment procedures can remove corrupt or incapacitated judges but are unlikely to be effective in getting judges to make the "right" decisions from the point of view of the citizenry. The opportunity to substitute someone nominated for a judgeship by the members of the judiciary at that level, if the substitute can secure a substantial fraction of the votes of the parliament, is one way the citizens, through their representatives, can keep a check on the judiciary. But if the citizens are "to remain their own masters" ultimately they must be prepared to remove their agents if the need arises. Under the judicial structure described here, the first constitutional convention would have to appoint the first highest level court, which in turn could fill the lower levels. The ultimate check on the judiciary under this structure would be the possibility to reconvene a constitutional convention and appoint a new court.

9 The amendment of the constitution

In addition to possibly replacing the judges on the highest court on some occasion, the citizens may wish to reconvene the constitutional convention from time to time to amend it, or to replace it *in toto*. The original constitution could

---

[28] Statement from Lincoln's first inaugural address, as quoted by Corwin (1906, p. 40).

[29] Real financial security requires that judicial salaries be automatically adjusted for inflation and geographic cost of living differences. Otherwise the judiciary's financial independence is at the mercy of whomever sets judicial salary increases and the rate of inflation.

allow for this in one of two ways: (1) Provision is made for the periodic convening of a constitutional assembly with the authority to amend or replace the existing constitution. This assembly could be governed by the same rules as the first convention, or one could establish new rules. (2) Provision is made for calling a new convention upon some fraction of the citizens or parliament or states demanding it. Once convened, it has the same powers to amend or replace the existing constitution. Another two procedures for amending the constitution that do not require a reconvening of the citizenry are: (3) The constitution can be amended by referendum. (4) The constitution can never be changed and all ambiguities and boundary disputes are settled by the judiciary.

If the consensual nature of the constitution rests on the size of the majority that ratifies it, the same supramajority should be required to amend it as was originally required to ratify it.[30] This requirement, coupled with the inability to amend a referendum proposal once made, makes amendment by referendum an unlikely occurrence.

Another potential disadvantage of amendment by referendum arises from the likelihood that the original set of rights obtained their supramajority as a package, that is, as a result of vote trades. If B traded her vote on free speech for A's vote on abortion and the article on abortion is subsequently amended to B's disapproval, B will have given A her vote rather than traded it. If B anticipates such a successful referendum effort, she will be unwilling to trade her vote in the constitutional convention, and the likelihood of obtaining the required majority on a package of rights falls. This consideration favors the reconvening of a full convention to amend the constitution rather than piecemeal amendments by referendum[31] so that whole packages of changes involving new trades replace previous packages.[32] Entrusting all changes to their agents in the judiciary is the simplest and potentially quickest procedure that the citizens can adopt to keep the constitution up to date. But this procedure suffers from two main defects. First, the court with final authority to settle constitutional disputes must consist of but a handful of individuals and is thus a very small sample of the population. Its judgment may diverge from that of the larger population, just as any small sample mean can diverge from the population mean.

---

[30] Charlotte Twight (1992) demonstrates that constitutional revisions in practice are seldom consensual.

[31] The Swiss hold the record for constitutional amendments (eighty-nine through 1980), and as a consequence their constitution gets "longer, more chaotic, in places more ridiculous each year" according to Christopher Hughes (1988, p. 279). The Swiss amendment procedure requires a majority of voters *and* a majority of cantons to approve an amendment before it passes. Although this rule is stronger than a straight simple majority requirement, it is considerably weaker than the seventy-five percent or so required majority envisaged here and thus leads to more successful amendment efforts.

[32] An interesting example of how compromise can and does occur in the writing of a constitution is presented by Przeworski's (1988) account of Sweden's first constitution.

Second, even if a decision made by the court is exactly the decision that a newly convened convention, or the citizens by referendum, would have made, there may be an advantage in reaching this decision by one of the more circuitous routes. If the constitutional convention is properly constituted, the citizen *knows* that she has been fairly represented. She can observe and consider the arguments on all sides of the issue as it is debated; debates among members of a court are never observed. The citizen knows, and presumably accepts, that the original constitution was ratified by a substantial majority and that any changes in it require the same majority. Changes cannot be made by simple majorities, as must be true of courts of last appeal. In a referendum the citizen participates directly and is exposed to arguments on all sides of the issue. The more time-consuming amendment procedures should generate a better understanding of the decisions made and thereby generate a conviction that the correct decision has been made. In so doing, these procedures are more likely to maintain citizen consensus on the provisions of the constitution and compliance with its provisions.[33]

10   Conclusions

Within the family of political systems that are democratic in some fundamental sense, one can identify a broad spectrum. At one pole there is an extreme form of majoritarian democracy. The majority is sovereign in all realms of government decision making. A normative rationale for such a system can be constructed under the assumption that on any pair of issues x and y, the gains to those who favor x if it wins are equal to the gains those who favor y will experience if it wins (May, 1952; Rae, 1969). The gains from a high limit being imposed to those who favor a high speed limit equal the gains to those favoring low limits if such are imposed. If this equal intensity assumption holds, then the net gains from collective actions are maximized through the use of the simple majority rule.

The logic of majoritarian democracy extends to all dimensions of collective life. Just as net social gains are maximized if the majority sets the speed limits, net social gains are maximized if the majority determines whether a judge who is tough or easy on speeders tries speeding cases. Judges should be popularly

---

[33] Bruce Ackerman (1991) argues that the Supreme Court has amended the U.S. Constitution fundamentally in the 1860s and the 1930s by changing its interpretation of the Constitution's language. The "amendments" have been precipitated at these two junctures of American history by significant shifts in the thinking of large majorities of Americans as to what the Constitution should be.

As a positive analysis of U.S. history, Ackerman's interpretation is most convincing. But it raises serious normative questions. How large a majority of the popular vote in presidential elections suffices for the Court to amend the Constitution? What should be done if the Court fails to heed the majority? To what extent does a minority remain party to the constitutional contract if the contract can be amended whenever a substantial majority so chooses?

elected in a majoritarian democracy to ensure that they are responsive to the, possibly shifting, preferences of the majority. The logic of majoritarian democracy, taken to the extreme, allows no person or institution to thwart the will of the majority. The country that comes closest to the majoritarian model of democracy is Great Britain. Neither the Crown nor the courts nor a constitution can prevent the British Parliament from undertaking any action should it so choose. Its only real constraint is public opinion and the threat of the governing party's defeat at the next general election.

At the opposite pole from unbridled majoritarian democracy is the kind of constitutional democracy outlined here. Ultimate sovereignty resides with the citizens – *all* of the citizens. It can be exercised only when all agree on how it should be exercised.

Both Russell Hardin (1989, p. 119) and Peter Ordeshook (1992) have objected to conceptualizing the constitution as a contract, and their objections would certainly apply to the interpretation of constitutional democracy offered here.

Ordeshook notes that if the constitutional contract is to solve the various social dilemmas a community encounters, it must somehow be enforced. "But if contracts ensure that people do things that they would not otherwise do, it is difficult to isolate the ultimate source of a constitution's durability. Are its provisions enforced by yet a second contract, that is enforced by a third, and so on? Are they enforced from within, by the police, the courts and the military? Or must they be enforced by force to be administered by an oligarchy that stands removed from constitutional limits? The answer to the first question is obviously 'No,' the second question merely pushes the problem back a step so that we must ask, 'How are the provisions enforcing those enforcement mechanisms enforced?' " (Ordeshook, 1992, p. 144).

This infinite-regress problem is "solved" by the two-stage nature of constitutional democracy and the ultimate sovereignty of the citizens as unanimously exercised in the constitutional contract. When the contract is first written, all citizens favor provisions that require and induce cooperation among them. All wish that the provisions of this contract will be enforced. They design institutions to the best of their ability to bring about this goal. These institutions are likely to entail the appointment of agents of the citizens, the design of mechanisms to control the agents, and incentives to induce agents to advance the citizens' interests.

We have described several options in this paper: constraints on the issues that can come before the parliament, a supramajority parliamentary voting rule, federalism, constitutionally defined rights, an independent judiciary to protect them, and the decisive constraint – the willingness of the citizenry en masse to reclaim their sovereignty and overrule or replace the agents or institutions it has created.

The potential importance of constitutional rights, federalism, and a supramajority rule in protecting individuals from government has been well recognized in public choice and political science literature and of course was part of the debate surrounding the drafting and ratification of the U.S. Constitution. Less well appreciated is the crucial role of a truly independent judiciary in this process and the necessity of the citizenry's willingness to reclaim and exercise their sovereignty if required.

In the kind of constitutional democracy described here, the parliament serves as agent of the people in determining what government actions should be undertaken, the executive serves as agent of the parliament to see that its decisions get carried out. The judiciary serves as impartial arbitrator of the constitutional contract and as agent of the citizens to ensure that those in the legislative and executive branches carry out their constitutionally assigned tasks for the benefit of the citizen sovereigns, and not primarily for themselves.

If the judiciary is to police the other two branches effectively, it must be truly independent of them with regard to its appointment and compensation. But if it is truly independent of them, who (what) ensures that the agents in the judiciary do not turn against the citizenry? We have argued that the citizenry must fill this role, either indirectly through their representatives in the parliament, *when they are united in the view that members of the judiciary must be replaced*, or directly by reconvening a constitutional convention.

This aspect of constitutional democracy underscores the importance of having a *written* constitution and ideally one written in a meaningful sense by the citizens. For only a written constitution can be rewritten. The citizens maintain their ultimate sovereignty and their control over their agents in government by standing ready to replace them and to redesign the institutions of government.

The ideal constitution *would be* a self-enforcing contract in that it would solve this principal–agent problem between the citizens and the government once and for all. But this is obviously a difficult ideal to achieve. If it becomes apparent that it has not been achieved, that the agent is overstepping its authority under the constitution, the citizens can exercise their ultimate sovereignty and rewrite the constitutional contract, placing new constraints and incentives on the (perhaps new) agent. Thus the constitution in an ideal constitutional democracy need not be thought of as a self-enforcing contract, but rather the *process* of constitution writing must be an ongoing, *self-correcting* process.

Enforcement of cooperation as specified in the constitution is a (difficult) principal–agent problem, not an infinite regress problem, *if* the constitution is a set of institutions designed and agreed on by the citizens, and they retain the authority to redesign them. Authority regresses back only as far as the body of citizens acting in unison. They must design and be prepared to redesign institutions that best advance their long-run interests.

References

Ackerman, B. A. 1991. *We the People*, Belknap Press, Cambridge, Mass.

Breton, A., and A. Scott. 1978. *The Economic Constitution of Federal States*, University of Toronto Press, Toronto.

Buchanan, J. M., and G. Tullock. 1962. *The Calculus of Consent*, University of Michigan Press, Ann Arbor, Mich.

Carstairs, A. M. 1980. *A Short History of Electoral Systems in Western Europe*, Allen & Unwin, London.

Corsi, J. L. 1984. *Judicial Politics*, Prentice-Hall, Englewood Cliffs, N.J.

Corwin, E. S. 1906. The Supreme Court and Unconstitutional Acts of Congress, *Michigan Law Review*, **4**, 616–30. Reprinted: R. Loss, ed., *Corwin on the Constitution*, Vol. II, Cornell University Press, Ithaca, New York, 1981, pp. 27–40.

Dahl, R. A. 1967. The city in the future of democracy, *American Political Science Review*, **61**, 953–70.

Dicey, A. V. 1915. *The Law of the Constitution*, 8th ed., Macmillan, London. Reprint, Liberty Classics, Indianapolis, Ind., 1982.

Dubois, P. L. 1980. *From Ballot to Bench*, University of Texas Press, Austin, Texas.

Eyck, E. 1962. *A History of the Weimar Republic*, vol. 1, Harvard University Press, Cambridge, Mass.

Fisher, L. 1972. *President and Congress: Power and Policy*, Free Press, New York.

Federalist (The), 1937. [original edition 1787–88]. Random House, The Modern Library, New York.

Frankfurter, F. 1957. The Supreme Court in the mirror of justices, *University of Pennsylvania Law Review*, **105**, Excerpts reprinted in *Courts, Judges, and Politics*, Murphy and Pritchett, eds., pp. 151–3, Random House, New York, 1979.

Friedrich, C. J. 1968. *Trends of Federalism in Theory and Practice*, Praeger, New York.

Goldman, G. 1973. The German political system in *Patterns of Government*, 3rd ed., Beer et al., eds., pp. 473–589, Random House, New York.

Gwyn, W. B. 1986. The separation of powers and modern forms of democratic government, in *Separation of Powers – Does It Still Work?*, R. A. Goldwin and A. Kaufman, eds., pp. 65–89, American Enterprise Institute, Washington, D.C.

Hardin, R. 1989. Why a constitution? in *The Federalist Papers and the New Institutionalism*, B. Grofman and D. Wittman, eds., Agerthon Press, New York.

Hughes, C. 1988. Switzerland (1875): Constitutionalism and democracy, in *Constitutions in Democratic Politics*, V. Bogdanor, ed., pp. 277–89, Gower, Aldershot, U.K.

Huntington, S. P. 1968. *Political Order in Changing Societies*, Yale University Press, New Haven, Conn.

Inman, R. P., and D. L. Rubinfeld 1996. The political economy of federalism, in *Perspectives on Public Choice*, D. C. Mueller, ed., pp. 73–105, Cambridge University Press, Cambridge.

Lamounier, B. 1990. Brazil: Inequality against democracy, in *Politics in Developing Countries*, Diamond et al., eds., pp. 87–134, Westview Press, Boulder, Colo.

Langbein, J. H. 1985. The German advantage in civil procedure, *University of Chicago Law Review*, Fall, **52**, 823–66.

Lepsius, M. R. 1978. From fragmented party democracy to government by emergency decree and national socialist takeover: Germany, in *The Breakdown of Democratic Regimes*, Part II, J. L. Linz and A. Stepan, eds., pp. 34–79, Johns Hopkins Press, Baltimore, Md.

Marlow, M. L. 1992. Intergovernmental competition, voice and exit options and the design of fiscal structure, *Constitutional Political Economy*, Winter, **3**, 73–88.

May, K. O. 1952. A set of independent, necessary and sufficient conditions for simple majority decision, *Econometrica*, Oct., **20**, 680–4.

Mueller, D. C. 1989. *Public Choice II*, Cambridge University Press, Cambridge.

1991. Constitutional rights, *Journal of Law, Economics, and Organization*, September, **7**, pp. 313–33.

1996. *Constitutional Democracy*, Oxford University Press, Oxford.

Mueller, D. C., R. D. Tollison, and T. D. Willett. 1975. Solving the intensity problem in a representative democracy, in *Economics of Public Choice*, R. D. Leiter and G. Sirkin, eds., pp. 54–94, Cyro Press, New York. Reprinted in *Political Economy and Public Policy*, R. Amacher et al., eds., pp. 444–73, Cornell University Press, Ithaca, N.Y., 1976.

Murphy, W. E. and C. H. Pritchett, eds. 1979. *Courts, Judges, and Politics*, 3rd ed., Random House, New York.

Neustadt, R. E. 1960. *Presidential Power: The Politics of Leadership*, Wiley, New York.

Niskanen, W. A. 1992. The case for a new fiscal constitution, *The Journal of Economic Perspectives*, Spring, **6**, 13–24.

Oates, W. E. 1972. *Fiscal Federalism*, Harcourt Brace, London.

Ordeshook, P. C. 1992. Constitutional stability, *Constitutional Political Economy*, Spring/Summer, **3**, 137–75.

Przeworski, A. 1988. Democracy as a contingent outcome of conflicts, in *Constitutionalism and Democracy*, J. Elster and R. Slagstad, eds., pp. 59–80, Cambridge University Press, Cambridge.

Rae, D. W. 1969. Decision-rules and individual values in constitutional choice, *American Political Science Review*, March, **63**, 40–56.

Schlesinger, A. M., Jr. 1989. *The Imperial Presidency*, Houghton Mifflin, Boston.

Sigmund, P. W. 1990. Chile, in *Latin American Politics and Development*, H. Wiarda and H. Kline, eds., pp. 201–30, Westview Press, Boulder, Colo.

Smith, D. 1989. Big-Show, No-Go Weapons, *The Washington Post*, July 31, p. C2.

Smith, G. 1989. *Politics in Western Europe*, 5th ed., Holmes and Meier, New York.

Starrett, D. A. 1988. *Foundations of Public Economics*, Cambridge University Press, Cambridge.

Sundquist, J. L. 1986. *Constitutional Reform and Effective Government*, Brookings Institution, Washington, D.C.

Tocqueville, Alexis de, 1945. *Democracy in America*, vol. I. Vintage Books, New York. (originally published in Paris in 1835).

Tullock, G. 1967. *Toward a Mathematics of Politics*, University of Michigan Press, Ann Arbor, Mich.

1969. Federalism: Problems of scale, *Public Choice*, Spring, **6**, pp. 19–30.

1991. The new federalism, mimeo, University of Arizona, Tucson, Ariz.

Twight, C. 1992. Constitutional renegotiation: Impediments to consensual revision, *Constitutional Political Economy*, Winter, **3**, 89–112.

Valenzuela, A. 1990. Chile: Origins, consolidation, and breakdown of a democratic regime, in *Politics in Developing Countries*, Diamond et al., eds., pp. 37–86, L. Reinner, Boulder, Colo.

Watson, R. A., and R. C. Downing. 1969. *The Politics of the Bench and the Bar*, Wiley, New York.

Weingast, B. R. 1992. Federalism and the Political Commitment to Sustain Markets, mimeo, Hoover Institute, Stanford University, Stanford, Calif.

Wilson, F. L. 1990. *European Politics Today*, Prentice-Hall, Englewood Cliffs, N.J.

CHAPTER 4

Necessary and sufficient conditions for a viable democracy

Peter Bernholz

1   Introduction

Let me warn the reader at the very beginning that this is not a formal essay, though the title might suggest it. The verbal reasoning will, however, be as rigorous as possible.

The definition of "democracy" has been a matter of contention for decades. Some scholars have limited the characteristics used for the definition to electoral competition among politicians and parties for governmental powers. Others have included the rule of law and the separation of powers as well as other elements in the definition. Now, whereas everybody is free to select definitions at his discretion, one should keep in mind that definitions do not make much sense without being applied in the framework of a theory. Also, it should always be clear which definition is used.

In the present essay I want first to discuss some factors eroding the stability of democracy as it is defined in the second, broader sense mentioned above (Sections 2–4). This means also that some questions concerning the preconditions for the existence and development of such democracies have to be raised (Section 5). Specifically, the following hypotheses will be discussed:

1. Apart from a system of self-sufficient farmers, a free-market economy with private property rights is a necessary, but not sufficient condition for the existence of stable democracies.
2. Democracies with unlimited or nearly unlimited jurisdiction for simple majorities of the population (direct democracy) or representative parliaments tend to erode the safety of property rights and the rule of law and to steadily increase government activity.
3. In time these processes diminish efficiency, saving, productive investment, and innovativeness in the market economy and lead to situations perceived as crises by the population.

4. During crises, ideologies and ideas (including economic and political theories) contend for the support of disillusioned voters. If more-or-less correct theories win the day, reforms restricting the influence of government and limiting state activities will be initiated. Otherwise, ideologies with supreme values promising easy solutions will win the day and restructure the economic and political system according to the implied goals. Democracy will be abolished or eroded. Its base, the free-market economy, may be transformed into a more-or-less planned economic system.

After discussing these hypotheses we will turn to the conditions that favor the evolution of democratic systems out of different political regimes. It will be shown that international political competition plays a leading role in this respect (Sections 6–7).

2 Free market economies as a necessary condition for democracy

Let me begin by quoting the sociologist Stanislav Andreski (1965, p. 357): "Up till now representative government has flourished only where there was in existence a large class of economically independent persons, not necessarily independent in the sense of enjoying unearned incomes but in the sense of having no boss. Whenever democratic institutions were promulgated in countries where wealth was concentrated in the hands of the few, they existed only on paper. In districts dominated by one large estate, whose owner could deprive of their livelihood even the persons who were not in his employment, there could be no free elections. An industrialized country in which the means of production would be monopolized would provide a more complex and sophisticated equivalent of the large estate."

In an economy in which all property is owned by the state and directed and controlled by the government, everybody is dependent on the ruling elite for his employment and his livelihood. Thus to take action or even to vote against the wishes of the government, its functionaries, and bureaucracy is only possible if tolerated by them. But why should the ruling elite agree to a limitation of its powers or to its tenure as government? Also, for the same reasons, an independent press, radio, and television are scarcely possible if even the means of production such as printing presses and paper are owned by the state. An exception would only be possible during passing periods in which a balance of power between different groups within government took place.

Similar considerations would be true for a market economy in which a few giant firms controlled the labor market and were able to influence the decisions of government.

By contrast, look at a market economy with safe property rights, sufficient competition, and rule of law. In such a system, people have several possibilities for finding employment and earning their livelihood, even if they are employees. Moreover, there are quite a number of independent farmers, entrepreneurs, professional persons, and wealthy people. All of them can engage in political activities, whether these are frowned on by the governing politicians or not. Moreover, every individual or group able to command the necessary finances can find newspapers, radio, and television stations in competition with others. Thus different opinions and ideas diverging from those in political power can compete.

If, on the other hand, property rights are not safe and the rule of law does not protect persons and contracts, the government or other groups are able to punish people who take actions that conflict with or do not promote governmental or group goals. Property can be confiscated, taxes levied at discretion, and contracts broken or not enforced.

It thus follows that only a market economy with safe property rights, rule of law, and competition can preserve the freedom and independence of a sufficient number of individuals necessary to maintain democracy.

3   The erosion of free market economies as a consequence of unlimited democracy

Democracy is no precondition for a capitalist market economy, as can be seen from the examples of Hong Kong, Chile under Pinochet, and South Korea under Park. Moreover, democracy may even endanger a free-market economy in the long run and thus, if the deliberations of Section 2 are true, even threaten its own existence. This usually occurs in unlimited or scarcely limited total democracies. By a total democracy I mean a democratic regime that is not restricted in its jurisdiction by constitutional or other safeguards. Thus shifting majorities in parliament, that is, small minorities of the population that are inadequately controlled by rationally uninformed voters can enforce their goals on the rest of the population. Because several parties compete for votes and need financial support to cover the expenses for their organizations and for election campaigns, one has to expect in time an ever-increasing sphere of government activities. Thus growing public expenditures, more and more regulations by government, and tax loopholes and subsidies to special minority interests and pressure groups flow from the incessant activity of legislative bodies (Figure 4.1). Such developments can occur because the majority of voters is rationally uninformed about issues. This is true for issues in which decisions impinge only marginally on the situation of consumers or taxpayers, because they then have little reason to incur the costs of informing themselves given the negligible effect of individual votes on election outcomes. Thus protection of certain industries against foreign competition, the fixing of agricultural

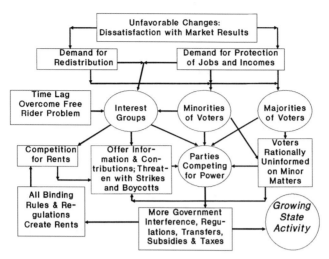

Figure 4.1. Growth of government in market economies.

prices above market clearing levels, subsidies to coal or steel industry, and the toleration or even promotion of cartels can be observed, though a majority of voters is hurt by the resulting higher taxes and/or prices. On the other hand, whenever changes like rent increases for housing are perceived by a majority of voters, because the expenditures for rent amount to a substantial part of their budgets, the government will take action in favor of the majority, for instance by introducing rent controls (Downs, 1957; Bernholz, 1966).

If the above arguments are correct, why is it that government activities are not increased at once under the pressure of political competition to a Nash equilibrium level in which each party maximizes votes, if such an equilibrium exists? Why does it take decades for government activity to rise to ever higher levels? Several reasons have been given to explain this empirical fact. Olson (1965, 1982) points out that since it is difficult to form interest groups because they provide public goods to their members, it takes time to organize them (see also Bernholz, 1969). The more diverse the interests and the greater the number of potential members, the more difficult the task and the longer the time needed to organize an interest group. As a consequence, cartels can only be formed and influence on the political system be exerted by potential groups after they have found enough time to be organized.

Bernholz (1986) has pointed out a second reason for the gradual extension of government, namely, changes of the industrial structure brought about again and again by economic development. These changes threaten old industries, their capital owners and managers, and the jobs and the wage level of the people employed by them. This leads to voter dissatisfaction and thus, under

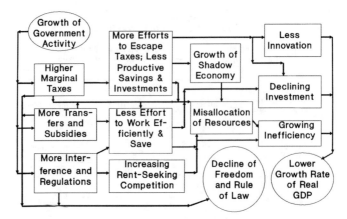

Figure 4.2. Consequences of growing government activity in democratic market economies.

the pressure of political competition, to government intervention to maintain or win the support of those voters and of their families who suffer from the changes in the industrial structure. A third reason sometimes mentioned in the literature is more or less closely related to the second: "The need to keep in check the forces which might produce unemployment is not the only root of the expansion of government control over industry and trade, because the sheer growth of complexity of economic structures requires more co-ordination, and the number of tasks which cannot be left to private initiative – such as prevention of soil erosion, traffic control, smoke abatement and so on – grows incessantly" (Andreski, 1965, p. 355). Finally, time is obviously needed to invent new governmental measures and to introduce and pass new legislation, taxes, and subsidies.

If our analysis is correct, state activity will grow in time in democracies. A democratic system with competing parties reacts to the demands of different minorities and majorities of voters and special interest groups that arise over time. As a consequence, the older and the less disturbed a democracy is by wars, revolutions, and other crises enforcing a restructuring of the political economic system, the higher the level of regulations, subsidies, transfers, and taxes one would expect to find at comparable levels of per capita incomes (Olson, 1982, 1983). But because excessive state activity also makes for less efficiency, savings, and innovation (Figure 4.2) one would also expect negative consequences for real economic growth, as measured, for instance, by the real growth rate of GDP per capita. This expectation seems to be supported by empirical evidence (Figures 4.3 and 4.4) (Bernholz, 1986, 1990; Marlow, 1986; Peden and Bradley, 1989; Weede, 1984, 1990).

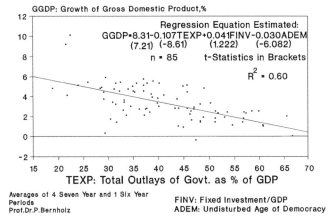

Figure 4.3. Growth of real GDP 1960–93 for seventeen OECD countries.

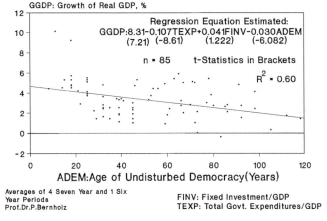

Figure 4.4. Growth of real GDP 1950–93 for seventeen OECD countries.

4   The influence of ideologies on the political economic system during crises

We have just discussed the tendency of democracies with free markets and private property toward more and more interventions and redistribution. This development, however, leads in time to decreasing efficiency and freedom and reduces productive investment and innovative activity. Resources are misallocated and the growth rates of GDP fall. As a consequence, after some time the political-economic system moves into a crisis engendering widespread voter dissatisfaction. It seems that Sweden experienced such a situation in the 1980s and may (as of 1994) not have left it behind.

There exist, moreover, other reasons for crises, namely wars, religious and ethnic strife, hyperinflations, depressions, etc. Obvious examples are the consequences of World War I, especially for the defeated countries under the harsh peace treaties of Versailles, St. Germain, Trianon, and Neuilly. Further examples are the Great Depression, beginning in 1929, and the hyperinflations in Germany, Austria, Hungary, and Poland in the 1920s, in China and Greece in the 1940s, and during the last decades in Bolivia, Argentina, and Brazil.

Crises provide a fertile ground for reform plans proposing new political-economic regimes. They are thus also favorable for the success of ideologies claiming to have the right recipe for solving the perceived problems. The same is true for the application of correct ideas like, for instance, those of the neoliberals after World War II in Western Germany. In this case, men like Eucken, Böhm, Röpcke, and Müller-Armack had already prepared their theoretical concepts concerning a new free-market system during the Nazi regime and the war (Peacock and Willgerodt, 1989). Their ideas were available in 1948, when the German currency reform took place, and were implemented by Ludwig Erhard, Müller-Armack, and others. Thus a successful change from a degenerating planned economy to a free-market regime took place.

Taken generally, different theories and ideologies with their often widely diverging proposals for problem solutions compete during crises. An ideology is to be understood here as a worldview, a Weltanschauung, an attempt to interpret major aspects of the world and their interrelationships. Many such ideologies contain supreme values whose pursuit is claimed to solve the problems of individuals and/or society. Ideologies thus respond to widespread human demands for spiritual goods. The implied Weltanschauung offers safety and provides meaning in an otherwise incomprehensible world. As far as it is shared with others, it offers feelings of warmth and belonging, of safety in the womb of collectivity. Major religions, as well as communism and national-socialism are examples of such ideologies.

It is not surprising that ideologies become most attractive to people disoriented and suffering during crises. This is especially true if such ideologies seem to offer simple and appealing solutions to the problems perceived by the masses. It was only during the crisis of the Great Depression that both Nazis and communists gained strong voter support in Germany (Frey and Weck, 1981), after they had widely lost such support with the end of the German hyperinflation in November 1923. Lenin and his supporters also gained power in Russia in 1917 as a consequence of the defeats and suffering brought about by World War I. And it is also doubtful that the communists under Mao's leadership would have defeated the Kuomintang in 1948–49 without the dismal economic situation, hyperinflation, and corruption in China.

It follows that ideological movements enjoy a good chance to grasp power during crises, provided they are perceived by the masses of the population as offering solutions to their problems. But if ideologies succeed in democracies, it is highly probable that they will transform not only the economic but also the political system, for their supreme values are usually in conflict with a substantial part of democratic institutions. These ideological supreme values have to be implemented either by constitution or law and have to shape many organizations of the state, because by the very definition of supreme values, they have to dominate all other goals. As a consequence, an ideological movement may thus even turn the nation into a totalitarian state if the supreme values of the new creed demand it (Bernholz, 1991, 1993).

The supreme values of ideologies, moreover, often contain rules referring to the economic regime wanted. Christianity forbade usury and Islam does not allow interest; nazism and communism implied a more or less centrally planned economy, the latter, additionally, a socialist or state property. Thus, as far as the supreme values of the respective ideology contain comprehensive rules referring to the organization of the economy, the success of an ideological movement to grasp power necessarily leads to a change of the economic regime. This is exactly what happened in Nazi Germany, the Soviet Union, Eastern Europe after World War II, communist China, Cuba, Vietnam, and Cambodia.

But if such a transformation of a former market economy with private property takes place, what consequences would this have for a democratic system? Assume for a moment that the victorious ideology did not contain any supreme values contradicting the political system of a democracy. Even then, if proposition 1 is true, the democratic regime would be eroded in time. For proposition 1 states that a free-market system is a precondition for democracy, and exactly this system would be transformed because the supreme values of the creed call for a different economic regime. Of course, in reality, the changes called for by the ideology may be so limited that the main characteristics of a market economy can be preserved. This shows that whether the democratic system will be eroded or can be preserved may be a matter of the intensity and scope of the transformation.

5   The control of rulers and the stability of restricted democracy

From the considerations in Section 4 we can draw some important conclusions. Government jurisdiction including the jurisdiction of simple parliamentary and popular majorities (in referenda and initiatives) has to be strongly restricted to preserve democracy in the long run. This applies not only to human rights but also to the safety of property, to government intervention in the economy, and to the power to tax and to create fiduciary money.

On the other hand, a strong government is needed to guarantee the rule of law, to control cartelization and concentration of industry, and to introduce measures to protect the environment, preferably by taxing polluters and by establishing property rights with the right to be compensated for environmental damages.

Moreover, possible dangers of ideologies striving for supreme values that contradict democratic and free-market principles should be taken into account. A first necessary step to reach this aim is the separation of church and state. Also outlawing ideological movements with goals conflicting with democracy and free markets may be another necessary measure.

These proposals, however, lead to another difficult question, namely, how the constitutional, institutional, and organizational safeguards for a stable democracy can be introduced and maintained, given the inclination of rulers to expand rather than to restrict their powers. We are thus faced with the Hobbesian problem of how to control the rulers who have to be accepted in order to overcome, or not return to, anarchy.

The first, more simple question, refers to how to maintain the rule of law and democracy once they have been won. The proposals just mentioned state some necessary but not sufficient conditions to reach long-run stability of democracy. They are not sufficient because they do not, for instance, say anything about how to control the army. I do not want to delve into this problem but would like to quote Andreski (1965, p. 132) who, himself, follows Gaetano Mosca: "Unless an army is too weak to be able to impose its will on the civilian population, as in the United States in the last century, the integration of the officers' corps in the ruling layer appears to be a necessary measure of its political neutralization." It is admitted, however, by Andreski himself that this is only a necessary but not a sufficient condition.

Another safeguard against the threat to freedom and rule of law that stems from power holders bent on extending their power has been proposed by Montesquieu, namely, the separation of legislative, executive, and juridical power within the government. Now it is obvious, for instance, that a constitutional court must exist if a constitutional limitation of the jurisdiction of the state as proposed above is present. In such a case an independent authority is necessary to control whether the legislature and executive live up to the constitution. Otherwise, though the legislature could control the compliance of the executive, only the population could monitor that of the legislature through referenda or initiatives, as is the case in Switzerland. But both institutional arrangements have their limits. What happens if the population is not aware of or agrees to the violation of the constitution? Or if the constitutional court reinterprets and thus erodes the constitution according to its own aims or according to new fashionable ideas widely accepted by the public? Moreover, will the judges of the constitutional court always be independent enough from the executive and/or the legislature, or the legislature from the executive? It seems, then, that the separation of powers may help to maintain freedom, rule of law, and limited democracy, but that it is certainly not sufficient to do so. Thus Mosca substituted a balance of social forces for Montesquieu's separation of governmental powers. But the balance of social forces may also be eroded by economic and political developments, as shown above. "However, the lack of a predominant centre of power does not need to produce a viable equilibrium: disintegration through strife or paralysis of the body politic are more probable outcomes. A political system based on an equilibrium of forces must generate conflicts, and at the same time contain them within narrow limits compatible with effective collective action" (Andreski, 1965, p. 120).

6   Reasons for the evolution of free, prosperous, and democratic societies

We turn now to the second problem announced in Section 1: How can free-market economies with rule of law and limited democracy develop? The answer to this question will reveal some forces outside democratic nations that also work to maintain the stability of existing democracies by redressing the growth of government and by imposing limitations on governmental jurisdiction.

It seems to be rather clear today that widespread prosperity based on an efficient and innovative economic system can only develop in free-market economies that rely on safe property rights, rule of law, and limited taxes and government interventions in the economy. Other conditions like stable money, relatively free trade with the outside world, absence of exchange controls, and a sufficient degree of competition should also be mentioned.

However, given an oligarchic, totalitarian and/or despotic regime, why should the ruling elite agree to strong and safe property rights for everybody, to minimal state intervention and regulation, or to a strong limitation of taxes and thus of its own powers to command and to take away goods and resources at its discretion? This question is particularly important because despotic regimes have ruled for the greatest part of history in most countries, and, in fact, do so even today. Dictatorships, oligarchy and despotism as regimes have been rather stable systems in the course of history. Freedom, rule of law, safety of property rights, democracy, etc., have been the exception, and not the normal state of affairs in history.

Fortunately, well-known explanatory sketches of "the rise of the West" by new economic historians (North and Thomas, 1973; North, 1981; Jones, 1981) are now available to answer our question. One should not forget, however, that the main ingredients of these authors' answers were already developed by earlier scholars like Andreski (1965, Chapters 15 and 16).

As Erich Weede (1987, p. 2) summarizes, "European *disunity* has been our good luck." After the breakdown of the Roman Empire, feudalism with its many

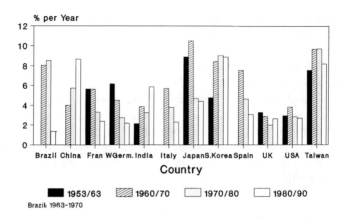

Figure 4.5. Average annual growth of GDP for several countries, 1953–90.

power centers developed, and a split opened up between religious and temporal power (Pope and emperor and kings). A strong rivalry arose between these emerging states and their rulers to gain, to preserve, and to extend their powers. This forced European rulers to become interested in the well-being and loyalty of their subjects and above all in economic development to secure a greater tax base and thus stronger armies. But economic development itself depended on the development of adequate property rights and on free markets. As a consequence, competition among states forced on reluctant rulers a limitation of their domestic powers. The development of competing legal systems and the rule of law, of property rights, and of due process of law was helped, not only by interstate competition, but also by the separation of church and state, thus preventing a theocracy (Berman, 1983). Limited government and pluralistic society were thus a predemocratic achievement. They were not planned by anybody but emerged and proved to be successful. First capitalism and later democracy were their progeny.

The motivation of rulers to limit their domestic powers and to strengthen economies to increase their power in the international system is also present today. It is highly probable that the efforts to decentralize and to move toward market economies since 1979 in China and recently in the former Soviet Union and Eastern Europe have more to do with the aim of China and the former Soviet Union to build up or to maintain a great power status (Figures 4.5 and 4.6) than with the wish to supply the population with more and better goods or even to grant them greater freedom.

We can now understand why Gorbachev tried to move the Soviet Union to undertake far-reaching institutional and economic reforms. Before he became Secretary General of the Politbureau, he was already stressing the necessity for

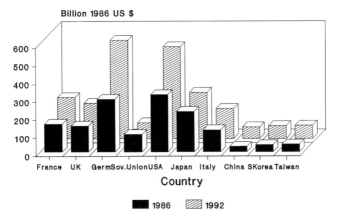

Figure 4.6. Value of exports of several countries.

reform in the Soviet Union. According to the *Neue Zürcher Zeitung* (December 12, 1984), which referred to reports in the Soviet press "The youngest member of the Politbureau was the main speaker at a (Communist Party) conference on ideology." The article reports that Gorbachev stated that "it was inescapable to transform the Soviet economy and to raise its technical and organizational performance to a qualitatively higher level. . . . Only such a modernized economy could meet the needs of the population, allow a strengthening of the position of the USSR on the international stage, and make it possible for her to enter the new millenium as a powerful and flourishing state." The article goes on to say "One could not learn from the presentation, in which way the Soviet economic production should be modernized and which reform ideas Gorbachev would like to apply."

Gorbachev's statement makes the reasons underlying reforms from above particularly clear. Note also that only reforms by rulers seem to be possible in dictatorships and/or totalitarian regimes. For, as Gordon Tullock (1974) has argued convincingly, a free economic and democratic regime are public goods, and the risks for life and family implied in a revolution or coup d'état far outweigh the possible gains for the ordinary person not in control of at least part of military or police power. Also, the wish of rulers to grant more economic freedom to realize a more successful economic regime does not mean that the reforms are adequate and will be successful.

An example of a successful reform of a constitutional, legal, and economic regime is provided by Japan during the second part of the nineteenth century, a reform which, in a sense, was fully completed only with the new Japanese constitution introduced by General McArthur in the wake of World War II. The Meiji Restoration of the 1860s was also a revolution from above. It was led by parts of the nobility against the weakened power of the shogun and skillfully used the device of restoring factual power to the Tenno. The restoration was decisively shaped, or even caused, by the realization of the superiority of the Western states' power after the forced opening of Japanese harbors to Western trade, beginning with Commodore Perry in 1854. Thus the new slogan of the day became "fukokukyohei," "rich country, strong arms" (*Encyclopaedia Britannica*, s.v. "Japan"). The reforms took the form of a wholesale adoption of Western constitutional, legal, educational, economic, technical, administrative, and military systems, which has proved quite successful in the long run.

If we turn to the cases of South Korea and Taiwan, it seems also that the foreign policy situation vis-a-vis North Korea and Red China may have been the most important consideration that swayed leaders to give capitalism a chance. The international position of their countries would thus have been the reason causing the rulers of South Korea and Taiwan to allow and even to further capitalist development, to limit their own powers, and thus to indirectly motivate their populations to also ask for more political rights and even for democratic regimes. Similarly, Communist China, which has been rather successful with its stepwise economic reforms toward a market economy since 1979, probably wanted to reach a stronger position as a big power in international competition.

What other reasons exist for motivating the rulers in oligarchies or even in democracies to limit their own powers and to allow safe property rights, free markets, and low taxes? It seems that only some kind of crisis can bring about such a response. For instance, the United Kingdom's economic performance had durably fallen behind France's and West Germany's. This may have been a more important factor explaining the Thatcher turnaround than the fact "that by 1979, the British had experienced the practical consequences of all the ideas propounded by the politicians in all the parties." (Seldon, 1988, p. 19). Similarly, Hong Kong and Singapore faced the challenge of supporting a big inflow of refugees and of the separation from their hinterlands in China and Malaysia.

7   Foreign policy and democracy

Autocratic regimes are more efficient and consistent than democracies in the formulation and execution of foreign and military policy. They are also able to divert more resources to their armed forces, for they have less reason to respond to the wishes of the population than do democratic governments with competition for votes between parties. It thus follows that autocracies are in a better position than democracies to follow expansionary aims through threats or even wars. Similarly, they can more easily prepare against and, as a consequence, prevent aggression by foreign states.

Given these relationships it must be expected that nations that are essential actors in the international system, like the great powers in the balance-of-power system before 1914, may be under pressure not to develop a democratic regime or to abolish one in order to secure their power position or even their survival. The famous German historian Leopold v. Ranke stressed this tendency and formulated it as the dictum of the priority of foreign over domestic policies. We conclude from this that nations that are essential international actors should have difficulties developing or maintaining democratic systems. But this conclusion would not hold for inessential actors like small states or for essential actors who are safe against foreign aggression because they are isolated by oceans or vast distances, dependent on the military technology of the age. This may explain why democratic regimes had a better chance to succeed in England, the United States, and the smaller countries of continental Europe than in the big European powers.

On the other hand, empirically supported theoretical reasoning shows that democracies are peaceful among themselves (Organski and Kugler, 1980; Rummel, 1983; Russett, 1993; Weede, 1992, 1996). This would imply that the introduction of democratic regimes by essential powers might not only favor aggression by autocratic states but also further the development of democracies in other big nations.

8   Conclusions

It has been argued in this essay that a free-market economy with private property rights is a necessary, though not sufficient condition for the existence of stable democracies in complex societies. It is not sufficient because democracies with (nearly) unlimited jurisdiction for simple majorities tend to erode the safety of property rights and the rule of law and to steadily increase government activity. This leads, in time, to decreasing efficiency, savings, investments and innovations, and as a consequence to crises that are perceived by the population. During crises, ideologies and ideas (including economic and political theories) contend for the support of disillusioned voters. If more or less correct theories win the day, reforms restricting the influence of government and limiting state activities will be initiated. Otherwise, ideologies with supreme values promising easy solutions will win the day and restructure the economic and political system according to the implied goals. Democracy will be abolished or eroded. Its base, the free-market economy, may be transformed into a more or less planned economic system. It follows that only a constitutionally or institutionally restricted democracy can remain viable and be maintained in the long run.

It has also been argued in this essay, however, that free-market economies with safe property rights and rule of law evolve as a consequence of international political and military competition between states. Because market economies further the development of pluralism and democracy, and because democracies tend to be peaceful among themselves, this means that there exists a chance for evolution into a peaceful democratic world if the forces eroding democracy can be restricted.

References

Andreski, S. 1965. *On the Uses of Comparative Sociology*, University of California Press, Berkeley and Los Angeles, Calif.

Berman, H. J. 1983. *Law and Revolution*, Harvard University Press, Cambridge, Mass.

Bernholz, P. 1966. Economic policies in a democracy, *Kyklos*, **19**, 48–80.

1969. Einige Bemerkungen zur Theorie des Einflusses der Verbaende auf die politische Willensbildung in der Demokratie, *Kyklos*, **22**, 276–287.

1986. Growth of government, economic growth and individual freedom, *Journal of Institutional and Theoretical Economics* (Zeitschrift fuer die gesamte Staatswissenschaft), **142**, 661–683.

1990. The completion of the internal market: Opportunities and dangers seen from an international perspective, in *The Macroeconomics of 1992*, pp. 59–105, Centre for European Policy Studies, Brussels.

1991. The constitution of totalitarianism, *Journal of Institutional and Theoretical Economics*, **147**(3), 425–440.

1993. Notwendige Bedingungen fuer Totalitarismus: Hoechste Werte, Macht und persoenliche Interessen, in *Ordnungstheorie und Ordnungspolitik*. G. Radnitzky, and H. Bouillon, eds., pp. 241–284, Springer, New York.

Downs, A. 1957. *An Economic Theory of Democracy*, Harper and Row, New York.

Frey, B., and H. Weck. 1981. Hat Arbeitslosigkeit den Aufstieg des Nationalsozialismus bewirkt? *Jahrbuch fuer Nationaloekonomie und Statistik*, **196**(1), 1–31.

Jones, E. L. 1981. *The European Miracle*, Cambridge University Press, Cambridge.

Marlow, M. L. 1986. Private sector shrinkage and the growth of industrialized economies, *Public Choice*, **49**(2), 143–154.

Neue Zürcher Zeitung. 1984. Das Modernisierungsbeduerfnis der UdSSR. Klare Sprache des Politbueromitglieds Gorbatschew. 12.12.1984, No. 290, p.1, signed A. O., Moscow 11.12.1984.

North, D. C. 1981. *Structure and Change in Economic History*, W. W. Norton and Co., New York.

North, D. C., and R. Thomas. 1973. *The Rise of the Western World: A New Economic History*, Cambridge University Press, Cambridge.

Olson, M. 1965. *The Logic of Collective Action*, Harvard University Press, Cambridge, Mass.

1982. *The Rise and Decline of Nations: Economic Growth, Stagflation, and Social Rigidities*, Yale University Press, New Haven, Conn.

1983. The political economy of comparative growth rates, in *The Political Economy of Growth*, D. C. Mueller, ed., Yale University Press, New Haven, Conn.

Organski, A. F. K., and J. Kugler. 1980. *The War Ledger*, University of Chicago Press, Chicago.

Peacock, A., and H. Willgerodt. 1989. *German Neo-Liberals and the Social Market Economy*, Macmillan, London.

Peden, E. A., and M. D. Bradley. 1989. Government size, productivity, and economic growth: The post-war experience, *Public Choice*, **61**, 229–245.

Rummel, R. J. 1983. Libertarianism and international violence, *Journal of Conflict Resolution*, **27**(1), 27–71.

Russett, B. M. 1993. *Grasping the Democratic Peace*, Princeton University Press, Princeton, N.J.

Seldon, A. 1988. Paper presented at the Meeting of the Mont Pelerin Society, 5–9 September, Kyoto, Japan.

Tullock, G. 1974. *The Social Dilemma: Economics of War and Revolution*, Center for Study of Public Choice, Blacksburg, Va.

Weede, E. 1984. Democracy, creeping socialism, and ideological socialism in rent-seeking societies, *Public Choice*, **44**(2), 349–366.

1987. The rise of the West to Eurosclerosis: Are there lessons for the Asian-Pacific region?, *Asian Culture Quarterly*, **15**(1), 1–14.

1990. *Wirtschaft, Staat und Gesellschaft*. J. C. B. Mohr (Paul Siebeck), Tübingen, Germany.

1992. Some simple calculations on democracy and war involvement, *Journal of Peace Research*, **29**, 377–383.

1996. *Economic Development, Social Order, and World Politics*, Lynne Rienner, Boulder, Colo.

PART II

Democracy and economic growth

CHAPTER 5

Government spending and economic growth under democracy and dictatorship

José Antonio Cheibub and Adam Przeworski

1   Introduction

Our purpose is to assess whether the economic size of the public sector is too small or too big to promote economic growth, first in general for all countries in the world and then for political regimes dichotomized as democracies and dictatorships. Even if many believe that, as Rodrik (1992, p. 331) puts it, "it is the quality of intervention that matters, not its quantity," we show that mere quantity does have consequences. Our econometric analysis extends and modifies that of Ram (1986), but we also seek to place the econometric analysis in a broader theoretical context.

Section 2 is an introduction to the perennial discussion of the relation between the state and the market. Section 3 summarizes alternative ways of thinking about the economic role of government. Section 4 sets up the econometric analysis, the results of which are presented in Section 5. Finally, Section 6 examines the impact of regimes.

2   The state and the market

Capitalism is a system in which most productive resources are owned privately. Yet under capitalism, property is institutionally distinct from political authority. As a result, there are two mechanisms by which resources can be allocated to uses and distributed among households: the market and the state. The market is a mechanism in which scarce resources are allocated by their owners: Individuals cast votes for allocations with the resources they own and these resources happen to be always distributed unequally. The state is also a system that allocates

We appreciate comments by Jean-Dominique Lafay and Mike Alvarez. This work was supported in part by a grant from the National Science Foundation, SES-9022605.

resources, including those it does not own, with rights distributed differently from the market.

The market is a decentralized mechanism: households and firms decide how to allocate the resources they own. Depending on market structure, their decisions may or may not be independent, but they affect each other only via the consequences of actions of one agent for the welfare of another. The state is a centralized mechanism: It coerces economic agents to do what they would have not chosen to do voluntarily. Once reached, state policies are binding, even if not always perfectly enforced.

The tension between the state and the market perennially generates blueprints to resolve it once and for all. The project of the political right is to render the state ineffective; the project of at least one political left was to centralize economic decision making completely. Yet neither blueprint is feasible. The state is necessary for markets to exist. Yet the very separation of political authority from property permits the state to intervene in the allocation of resources, including those it does not own. This is the fundamental dilemma of economic liberalism: As Posner (1987, p. 21) bemoans, "The economist recognizes that government can do some things better that the free market can do but he has no reason to believe that democratic processes will keep government from exceeding the limits of optimal intervention." In turn, subjecting all resource allocation to centralized command encounters informational and motivational problems that generate disasters. The social democratic project was a reasonable compromise: let the market allocate what it allocates better and the state the rest. But the liberal dilemma haunts the social democratic project as well: how to allow the state to do what it should while preventing it from doing what it should not?

The allocation of resources that would result from an unfettered operation of the market differs from that resulting from a political process for two reasons that need to be distinguished: (1) The state may decide to pursue different goals than those that would be maximized when individuals act as economic agents, and (2) market allocation may be inefficient.[1] Let us discuss these reasons in turn.

Individuals are simultaneously market agents and citizens. Their preferences expressed through the political process may differ from those actualized via the market because of considerations of distributive justice. The distribution of income generated by the market depends on the initial endowments, and this distribution may be collectively deemed unjust on a number of different grounds. Security may be another reason for this divergence. Markets do not and cannot insure against all risks because some forms of insurance involve too much moral hazard. There is no private market for unemployment insurance

---

[1] We rush to emphasize that centralized allocation can be and is inefficient as well.

because the moral hazard entailed in such insurance requires coercive monitoring (Ganssmann and Weggler, 1989). Yet people may want to have more security than markets can provide: A Polish survey conducted in 1990 showed that although 72.2 percent of respondents supported privatization, 52.3 percent preferred to work for state enterprises (*Zycie Warszawy*, 25 June 1990, p. 4).

Although justice and security are obvious candidates for collective goals that would not be satisfied by markets, there is no reason to restrict such goals to economic ones. Beauty is as good a goal as justice: The people may want to preserve opera as an art form even if economic agents are not willing to pay what it takes. Opera may be an ecological good: a cultural stock people may not want to deplete out of respect for the potential tastes of future generations.

Justice, security, or beauty are goals people may decide to pursue even if markets were efficient in the standard sense and even if their pursuit was economically costly. But markets are not efficient. The standard neoclassical model is a poor instrument for analyzing the role of the state in the economy. Because under the Walrasian assumptions the market generates a first-best allocation of resources, there is no place for the state in this framework. State intervention, in any form or fashion, is but a transfer of income and, in turn, all transfers of income, by making rates of return diverge from the competitive allocation, reduce incentives and distorts information about opportunities. The function that relates output (or, often confusedly in this literature, welfare) to government intervention is thus monotonically downward sloping.

However, the conclusion the standard neoclassical model leads to follows directly from precisely those simplifying assumptions that were required to make the model tractable:[2] In a Walrasian economy, markets are complete, information is perfect, and there are no public goods, no externalities, and no increasing returns. The idea that everything governments do is pernicious for private agents is too farfetched to be taken seriously. Even the most ardent neoliberals think that governments should provide law and order, safeguard property rights, enforce contracts, and defend from external threats. And the moment these functions are treated as an input to private production, the entire framework of analysis becomes transformed. Some productive role for the state is optimal for maximizing efficiency, growth, or welfare. And if there is at least something the state needs to do for markets to function, then the optimal size of the state is not zero: it is somewhere partway between anarchy and communism.

---

[2] For example, Rebelo (1991) declares that "To isolate the effects of taxation from those of government expenditures, I assume throughout the paper that this revenue is used to finance consumption of goods that do not affect the marginal utility of private consumption or the production possibilities of the private sector." (p. 505) only to discover that "All the models studied in this paper have the implication that the growth rate should be low in countries with high income tax rates. . . " (p. 519). These are but prior beliefs mathematically adorned.

3   The state and the economy: Alternative conceptualizations

There are four basic ways to think about the (always aggregate) role of the state in the economy. Let us first provide the notation used throughout:

Y stands for gross output.
$F = F(.,.)$ stands for output of the private sector.
$S = S(G)$ stands for output of final-demand goods by the public sector.
$H = H(G)$ stands for output of intermediate goods by the public sector.
P stands for private capital stock.
G stands for public capital stock or purchases of capital services by the public sector.

It will also be true throughout that for all $t = 0, 1, \ldots$

$$Y = F + S. \tag{1}$$

$$K = P + G. \tag{2}$$

Note that if only the private sector produces final demand goods, then $Y = F$. Here are four ways to think about the state and the economy:

(1)   There are two sectors, private and public, both of which produce final-demand goods of a different kind, using their own capital (or purchasing capital services). Private firms produce F out of P:

$$F = F(P), \tag{3}$$

and the state produces S out of G:

$$S = S(G). \tag{4}$$

The efficient size of the public sector is given by[3]

$$Y_G = F_P(dP/dG) + S_G = 0$$

---

[3] Note that the maximand that we use to find the efficient size of the government is *gross* output. Olson (1991) and McGuire and Olson (1996) take output net of government expenditures as the criterion for efficiency. Olson's (1991, p. 140) argument goes as follows: "This increase in 'true gross income' must be compared with the cost of the public expenditure that generated it. 'True net income' is then obtained by *subtracting* public expenditures from true gross income, which is essentially income as defined in national accounts. . . . The true gross income is then analogous to an individual's true pre-tax income, and the true net income for the society then is equivalent to true post-tax income for the individual. For the society as well as the individual, it is post-tax income that is relevant for welfare." Now, this is obviously mistaken. Let the pre-fisc income of an individual i be Y_i. The post-tax income of this individual is $(1 - \tau_i)Y_i$. But the total, post-fisc, that is tax and transfer, income of this individual is $(1 - \tau_i)Y_i + \delta_i \sum \tau_i Y_i$, where δ is this individual's share of transfers or benefit from public goods. Hence the analogy fails: Taxes are somehow completely dissipated. Moreover, if government is a separate sector producing final demand (including public) goods, then people employed in the public sector earn income, so

or

$$S_G = F_P.^4 \tag{5}$$

Efficiency requires both sectors to be equally productive at the margin.

(2) There is one composite good produced by a combination of private capital, P, and public capital, G. The production function is

$$Y = F(P, G). \tag{6}$$

Barro and Sala i Martin (1990) present several versions of this model in which public capital is a private good supplied in a rival way to each firm, a public good supplied to all firms, or a public good subject to congestion.

The efficiency condition is

$$F_G = F_P.^5 \tag{7}$$

Condition (7) is the same as (5) in the sense that the marginal products of the private and the public sectors are equal, but the interpretation is different: In Model 1, there are two sectors that must be equally productive at the margin, whereas in Model 2 the production in the single sector must mix private and public inputs in such a way that their marginal product is the same. The only reason to distinguish these two models is that goods produced publicly may be valued differently than the goods produced privately, for example, when the government produces goods that offer more material security or satisfy basic needs. Then we have to define efficiency in terms of utility, and the optimality condition would be $U_F F_P = U_G F_G$. We will not pursue this line.

(3) There are two sectors, each producing distinct goods out of their capital stock and with different technologies, but the output of the public sector

---

that if $Y = F + S$, S is a part of the maximand for the *society*. The same is true if government provides productive inputs, $Y = F(P, G)$: People get paid for producing G and the maximand of the society should be Y, not $Y - G$. Only if government produces exclusively intermediate goods, $Y = F(P, H)$, should H not be counted. But it already is not counted in the gross national income, $Y = F$. Hence Olson is engaged in "double discounting." For an excellent discussion of "net income" that should serve to evaluate welfare maxima see Dasgupta (1993).

[4] Note that from equation (2) $dP/dG = -1$.

[5] Findlay and Wilson (1987) and Findlay (1990) present this model with labor as the distinct input into production. Their production function is $Y = A(L_G)F(L_P, K)$, with $L_G + L_P = L$, the total labor supply, employed by the government and the private sector, respectively. They derive equation (7) as the condition for efficiency, with the marginal products defined as functions of labor rather than capital.

enters as an externality into production the of the private sector. This is the Ram (1986) model. In our notation

$$F = F(P, S),\tag{8}$$

$$S = S(G),\tag{9}$$

$$Y = F + S,\tag{10}$$

$$K = P + G.\tag{11}$$

This model calls for a comment. Note that S must enter in equation (8) as an externality, not as an intermediate good: Otherwise we will be double counting the contribution of the public sector to output. Carr (1989) provides the following example: Suppose that the government builds a road that permits a shoe factory to deliver its product to the market and taxes the factory for the road. Then the price of shoes will contain the effect of the tax and the value of the shoe output, F, will include the road. This can be seen if we imagine that the factory builds the road itself and includes the cost in the price of shoes. Hence, the Ram model assumes that S is a final-demand good, say public order, that enters into private production only as an externality.

The efficiency condition for the Ram model is

$$Y_G = F_P(dP/dG) + F_S S_G + S_G = 0,$$

which implies that

$$S_G(1 + F_S) = F_P.\tag{12}$$

Because $F_S > 0$, equation (12) implies that the government sector should be less productive than the private sector. The reason is obvious: Government production is valued by itself and as a contribution to the private sector.

(4) Finally, suppose that the private sector produces final-demand goods out of private capital stock and an intermediate input supplied by the government, H.

$$F = F(P, H),\tag{13}$$

$$H = H(G),\tag{14}$$

$$Y = F\tag{15}$$

$$K = P + G.\tag{16}$$

The efficiency condition is

$$Y_G = F_P(dP/dG) + F_H H_G = 0$$

or

$$F_H H_G = F_P. \tag{17}$$

This is the same condition as equation (5) or (7): It says that the marginal contribution of public capital to the final output should equal the marginal product of private capital. The difference between this model and Barro's is that here public capital is produced with a different technology than private capital (which is produced by the same technology as final-demand goods).

4 Estimating equations

Note that three concepts of "government size" appeared in the models distinguished above: G is public capital stock (or government capital services if these are purchased from the private sector), S is the government output of final-demand goods (or government consumption of goods and services if these are purchased from the private sector), and H is the government input of intermediate goods. Let us now develop specifications of growth equations under each model, assuming à la Ram that S_G or F_G, depending on the model, is equal to $(1 + \delta)F_P$, and $\dot{P} + \dot{G} = \dot{K} = I$ ($\dot{\ }$ denotes time derivatives).

Model 1 (two independent sectors)

$$Y = F(P) + S(G),$$

$$\dot{Y} = F_P \dot{P} + S_G \dot{G} = F_P \dot{P} + (1 + \delta)F_P \dot{G} = F_P I + \delta F_P \dot{G},$$

$$\dot{Y}/Y = F_P(I/Y) + \delta F_P(\dot{G}/Y) = F_P(I/Y) + \delta F_P(\dot{G}/G)(G/Y). \tag{18}$$

Model 2 (one sector with two kinds of capital)

$$Y = F(P, G),$$

$$\dot{Y} = F_P \dot{P} + F_G \dot{G} = F_P \dot{P} + (1 + \delta)F_P \dot{G} = F_P I + \delta F_P \dot{G},$$

$$\dot{Y}/Y = F_P(I/Y) + \delta F_P(\dot{G}/Y) = F_P(I/Y) + \delta F_P(\dot{G}/G)(G/Y). \tag{19}$$

Hence, models 1 and 2 are econometrically indistinguishable, but the interpretation of δ is different. In fact, if we have data for private and public investment, which this model presupposes anyway, it is sufficient to estimate

$$\dot{Y}/Y = F_P(\dot{P}/Y) + F_G(\dot{G}/Y) \tag{20}$$

with the optimality condition $\delta = 0$ in equation (19) or $F_P = F_G$ in equation (20). Note that if $F_G < F_P$, this does not imply that the government is less efficient but only that public investment is too large in relation to private investment. Government is less efficient if the function $F(G)$ is dominated by the function $F(P)$, or at least if $F_G < F_P$ at $G = P$. Hence the assertion that the marginal product of the public sector of some size is smaller than that of the private sector of some other size should not be confused with the claim that the public sector is less productive at every size.[6]

Model 3 (two sectors with government output as externality)

Here we need to do some algebra, so we reproduce the development of the Ram model, in our notation and without a variable for labor.[7]

$$Y = F(P, S) + S(G);$$

it follows that

$$\dot{Y} = F_P \dot{P} + F_S \dot{S} + S_G \dot{G}.$$

Let $S_G = F_P(1 + \delta)$, where δ is the difference in productivity of capital in the two sectors. If $\delta > 0$, productivity is higher in the government sector (or the sectors from which the government purchases goods and services). Then

$$\dot{Y} = F_P \dot{P} + F_S \dot{S} + F_P(1 + \delta)\dot{G}.$$

Let $\dot{P} + \dot{G} = \dot{K} = I$, total investment. Then

$$\dot{Y} = F_P I + F_S \dot{S} + F_P \delta \dot{G}.$$

But $F_P = S_G/(1 + \delta)$, so that

$$\dot{Y} = F_P I + F_S \dot{S} + S_G[\delta/(1 + \delta)]\dot{G}.$$

In turn,

$$S_G \dot{G} = \dot{S}.$$

Substituting and dividing through by Y yields

$$\dot{Y}/Y = F_P(I/Y) + F_S(\dot{S}/Y) + [\delta/(1 + \delta)](\dot{S}/Y).$$

Collecting terms yields

$$\dot{Y}/Y = F_P(I/Y) + [\delta/(1 + \delta) + F_S](\dot{S}/S)(S/Y). \tag{21}$$

---

[6] This point may appear obvious. We were nonetheless prompted to make it, having read Khan and Reinhart (1990), who are not even bothered by finding a negative (even if statistically not significant) marginal product of public investment.

[7] We estimate all the Ram models with a term $(1 - \beta)(\dot{L}/L)$, where β is the marginal elasticity of output with regard to the labor input.

The term $[\delta/(1+\delta)]$ shows the, positive or negative, contribution of government owing to the potentially different productivity in the two sectors. The term F_S indicates the externality effect of government consumption for private production. (Note that public investment is included in the term I/Y and is implicitly assumed to have the same marginal product, F_P, as private investment). The efficiency condition (12) implies that when the size of the government is optimal, the term $\delta/(1+\delta)+F_S = 0$: The lower productivity of the public sector is compensated exactly by the externality effect of the public on the private sector.[8] If this term is positive, the government is too small: Increasing the public sector would lower its marginal productivity but would increase the rate of growth by providing larger externalities for the private sector. If this term is negative, the government is too large.

Whereas the impact of government can be estimated and inferences about the size of government can be derived from equation (21), the impact of productivity differentials cannot be distinguished from the impact of public externalities. To identify these two impacts, Ram writes the production function of the private sector as $F(P, S) = S^\theta F(P)$, which after some manipulation leads to

$$\dot{Y}/Y = F_P(I/Y) + [\delta/(1 + \delta) - \theta](\dot{S}/S)(S/Y) + \theta(\dot{S}/S). \quad (22)$$

The coefficient θ shows the externality effect of public consumption for the private sector production, and the coefficient δ shows the productivity differential between sectors. Both are now identified. If the externality effect is positive, as one would expect it to be, then the optimal size of government implies that $\delta < 0$.

Ram's central point, and one reason we reproduce his development, is that models that use only government share in output to indicate the size of government are misspecified. Properly specified models, whether in the Ram or Barro formulation (equations (21) and (19), respectively) always related growth of output to the *growth* of government. To show the effects of misspecification, we follow Ram by estimating a model of the form

$$\dot{Y}/Y = F_P(I/Y) + \alpha(S/Y). \quad (23)$$

The conclusion is the following. Models 1 and 2 are identical: model 1 is interesting only if utilities derived from publicly and privately supplied goods are not the same. Hence we have two models: Barro's, which is Model 2, and Ram's, which is Model 3 (Model 4 is uninteresting by itself). Barro's model is specified in terms of public investment, Ram's model in terms of public output.

---

[8] The optimality condition is $S_G(1 + F_S) = F_P$, which implies that $F_S = -\delta/(1 + \delta)$.

Table 5.1. *Panel estimation: government variables only*

Equation	(21)	(22)	(23)
Constant	0.48872	0.61431	2.84460
	(1.291)	(1.592)	(4.428)
F_P	0.13321	0.12893	0.15263
	(6.418)	(6.184)	(6.603)
$(1 - \beta)$	−0.47519	−0.49736	−0.62159
	(−8.00)	(−8.19)	(−9.35)
$\delta/(1 + \delta) - F_S$	0.96092		
	(28.09)		
$\delta(1 + \delta) - \theta$		0.95996	
		(13.61)	
θ		−0.00370	
		(−0.24)	
δ		21.86240	
α			−0.11120
			(−4.42)
R^2	0.26	0.27	0.12
Method*	2F0	2F1	2F1

*Method: 2F0 = Fixed effects model with group and time effects; 2F1 = Fixed effects model with group and time effects correcting for first-order autocorrelation.

Equation (21): $\dot{Y}/Y = \beta_0 + F_P(I/Y) + (1 - \beta)(\dot{L}/L) + [\delta/(1 + \delta) + F_S](\dot{S}/S)(S/Y)$.

Equation (22): $\dot{Y}/Y = \beta_0 + F_P(I/Y) + (1 - \beta)(\dot{L}/L) + [\delta/(1 + \delta)] + [\delta/(1 + \delta) - \theta](\dot{S}/S)(S/Y) + \theta(\dot{S}/S)$.

Equation (23): $\dot{Y}/Y = \beta_0 + F_P(I/Y) + (1 - \beta)(\dot{L}/L) + [\delta/(1 + \delta)] + \alpha(S/Y)$.

5   Results

Our econometric analysis extends that of Ram by (1) using a larger data set and (2) applying panel techniques to estimate the coefficients. Our data set covers 139 countries between 1950, or the year of independence, or the first year data are available ("entry" year) and 1990 or the last year data are available ("exit" year). The data are derived from the World Penn Tables 5.6.

Table 5.1 shows the results for the entire sample during the entire period:

(1)   The size of the government was on the average too small: the term $[\delta/(1 + \delta) - F_s]$ in equation (21) is positive and significant.

(2)   On the average, the public and the private sectors were almost independent: the value of θ in equation (22) is very small. The value of δ

Table 5.2. *A comparison of all countries with those existing before 1960: panel estimation*

Equation (21)	$\delta/(1 + \delta) - F_S$ (*t*-stat.)	S/Y	N	Method*
All Countries				
1950	1.05789 (7.730)	14.92	568	1RT
1960	1.47740 (16.39)	16.57	1038	1FG
1970	0.91881 (15.04)	18.87	1226	2F0
1980	0.85724 (16.37)	20.20	1294	1FT
Old Countries				
1950	1.12120 (8.053)	14.93	541	1RT
1960	1.46860 (11.61)	15.45	660	1FG
1970	0.94137 (11.12)	16.29	690	2F0
1980	1.22070 (10.86)	17.11	685	1FT

* Method: 1RT = Random effects model with time effects; 1FG = Fixed effects model with group effects; 1FT = Fixed effects model with time effects; 2F0 = Fixed effects model with group time effects.

is positive, indicating that the government sector was on the average more productive. However, there are reasons, discussed below, to think this value is incorrectly identified.

(3) When the model is misspecified, that is, when the only government variable on the right-hand side is the share of government consumption in output (equation (23)), government appears to have no impact on economic growth. Hence we confirm that the Landau (1983), as well as the Barro and Lee (1993) results are due to misspecification.

(4) Results by decade, shown in Table 5.2, indicate that for the sample as a whole, the size of the government was too small in the 1950s, decreased in the 1960s, and increased in the 1970s and 1980s, thus getting closer to the optimum.

(5) Regional differences, presented in Table 5.3, show that Eastern Europe is the only region where the government was too large. Everywhere else it was too small. The differences in the externalities produced by governments are rather startling: They are negative in the OECD and in Africa and are positive in the Middle East and in South and East Asia. To the extent that these externalities indicate the quality of government intervention, these results confirm popular wisdom about state intervention in the Far East.

Because these results disturb the recent ideological mood, we may as well anticipate some obvious and perhaps some less apparent criticisms of the model, the data, and the method. Here then are some caveats:

José Antonio Cheibub and Adam Przeworski

Table 5.3. *By region: panel estimation: government variables only*

Equation (21)	$\delta/(1 + \delta) - F_S$	(t)	R^2	Method*
Latin America	0.87333	(14.23)	0.35	2F0
Middle East	1.21330	(7.485)	0.22	OLS
Eastern Europe	−0.15924	(−0.26)	0.28	1F1T
Africa	0.95124	(15.73)	0.20	OLS
South Asia	1.32040	(12.59)	0.62	OL1
East Asia	1.00890	(10.69)	0.23	2R1
OECD	1.44360	(14.88)	0.11	2R1
Asia	1.10360	(8.061)	0.30	2R1

Equation (22)	$\delta/(1 + \delta) - \theta$	θ	δ	R^2	Method*
Latin America	0.77564 (7.769)	0.02662 (1.151)	4.05713	0.35	2F1
Middle East	0.19435 (0.490)	0.26432 (2.807)	0.84729	0.24	OLS
Eastern Europe	−0.52260 (−0.59)	0.05818 (0.591)	−0.31713	0.27	1FT1
Africa	1.24190 (9.460)	−0.07117 (−2.49)	−6.85893	0.21	OLS
South Asia	1.21180 (3.008)	0.03108 (0.297)	−5.11800	0.61	OL1
East Asia	0.51266 (2.360)	0.13560 (2.518)	1.83810	0.26	2R1
OECD	2.42630 (3.762)	−0.13312 (−1.37)	−1.77326	0.11	2R1
Asia	0.61653 (3.324)	0.14441 (3.081)	3.18307	0.35	2R0

*t-statistic in parenthesis.
OLS = Ordinary least squares; OL1 = Ordinary least squares, correcting for
first-order autocorrelation; 1FT1 = Fixed effects model with time effects, correcting for first-order autocorrelation; 2F1 = Fixed effects model with group
and time effects, correcting for first-order autocorrelation; 2R0 = Random
effects model with group and time effects; 2R1 = Random effects model with
group and time effects, correcting for first-order autocorrelation.

(1) Direction of causality, a point made by Rao (1989), is a serious problem, which we did not explore. If there is simultaneity between economic growth and government growth, then our estimates are upward
biased: a likely possibility.

(2) Double counting is a problem. Ram's defense against Carr's accusation of double counting is that it does not make much difference in his estimates. But because we do not know what part of government expenditures enters into private production as an intermediate input and what part enters only as an externality, this is not a convincing defense.

This point deserves some attention. Assume that the Ram model is modified to distinguish the part, $0 < h < 1$, of government output that enters into private production as an intermediate good, and the part $(1 - h)$ that constitutes a final good and enters into private production as an externality. Going through the steps, we can write the modified version of equation (22) as

$$\dot{Y}/Y = F_P(I/Y) + [\delta/(1 + \delta) - \theta + h(\theta + F_H - 1)]$$
$$\times (\dot{S}/S)(S/Y) + \theta(\dot{S}/S), \qquad (22')$$

which implies that if $\theta + F_H < 1$, then δ is underestimated by equation (22), and otherwise it is overestimated. Yet we do not know what a reasonable guess for F_H may be. Hence our estimates of δ may be inaccurate.

(3) Rao argued that the omitted-variables bias leads to a misspecification of the Ram model for the 1960–70 period, as indicated by the RESET test. Our equations (21) and (22) pass the test for the 1960–70 and 1970–80 periods.

These statistical problems may reflect a major theoretical difficulty: The entire attempt to assess the marginal role of government in economic growth may be wrongheaded. Government is not like the private sector, and the system of national accounts, which is the only source of available data, cannot handle this difference. On the one hand, because many government goods and services are monopolistically supplied, their value is calculated at the cost of production, which in turn need not reflect the forsaken opportunities. On the other hand, because governments rarely trade their assets (privatization is a new phenomenon), national accounts do not incorporate changes in the value of government-owned stocks.

However, the difficulty is perhaps even more profound: It concerns the conceptual distinction between investment and consumption. From the economic point of view, any use of resources that increases the productivity of physical or human capital should be treated as an investment (Dasgupta, 1993). This is, by the way, not a new discovery: In 1938, Bertil Ohlin, a member of the Swedish Social Democratic government, observed that "the costs of the health services represents an *investment* in the most valuable productive instrument of all, the people itself. In recent years it has become obvious that the same holds true of many other forms of 'consumption' – food, clothing, housing, recreation." Indeed, Fogel (1994) estimated that about thirty percent of British economic growth since 1780 is due to improved nutrition, and the World Bank has extensively documented the growth-generating effects of education and health.

Hence "government consumption" in fact includes many expenditures that constitute investment. A machine guarded by policeman is more productive than one that is not: It is more likely to be in use. A human being who has enough to eat is more productive than one who does not: As Fogel forcefully reminds us, the first law of thermodynamics applies to human machines as well. What this implies in our context is that models such as ours may be misspecified in the following way: We treat capital and labor as homogeneous, and then investigate the marginal impact of government expenditures other than investment in physical stock. But in fact the quality of both physical and human inputs to production depends on the supply of goods and services by the government: whether it is police to guard physical machines or food to energize human ones. Although one can certainly learn more, this is not just a question of disaggregating public expenditures. The point is that both physical and human inputs already embody the government: machines are designed by engineers using government-sponsored research, people use machines that incorporate government-sponsored education. To assess the role of the government, one would want to know the marginal product of the "government content" of the productive inputs: Am I more productive today because last night I listened to a government-subsidized opera?

This is probably not a feasible research program. Yet in the meantime the controversies about the economic role of the government will not vanish from the political and the intellectual agenda. Hence, with all the caveats and subject to tests still to be run, we stand by our results. At least if one accepts the shaky premises on which this analysis is based, governments tend to be in general too small.

6   Political regimes, government spending, and economic growth

Is the size of government closer to the optimum under democracy than under dictatorship?

The reason democracies are often thought to generate better public decisions is the "Dahl theorem": Contested elections with widespread participation and a modicum of political rights and liberties are supposed to force governments to be accountable to the public. The argument is that, anticipating retrospective judgments of voters, democratic rulers must trade at the margin the private benefits they extract from holding office during the current term and the probability of losing office if they displease the voters. If voters can punish politicians who

Because the effect of deadweight losses enters into the coefficient of $\dot{S}/Y$, this coefficient still represents the total net effect of government. To compensate for deadweight losses, the government sector must be either more productive or must generate a larger technological externality for the private sector. But the net effect of government can be still read from this coefficient, whatever it hides. In turn, the coefficient δ is no longer identified in equation (22).

References

Alvarez, M., J. A. Cheibub, F. Limongi, and A. Przeworski. 1996. Classifying political regimes, *Studies in Comparative International Development*, Vol. 31, no. 2, in press.

Barro, R. J. 1990. Government spending in a simple model of endogenous growth, *Journal of Political Economy*, **98**, S103–S126.

Barro, R. J., and X. Sala i Martin. 1990. Public Finance in Models of Economic Growth, *Working Paper # 3362*, National Bureau for Economic Research, Cambridge, Mass.

Barro, R. J., and J. W. Lee. 1993. Losers and winners in economic growth, *Proceedings of the World Bank Annual Conference on Development Economics*, 267–314. The World Bank, Washington D.C.

Carr, J. L. 1989. Government size and economic growth: A new framework and some evidence from cross-section and time-series data: Comment, *American Economic Review*, **79**, 267–271.

Cheibub, J. A., and A. Przeworski. 1996. Democracy, Elections, and Accountability for Economic Outcomes. Paper presented at the conference on Democracy and Accountability organized jointly by the Department of Politics and the Law School at New York University and the Chicago Center on Democracy at the University of Chicago. New York University, April 26–28.

Dahl, R. A. 1971. *Polyarchy*, Yale University Press, New Haven, Conn.

Dasgupta, P. 1993. *An Inquiry into Well-Being and Destitution*, Clarendon Press, Oxford.

Findlay, R. 1990. The new political economy: Its explanatory power for the LDCs, *Economics and Politics*, **2**, 193–221.

Findlay, R., and J. D. Wilson. 1987. The political economy of Leviathan, in *Economic Policy in Theory and Practice*, A. Razin and E. Sadka, eds., St. Martin's Press, New York.

Fogel, R. W. 1994. Economic growth, population theory, and physiology: The bearing of long-term processes on the making of economic policy, *American Economic Review*, **84**, 369–395.

Ganssmann, H., and R. Weggler. 1989. Interests in the welfare state, in *Political Regulation in the 'Greate Crisis'*, W. Vaeth, ed., Sigma, Berlin.

Heckman, J. J., 1988. *The Macroeconomic Evaluation of Social Programs and Economic Institutions*, Institute of Economics, Academia Sinica, Taipei, Taiwan.

Khan, M. S., and C. M. Reinhart. 1990. Private investment and economic growth in developing countries, *World Development*, **18**, 19–27.

Landau, D. 1983. Government expenditure and economic growth: A cross-country study, *Southern Economic Journal*, **49**, 783–92.

Manin, B., A. Przeworski, and S. C. Stokes. 1996. Democracy and Accountability. Paper presented at the conference on Democracy and Accountability, organized jointly by the Department of Politics and the Law School at New York University and the

Chicago Center on Democracy at the University of Chicago. New York University, April 26–28.

McGuire, M. C., and M. Olson, Jr. 1996. The economics of autocracy and majority rule: The invisible hand and the use of force. *Journal of Economic Literature* **34**, 72–96.

Olson, M. Jr. 1991. Autocracy, democracy and prosperity, in *Strategy and Choice*, R. J. Zeckhauser, ed., pp. 131–157. MIT Press, Cambridge, Mass.

Posner, R. A. 1987. The Constitution as an economic document, *The George Washington Law Review*, **56**, 4–38.

Przeworski, A., and F. Limongi. 1993. Political regimes and economic growth, *Journal of Economic Perspectives*, **7**, 51–69.

Ram, R. 1986. Government size and economic growth: A new framework and some evidence from cross-section and time-series data, *American Economic Review*, **76**, 191–203.

Rao, V. V. 1989. Government and economic growth: A new framework and some evidence from cross-section and time series data: Comment, *American Economic Review*, **79**, 281–284.

Rebelo, S. 1991. Long-run policy analysis and long-run growth, *Journal of Economic Perspectives*, **99**, 500–521.

Rodrik, D. 1992. Political economy and development policy, *European Economic Review*, **36**, 329–336.

CHAPTER 6

Rent seeking and redistribution under democracy versus dictatorship

Ronald Wintrobe

1 Introduction

The idea that "too much" democracy is bad for economic development has resurfaced again in recent years. In the economic literature, the main reason advanced is that democracy is "plagued" by redistributional impulses. Perhaps the most famous work to advance this theme is Mancur Olson's (1982) *The Rise and Decline of Nations*, in which interest groups are reclassified as "distributional coalitions" that pursue their own selfish interests at the expense of overall economic efficiency. The older and more established the democracy, the larger the number of distributional coalitions that have a chance to form and the more the economic landscape is "rent" with inefficient laws, regulations, and other practices that hinder growth. In a similar vein, the vast literature on rent-seeking, originated by Tullock (1967), Krueger (1974), and Posner (1975), identified rent-seeking and its associated social costs with democratic government and thus made it possible, by a strange twist of logic in which democracy is identified with the proliferation of economic monopolies, for monopoly to be elevated to the status of a serious problem.

Although critical of democratic processes, none of the above-named authors has embraced the notion that authoritarianism can facilitate economic development, and indeed, Mancur Olson in particular has forcefully argued the opposite (Olson, 1993). However, the closely related idea that insulating economic policy from democratic processes – "a little bit"[1] of dictatorship – can be good for economic development has gained currency, especially in political science and among theorists of development from both economics and political science who specifically point to the capacity of authoritarian states to resist distributional pressures as the key to successful development. The most influential

---

[1] The case for massive dictatorship, for instance that communism is better able to promote economic growth than capitalism, is no longer fashionable.

contemporary exponent of this view seems to be Stephen Haggard (1990), although the argument is much older [see Przeworski and Limongi (1993) for a good list of earlier references]. Among development economists, Bardhan (1990, p. 5) is explicit on the redistributional issue:

> "Once developmental goals are centrally involved in the issues of the legitimacy of the regime, I think it is not so much authoritarianism per se which makes a difference, but the extent of insulation that the decision makers can organize against the ravages of short-run pork-barrel politics."

Perhaps more important than academic fashion is the striking success in economic terms of a number of countries under authoritarian regimes, commonly known as the Newly Industrializing Countries (NICs) – especially the East Asian economies of Singapore, South Korea, Taiwan, and Hong Kong. Most dramatic has been the success of "free-market communism" in contemporary China, in which extensive political authoritarianism combined with the opening of free markets has achieved dazzling economic growth. By contrast, the failures of "populist" governments in recent years, especially in Latin America, have been only too apparent. Dornbusch and Edwards (1990) have invented the derisive label "macroeconomic populism" to describe the policies of countries like Chile under Allende or Peru under Garcia where leftist governments attempted to respond to pressures for income redistribution through macroeconomic means. Dornbusch and Edwards (1990, p. 248) point out that these programs usually achieved the opposite of their objectives and ended when "foreign exchange constraints and extreme inflation forced a program of violent real wage cuts that ended in massive political instability, violence, and in the case of Chile, even in a coup."

Although their 1990 article uses Chile and Peru as examples of macroeconomic populism, their subsequent Dornbusch and Edwards' (1991) edited volume expands the list of "populist experiences" to include Argentina, Brazil, Mexico, and Nicaragua. The authors emphasize that they share the predilections of the policymakers who authored these episodes that income is distributed unacceptably in these countries; it is just that populism is no substitute for sound economics, fiscal conservatism, and (presumably) waiting for the next generation at least to improve the distribution of income.

Whereas the root of the success of the East Asian NICs could be vaguely attributed either to their relentless use of free markets and only to that [see Wade's (1990) Chapter 3 for a survey of neoclassical economic explanations of the success of Taiwan and other NICs in these terms], or to vague notions of oriental cultural inheritances, the most dramatic case of turnaround is probably contemporary Chile, where one of the most brutal periods of dictatorship seems to have given birth, after some false starts, to a dynamic and successful market economy, in which democracy has (mostly) returned and in which even the former enemies of the regime appear loath to abandon many of its policies.

Support for the Chilean achievement can even be found expressed by Guillermo O'Donnell, the original architect of the "bureaucratic authoritarian" model of Latin American dictatorships and one of their most important critics:

> "The sober fact is that the distributional consequences of more ambiguous and less harsh policies in countries such as Brazil, Argentina, and Peru have not been better than the ones under the Pinochet government. Furthermore, the resources presently available to the Chilean government for alleviating equity problems are relatively larger than the ones available to Brazil, Peru, and Argentina . . ." (O'Donnell, 1993, p. 1,366).

Presumably, however, Pinochet would not be pleased by the analogy O'Donnell draws between the effectiveness of some of Pinochet's policies and those of Lenin.

The argument that authoritarianism fosters growth has not gone uncriticized. In particular, scientific work on the connection between authoritarianism and growth has achieved decidedly mixed results. Przeworski and Limongi examine the statistical evidence. They review eighteen studies, each of which considered a number of countries over a period of time. The countries were classified as either democratic or authoritarian, and tests were performed to see which type of regime is more favorable to economic growth. As they summarize their findings, of the twenty-one results in the eighteen studies, eight found in favor of democracy, eight in favor of authoritarianism, and five discovered no difference.[2] One obvious problem with the methodology used in those studies is that the category "political regime" (democratic versus authoritarian) is simply too coarse. Thus such studies would end up lumping together countries like South Korea and Zaire or Haiti. Neither Papa Doc and his successors nor Mobutu have ever evinced much interest in promoting economic growth. On the contrary, they have succeeded in largely destroying their economies. Elsewhere (Wintrobe, 1997) I referred to these regimes as "immiserizing" dictatorships and showed some of the conditions under which that strategy is attractive to dictators. In any case, there is little doubt about the record of these regimes. Geoffrey Hawthorn (1993, p. 1305) describes the present state of the Zairean economy:

> "The country's outstanding debt is widely reported to be the same size as Mobutu's personal fortune. Half the present budget goes to debt servicing; a quarter to Mobutu's own political fund which he uses to pay off the politicians and officers he constantly rotates; and the remaining quarter to internal security . . . . Roads are 10% of what they were when the Belgians left in 1960, recorded

---

[2] Przeworski and Limongi (1993, p. 60).

wages, in real terms, 6% . . . – it is estimated that only about 1% of the country is now cultivated."

Another flaw in the theoretical case that capitalist–authoritarian regimes facilitate economic growth has been elaborated by Robert Wade (1990) and Alice Amsden (1989) and recently emphasized in the economic development literature by Dani Rodrik (1993): Many of the most prominent NICs, especially Korea, Singapore, and Taiwan, although authoritarian enough, do not fit the free-market model. Their economies are not particularly free of trade restrictions, and their states have been extensively involved in industrialization. Thus Rodrik notes that in Korea for example, "the average effective rate of protection . . . (for domestic sales only) actually rose from 30% in 1963 to 38% in 1978, after a dip to 24% in 1970. . . . The Korean state has used trade protection, selective credit subsidies, export targets (for individual firms!), public ownership of banking sector, export subsidies, and price controls."[3] Moreover, as Rodrik emphasizes, the policy instruments used in countries like Korea or Singapore that have been dramatically successful at achieving economic growth are no different from those that have apparently failed so miserably in Latin America, Africa, and the rest of Asia. The policies in question are import quotas and licenses, credit subsidies, tax exemptions, public ownership, and so on.[4]

What is most conspicuously absent in this literature – either from those who believe that there is a connection between dictatorship, at least in its author-itarian capitalist variant, and economic growth or from those who argue the opposite – is an adequate theoretical perspective.

This essay considers the popular idea that democratic governments inhibit growth because of excess redistributory activity or rent-seeking. I ask the ques-tion: on theoretical grounds, which type of regime can be expected to engage in more redistribution – democracy or dictatorship? The analysis proceeds by examining the equilibrium level of redistribution in a number of well-known models of democracy – that of Meltzer and Richard (1981), in which redistri-bution takes place from the mean to the median income voter, Becker's (1983) interest group model, and the probabilistic voting model of Coughlin, Murrell, and Mueller (1990). I then ask what would happen to the level of redistribution if a dictator took over the government. The analysis suggests that, in all these cases, we would expect more redistribution under dictatorship than democ-racy. Armed with this conclusion, I suggest an alternative explanation for the superior economic performance of capitalist–authoritarian regimes – it is not because they don't redistribute but because they do, and the redistribution in the case of these regimes happens to be toward groups who especially profit from economic growth.

[3] Rodrik (1993, p. 22).
[4] Rodrik (1993).

In the model, agents are rational and selfish. However, the dictator's formal monopoly of political power provides him with some unusual incentives or constraints, compared to those facing democratic politicians. To put it bluntly, his most basic dilemma, as I have discussed more extensively elsewhere, is that although today he is the dictator, tomorrow he could easily be dead (the most common method of removing a dictator is assassination). How can he ensure or at least prolong his survival in office? Section 2 compares the incentives facing dictators and democratic politicians with respect to redistribution and develops the main proposition of this paper: Other things being equal, dictatorships tend to engage in income redistribution (from a benchmark free-market distribution) more than democratic regimes. Section 3 suggests that there is an alternative way in which dictatorships can affect the functioning of markets and therefore the rate of economic growth. It derives from Coase's central proposition that, in the absence of the fiction of costlessly enforceable property rights, markets aren't free. One implication is that the intervention of the state is necessary to support property rights. More powerful implications emerge from the "efficiency wage" models to the effect that, when contractual enforcement is not costless, markets will not clear, and other mechanisms such as authority or power are necessary to make markets work. The functioning of the economy depends on the mechanisms used to enforce trade and therefore on the society's political and legal institutions. This provides an additional avenue whereby the political system affects the operation of the economic system and shows the flaw in the "Washington consensus" in which the nature of the political system plays no role. It also, in my view, explains the success of the capitalist–authoritarian system. However, in this way of thinking, the system is not successful because it *resists* redistribution, but because it redistributes power and property rights, and therefore income, to those who benefit most from growth-oriented policies.

2   Dictatorship, democracy, and redistribution

This section is devoted to a general comparison of the redistributive tendencies of democratic governments versus dictatorships. Although I do not present a formal proof, I develop and defend a simple proposition: *Dictatorships tend to redistribute income more than democracies do.* If the analysis is correct, it obviously casts doubt on the proposition that democracies are less efficient than dictatorships because they are more capable of resisting demands for redistribution. There could be other reasons for the superior performance of some dictatorships, which I discuss briefly in the concluding section. But, as discussed in Section 1, redistribution is the most common argument in the literature and therefore worth examining in some detail at a theoretical level, something that has not been done heretofore.

I conduct the analysis with reference to the standard economic theory of monopoly. In that model it is assumed that a monopoly takes over a competitive industry and that the cost curves of the firms, which now become the monopolist's plants, are unchanged. Here, I assume that a dictator "takes over" a democratic government and that this change does not affect the preferences of the people for public goods or public policies. To illustrate, I assume that if a left-wing dictator takes over, the preferences of the population do not shift either right or left simply because a democratic government has been replaced by a dictatorship. To be sure, some right-wing citizens shift left in order to obtain favors from the dictator or to avoid repression. Such changes are endogenous to the analysis. What I am ruling out by assumption is shifts in the preferences of the population in the absence of any change in public policies on the part of the government or any change in the distribution of the benefits and burdens of the state. Note that if this assumption was dropped, it is not obvious what would happen: One can make a case that some citizens would oppose the policies of the dictator, even if they are the same as the policies of the previous democratic government, simply because the regime is a dictatorship. But others can be expected to shift in the opposite direction.[5] So I will simply assume in what follows that shifts in support or opposition are undertaken in respect to changes in government policy and not to the existence of dictatorship per se.

Another issue that arises in conducting an analysis like this is the standard of comparison. If dictatorships are to be said to redistribute more than democracies do, the obvious question is Compared to what? The obvious standard of comparison is the free-market distribution of income, but this concept is itself ambiguous. It cannot be equated with what the distribution of income would look like in the absence of government, because in the absence of government, property rights would not exist, and the free-market distribution of income is that which would obtain through relying on purely private methods of enforcement and not on public enforcement of property rights or contracts.

One approach to this problem is to designate the "benchmark" case with the distribution of income that would prevail under the minimal government obtaining under a constitution where the provisions of that constitution are those that would be agreed to by the citizenry operating under a unanimity rule at the constitutional choice stage. In that case, even in the free-market or benchmark case, there would be redistribution of income for charity purposes of the Pareto optimal variety. But there would also be redistribution to the extent that the public provision of defense, police protection, protection of contracts, and other public goods would tend to favor one group or another. One good

---

[5] See Wintrobe (1997, Chapter 2) for a discussion of a related problem, that is, whether the increased use of repression by a dictator generates more or less loyalty on the part of the population.

definition of minimal government along these lines might be that provided by Buchanan (1975) in his *The Limits of Liberty.*

Fortunately, I will largely be able to avoid this problem in what follows because the argument proceeds essentially by taking existing models of the level of redistribution under democracy and then showing that, in a well-defined sense, the amount of redistribution in the model of dictatorship is larger than this. Specifically, suppose that, under the benchmark free-market case, the distribution of income is given by $x_1, \ldots, x_n$. Now suppose we assume a normal (not necessarily minimal) democratic government and ask what happens to this distribution. Of course, what happens depends on the model of democracy used, and there is at present no common agreement on the effect of democratic government on the distribution of income. In the standard, median-voter model, there is no solution to this problem, because, under majority rule, no majority coalition is dominant and the outcome simply cycles among the alternatives available. There are, however, other models that do obtain determinant results: Meltzer and Richard's (1981) model, in which income is redistributed from the mean to the median (in terms of income) voter; Becker's (1983) model of interest group pressure; and the probabilistic voting model of Coughlin (1986) and others. We will consider all three of these models. Each of them can be thought of as producing a vector of incomes $y_1, \ldots, y_n$.

The next step is to impose a dictatorship and see what happens to the distribution of income. Call the resulting distribution of income $z_1, \ldots, z_n$. Our central proposition is that the distribution of income under dictatorship $z_1, \ldots, z_n$ is "further away" from the benchmark free-market cases $x_1, \ldots, x_n$ than the distribution of income under any of the three models of democracy $y_1, \ldots, y_n$. Alternatively, and more formally, the proposition is that dictatorship is characterized by more redistributive "activity," that is,

$$\sum_{i=1}^{n}(z_i - x_i)^2 > \sum_{i=1}^{n}(y_i - x_i)^2 \tag{1}$$

Why would this be so? Before proceeding to a more formal analysis, let us consider a couple of reasons why we should expect this result. The first has to do with the origins of dictatorship. As discussed elsewhere, the simplest explanation for the rise of dictatorship is that in societies with polarized preferences, or low trust between the citizens and the parties, or where there is no willingness to compromise, there are really only two possibilities: Either the party that gains office in democratic voting tries to implement its preferred position, in which case large social conflict will ensue, or the society will be simply paralyzed by inaction. The "allure" of dictatorship under these circumstances is obvious; either the left or the right, if it takes power by force, will be able to eliminate its opposition through repression and in this way be able to implement its program.

Either alternative implies a massive redistribution of income compared to that typical under democracy.

A second explanation of the redistributive tendencies of dictatorship is implicit in Przeworski's (1991) analysis of "self-enforcing" democracy. Przeworski suggests that for democracy to be stable, it must be self-enforcing, and for that to be true, the competitive political process cannot result in outcomes highly adverse to any major group's interest. If it did, it would benefit that group to subvert democracy rather than support it. The dictator faces no such constraint.

A third line of thought concerns the rent-seeking process. To elaborate the process, we first have to discuss a serious flaw in the standard model of rent-seeking. Explaining this flaw will illustrate some of the ways in which the distribution of rents differs between democracies and dictatorships. In the standard model, citizens and interest groups compete for rents through "wasteful" activities such as lobbying, hiring lawyers, and so on. Thus in the case of a $10,000 "prize," with 10 groups competing, each of which has an equal chance of getting the rent, the expected value of the rent to each competitor is $1,000. If the competitors are risk neutral, each of them will waste up to $1,000 attempting to obtain the prize. The problem with this model is that the process is irrational *from the point of view of politicians.* They give out a monopoly rent worth $10,000 and receive nothing in return. A rational politician would organize the process differently. For example, she would suggest to the competitors that they should offer cash payments instead of wasting the time of politicians through their lobbying activities. (It is essential to the model that it makes no difference which of the competitors gets the prize; hence the lobbying activity is pure waste to the politicians as well as to society.) But if bribes instead of lobbying are used, the $10,000 that is received in bribes by the politicians is not waste, but a pure transfer to politicians from interest groups, which represents no *social* waste or deadweight loss at all.

To see some other ways in which the rent-seeking process can be organized consider what typically happens under dictatorship. Dictators, at least of the more "successful" (i.e., relatively long-lived) variety, often know how to organize things so that they get a substantial return out of the process of rent-seeking. Indeed, under many regimes the distribution of rents reached legendary proportions. Examples would include the Marcos regime in the Philippines [for details see Hutchcroft (1991), or for a more extensive treatment, Wurfel (1988)], Ghana (see Herbst, 1993), and the military regimes in Latin America in the 1970s and elsewhere, whose most concrete and lasting achievement has been to increase military salaries and the military budget (Nordlinger, 1977; Remmer, 1989). As I have suggested elsewhere (Wintrobe, 1990, 1997) and briefly alluded to above, the simplest explanation for the legendary "shortages" characteristic of Soviet-type systems is that the shortages create rents, the distribution of which is controlled by the Communist Party and that can therefore be used to garner political support. The South African system of apartheid provided job reservation for white workers and the institution of the pass for the benefit of white capitalists (black workers in the white manufacturing sector could only remain in that sector with a "pass." A black worker who lost his job lost the right to work in the white sector. So the system lowered black wages in the white sector). Finally, the creation and distribution of rents on ethnic grounds in a dictatorship like Nazi Germany can be mentioned simply to complete the list. One example will suffice: that of the medical profession, whose membership was disproportionately Nazi. German doctors and medical officials took the lead (i.e., they did not wait for "orders" from senior party officials) in expelling Jewish doctors from the profession and taking over their practices (see Kater, 1983). One might think that, as highly educated professionals, they could be expected to oppose the use of such nonsensical criteria as blood, skull type, etc., as indices of human worth. Instead, they largely took the attitude that they were experts on such matters, and if they were to be the basis for regime policy, they wanted to be in the forefront of policy implementation.[6]

In all of these systems, resources are not wasted bidding for the rents of the public sector. Rents are given out, and the dictator receives political support or money payments or other things (cash for the ex-president of Korea, young girls for Mao-Tse Tung) in return. In other words, there is *no waste*, in the economic sense. One explanation for the difference in the way rents are distributed under dictatorship versus under democracy is that dictators typically impose restrictions on entry into competition for the rents given out by the state. Sometimes the rents are reserved for specific groups, as is obviously clear from the examples we have been referring to: the Chicago Boys under Pinochet were not interested in the pleas of the old populist urban coalition (Constable and Valenzuela, 1991). Blacks were obviously restricted from competing with whites in South Africa: The job reservation system could obviously not have been converted into a program for overpaying blacks if they bid hard enough. Gypsies, homosexuals, Jews, and communists could not have gained ethnic preferences under the Nazis; these parties were the victims of the regimes' repression, and, even if they might offer more, were simply not allowed to compete for rents.

In part, the reason for this is obvious: If free competition for rents is allowed, and support depends on receiving net benefits from the state, then, because rent-seeking results in net *losses*, dictators would lose support by distributing rents through an openly competitive process!

How does democracy differ? Restrictions on entry into bidding processes for rights and privileges, goods, and services distributed by the state, which are characteristic of authoritarian governments, are clearly inconsistent with the

---

[6] I owe this point to a private conversation with Michael Kater.

very notion of democracy. A typical democracy will impose conditions like the following in any process of allocating public resources:

(1)   No restrictions are imposed on who can bid, except of a technical nature.
(2)   The winning bid should be selected on the basis of criteria involving net benefit to the public such as the worth of the project, costs, etc., and not on the political connections, race, ethnicity, status, and so on of the bidders.
(3)   The process of bidding should be as open as possible and be open to review by an independent judiciary.

The inefficiency of democracy, according to the rent-seeking model, is now exposed. All of these conditions imply that more resources will be wasted under the bidding process in democracy. In short, *democracy is a much more wasteful system than dictatorship.*

The problem with the theory is that losses from pure rent-seeking implies that there are gains from trade between politicians and rent seekers. To the extent that trade between these groups takes place (through bribery, corruption, extortion, etc.), the waste in the process will be eliminated. Consequently, if transaction costs between these groups are low, the equilibrium will not be as described in the rent-seeking model, but instead will be the "corruption" equilibrium with no waste but with a defrauded public. On the other hand, suppose that these transactions are prevented, because the rules against influence peddling, bribery, and extortion (the existence of which are characteristic of democracy everywhere) are well-enforced by alert and powerful independent authorities. This gives a second possible equilibrium, in which fair competition among bidders is enforced. If this bidding results in rents being distributed to those who bid the lowest or who offer the public the most in the way of benefits, then this process produces something useful. The natural name to give this equilibrium is "strong democracy."

The rent-seeking model rules out this outcome by assuming that it makes no difference who wins the contest and that no social benefits result from the bidding process. Combining these assumptions with the assumption that the rules against corruption and the enforcement of them are so powerful that corruption is eliminated gives a third possible equilibrium: waste. A more appropriate name for this equilibrium is "irrational" because it implies that political institutions are fundamentally irrational in design: They are there to ensure the persistence of waste. As the Coase theorem implies, one should be skeptical of such equilibria.

At this point, the reader may be tempted to ask, What difference does it make? Suppose that the losses from rent-seeking are not genuine waste in the economic sense, but "merely" unauthorized (in effect, fraudulent) transfers to politicians and bureaucrats. It is true that these are not waste in the sense of economic theory, but they are certainly not what the cost – benefit analysis promised! If the proper equilibrium involves corruption, not rent-seeking, isn't that bad enough?

One reason for insisting on the distinction between corruption and rent-seeking is that the solutions to these two problems can be vastly different. In particular, it is easy to imagine that a "little bit of authoritarianism" might possibly reduce rent-seeking (which after all is a form of political competition). It is much more difficult to believe that autocracy is the solution to corruption. Under autocracy, there are fewer or no constraints on the practice of rent distribution by independent courts or an inquisitory free press; political dictatorships have a significantly larger capacity to organize the distribution of rents in order to maximize their own "take" in the case of bribes or to generate the most political support. Moreover, the dictator is capable of sanctioning nonrepayment directly, solving the enforcement problem that is inherent in rent-seeking trades in a way that no democracy is capable of. In addition, as I have suggested elsewhere, the dictator lacks the alternative ways of creating trust or support characteristic of democracy. The distribution of rents in exchange for loyalty is therefore her major avenue for developing political support or trust.

This reasoning relies on the capacity of dictators to *repress* the political or economic rights of its citizenry as the key to its redistributive tendency. And indeed, the most common definition of dictatorship in the literature of political science essentially distinguishes dictatorship from democracy on this ground. In this third line of analysis we will hold to this definition but pursue the analysis in a bit more depth by looking at models of redistribution under democracy. As announced in Section 1, I ask a straightforward question: On theoretical grounds, which type of regime can be expected to engage in more redistribution – democracy or dictatorship? I proceed by examining the equilibrium level of redistribution in a number of well-known models of democracy: that of Meltzer and Richard (1981), in which redistribution takes place from the mean to the median income voter; Becker's (1983) interest group model; and the probabilistic voting model of Coughlin et al. (1990). I then ask what would happen to the level of redistribution if a dictator took over the government. The analysis suggests that, in all these cases, we would expect more redistribution under dictatorship than democracy.

The simplest model of political redistribution under democracy is probably Becker's (1983) model of competition among interest groups. Most of the analysis is conducted with just two homogeneous groups, s and t, who engage in political activity in order to raise the incomes of their members. Both groups produce political "pressure," and in equilibrium, group s receives a subsidy financed by taxes on group t. The size of the tax and subsidy is determined by deadweight losses (which rise as the tax or subsidy rises) and by the fact that the "loser" in the political game (the taxed group t) need not passively accept his losses but can limit them through lobbying, threats, disobedience, migration, and other kinds of political pressure. However, no model of the political system is presented; rather, the analysis is explicitly intended to apply to many different kinds of political systems including dictatorship (Becker, 1983, p. 375).

Suppose, however, that the equilibrium described by Becker corresponds to that under democracy. How would it change if this democracy were taken over by a dictatorship? There are two main forces that would affect the outcome. The first is that the dictator has the power to repress opposition to his policies; the second is that the dictator is more insecure about his political support, because, as discussed in the previous section, among other things, the overt proffering of support from those over which he has power is necessarily less reliable than offers of support to a democratic politician. If the preferences and constellation of power relations between the two groups is unchanged (the analysis would be unchanged if many groups were assumed), the most reasonable assumption to make is that the dictator achieves power with the support of the subsidized group. The dictator, however, has the power, which was unavailable to a democratic politician, to directly repress pressure by the taxed group by banning their political organizations, refusing to permit their views to appear in the media, refusing to allow them to meet or organize, and jailing, torturing, or even executing their leaders. Moreover, the dictator either maximizes power or consumption, subject to the power constraint. In either case, repressing the opposition is obviously beneficial to him. In terms of Becker's analysis, the effect of political repression is the same as if the taxed group experienced a reduction in its capacity to produce pressure, as described in Becker's Proposition 1. The result is an increase in the size of the subsidy to group s and an increase in the tax on group t, that is, more redistribution than in the democratic case.

This conclusion seems straightforward and obvious enough and is derived solely on the assumption that the dictator has an interest in power and possesses an instrument – the capacity for political repression – that is unavailable to a democratic politician. If, in addition, we were to consider the second characteristic of dictatorship discussed above – namely, his insecurity – this would only reinforce the conclusion just obtained. The dictator will want to increase the size of the subsidy to the winners of the political game in order to guarantee their loyalty. To put it differently, repressing the opposition would appear to raise the probability of the dictator's survival in office, as would the distribution of extra rents to keep her supporters loyal. Again, therefore, more redistribution (larger taxes on the losers and bigger subsidies to the winners) is to be expected.

A second, widely used model of redistribution is that developed by Meltzer and Richard (1981). In that model, the decisive voter in a democracy is the median voter, and so long as her income is less than the mean income, there is redistribution from the (more productive) rich to the (less productive) poor and middle-income voters. In one sense, the model is already a model of dictatorship because the tax rate is chosen by a "decisive voter" who, under democracy, is taken to be the median voter. The tax rate in turn determines the level of redistribution. If, on the other hand, the decisive voter was poor, he would choose a higher tax rate, resulting in more redistribution; but if rich he would choose a lower one, resulting in less redistribution.

However, the model simply does not allow for any mechanism by which re-distribution can be effected from the poor. Thus none of the strategies discussed in Stigler's (1970) famous paper on Director's law, which alleged that redis-tribution in a democracy was typically from both the rich and the poor to the middle classes, and included such practices as tax exemptions, minimum-wage laws, farm policy, regulation, licensing practices, and so on, can be introduced into the model, in which redistribution is financed by a single tax rate that ap-plies equally to everyone. Nor can any of the practices used by dictators who have drastically redistributed from the poor to the rich, such as land alienation (widely practiced by colonial regimes in Africa on the endogenous black popu-lation); labor regulations (such as the South African system of job reservation, in which certain jobs are reserved for whites); the pass system, by which black workers who lost their job in the white sector were "deported" to the homelands; or the ingenious schemes of Papa Doc Duvalier, who at one time "sold" workers to the neighboring Dominican Republic, be discussed within this model. So the model is not very useful for our purposes. However, given these qualifications, a genuine dictatorship could be introduced into the model by empowering the "decisive voter" with the capacity to repress opposition. In that case, provided only that this permits higher taxation than is possible under democracy at any given level of productivity, the dictator in the model would presumably repress the rich, leading, again, to more redistribution, in this case from the rich to the poor and middle-income members of society.

The third widely used model of income redistribution under democratic governments is the probabilistic voting model. In simplified form (Mueller, 1989), there are two candidates, each of which maximizes expected votes. Let P_{1i} equal the probability that voter i will vote for Party 1, and consider a pure redistribution problem in which the government is faced simply with the problem of distribution $\$X$ among the n voters. Each party's "platform" is then simply a proposed allocation of the $\$X$ among the n voters. So each party maximizes

$$\left[\sum_i P_{1i} = \sum_i f_i(U_i(x_{1i}) - U_i(x_{2i})) \right] + \lambda \left[X - \sum_i x_{1i} \right] \qquad (2)$$

Because Party 2 maximizes its expected vote total as well, the two parties propose a common platform, the equilibrium condition for which is

$$f_i' U_i' = f_j' U_j' \tag{3}$$

so in democratic equilibrium, each party maximizes a weighted sum of voters' utilities, where a voter's "weight" (and therefore the sum allocated to that voter) is proportional to her "responsiveness" (f_i) to an increase in $U_{1i} - U_{2i}$. In a sense, then, the more "disloyal" the voter to either party, the more that voter will receive as the result of democratic political competition.

This conclusion makes sense if voters are sensitive or responsive to changes in the utilities promised by the parties for nonpolicy reasons, that is, if a voter is a Democrat because his parents were Democrats, and he doesn't care about the policies of the Democratic party but cares about pleasing his parents. Voters like that can be "exploited" by politicians by actually giving them less than they would get if they were less loyal to the Democratic party. However, if the reason a Democratic voter will not easily switch to the Republican side is because the voter is relying on the reputation of the Democratic party to take care of him and others like him by giving him a disproportionate share of the spoils, then the party that attempts this strategy of exploitation will lose its reputation. Indeed, voters who would be tempted to be loyal to a particular party will anticipate that the parties will take advantage of them in this way, that is, they will realize that loyalty does not pay and will refuse to extend it. So the political strategy unravels.

An analogy may be drawn to the family (dictators often refer to themselves, and like to be referred to, as "fathers" of their people). Suppose a nuclear family with two children, one of whom is "loyal" to the family in the sense that he follows the approved norms of family behavior – dates the right girls, does his homework, doesn't smoke, is nice to his relatives, believes in the family religion, goes to church socials, etc. The other is disloyal in the sense that he does none of these things. The parents who decide to cope with this situation in the manner suggested by the probabilistic voting model would do so by buying better clothes for the disloyal child, giving him a nicer car, a bigger allowance, and so on in the hope of bringing the child to his senses. The likely effect would be to alienate the loyal child, and the parents would probably simply end up with generalized disloyalty ("rotten" kids). Of course, "caring" within the family disturbs the analogy to dictatorship, but if caring within the family were sufficient, presumably these problems wouldn't arise. In the absence of sufficient caring, presumably the parents will respond to the situation by using authority (repression) – orders or rules backed by sanctions – to control the disloyal child. Of course, dictators can use this instrument as well.

Coughlin et al. (1990) develop a model of interest group influence on democratic government that solves this problem in a different way. In the model each member of an interest group has a (nonpolicy) bias b_{ij}. If $b_{ij} > 0$, this implies a positive bias in favor of the government. The b_{ij} are not known to the government or the opposition, but are represented by a random variable distributed uniformly over the interval (ℓ_i, r_i) with density a_i. Candidates are assumed to know the distribution of bias terms, but not their individual values. So although they cannot know with certainty how a given individual will vote, they can predict that they will pick up a greater fraction of an interest group's vote, the greater the difference in the utility their platform promises the representative interest group member over that of their opponent. In our terms, this gives candidates an incentive to distribute rents to interest groups. Now f_i' can be interpreted as the probability of winning the vote of a member of interest group i. The greater the density of the distribution a_i the larger f_i' is and the more that interest group will receive from both the government and opposition in equilibrium.

Consequently, interest group influence is negatively related to the dispersion of the bias terms, that is, to the degree of uncertainty on the part of politicians about the preferences of the members of the interest group. In equilibrium, democratic politicians act as if they maximized a weighted sum of voters' utilities, where the weights are positively related to interest group influence, that is, negatively related to the dispersion of the bias terms.

Now suppose that a dictator takes over this democratic polity, as before. The dictator can be presumed to face some opposition and to be able to win support from interest groups to the extent that he can "credibly" promise more than the opposition. Assume that the distribution of the bias terms is unchanged, as before. The dictator is unlike a democratic politician in two main respects: (1) He has the power to repress opposition to his policies; and (2) he does not and is not driven by competition to maximize expected "votes" (support). Is there a way that the dictator can improve on the democratic equilibrium; that is, is there a way that funds can be reallocated among the citizens in such a way as to increase the dictator's power? It seems clear that he can, although a precise description of the optimal strategy is difficult. From his point of view, there are two dimensions along which the voters can be ordered: in terms of the size of their f', and in terms of the size of their b_{ij}. Thus imagine that the dictator is sitting at a table, and in front of him he has a list of the interest groups under his control, to each of which is attached estimates of that group's f_i' and b_{ij} (prepared by a consulting firm). The dictator wants to order these groups for the purpose of deciding whom to repress, and to whom to distribute rents so as to buy their loyalty. The problem he faces is that the ordering produced by the f' is not the same as the ordering produced by the b_{ij}. For example, some of those groups with low f' support the dictator (high, positive b_{ij}) whereas others favor the opposition (negative b_{ij}).

However, some decisions are easy to make. Those who rank low on the f' scale and who are opposed to his policies (negative bias) are obvious candidates for repression. They oppose him, and they cannot easily be turned around with the kind of rents he is prepared to distribute (low f'). So long as repression is not too expensive, the dictator can gain power by silencing these people. This also makes it easy to subject them to taxation and regulation. These funds can then be redistributed in the form of rents to those whose loyalty can be purchased more easily or assuredly, namely, those with high f'. They *can* be bought, and it is better to make sure they remain so by giving them more than they received under democracy. Through these gifts, the dictator again accumulates more power. Finally, those groups with low f' and positive bias will not be repressed (they support him, on the average) but need not be showered with gifts, because a low f' implies that the expected increase in loyalty from so doing is not large.

Of course, other factors besides those considered in this simple model might be relevant in determining the dictator's optimal choices, such as the nature of the regime's ideology or the degree of ideological "connectedness" among different groups.[7] If we ignore these and assume only two groups, the "winners" (high f') and "losers" (low f' and negative bias) in the analysis above, then it is clear that the benefits and burdens of the public sector will be distributed more unequally among these groups under dictatorship than democracy. Thus, letting a_i represent the weights on the utilities of different groups in the dictator's social welfare function, or in the social welfare function implicitly maximized in the probabilistic voting model of democracy, and specifying group 1 (high f') as the taxed group, the analysis implies

$$a_1^z < a_1^y \tag{4}$$

and if group 2 is the favored group (low f' and negative bias),

$$a_2^z > a_2^y \tag{5}$$

Proposition (1) above – that dictatorships tend to redistribute more than democracies – follows directly.

3   Redistribution in capitalist authoritarian states

So far in this paper I have argued that one popular explanation for the success of many developing countries with authoritarian political systems such as South Korea or Singapore – namely, that the authoritarian governments there redistribute less or are less subject to inefficiencies caused by rent-seeking than democracies – is misguided. I have tried to show, on the contrary, that *all* dictators can be expected to redistribute more than democracies do. As far as the facts are concerned, I know of no systematic evidence on this question, but it is well known that there is massive redistribution in totalitarian dictatorships

---

[7] Axelrod (1984, ch. 4) finds "minimum connected winning coalition" to be superior to the minimum winning coalition concept in explaining coalition formation in democratic politics.

and that most left-wing dictatorships tend to be redistributive in nature. It might appear more controversial to contend that the analysis applies also to "capitalist authoritarian" dictatorships, but I have no hesitation in suggesting that it applies to these countries as well. The point has been missed, in my view, because of the "fallacy of the free market," that is, the common assumption in this literature that markets operate costlessly, so that to have free markets, it is only necessary for the government to get out of the way. Once the central point of the efficiency wage literature is grasped, that power relationships are central to competitive market behavior, then it is clear that how markets work depends on how property rights are specified and enforced.

Dictatorships such as Pinochet's Chile or South Korea under Park essentially redistribute through shifting the property rights of labor to management backed by the state, raising the cost of job loss to workers, removing or not allowing collective bargaining rights, and in other ways by generating a labor force willing to work for low wages. Thus Dornbusch and Park (1987), examining the success of Korea, argued the "central point" that "Korean wages are exceptionally low by international standards, given the skill level of the labor force. . . ."[8] Pinochet at first banned unions and union activity and then severely restricted their freedom of action with the labor code promulgated in 1979 (the first of his "Seven Modernizations"). Related reforms in health care, social security, and other areas all had the effect of raising the cost of job loss to workers. When democratic government was restored, the area where it *did* make significant changes was to the labor code, and it did this shortly after it assumed office. Other measures redistributed more directly.[9] Moreover, political measures such as the widespread planting of spies in factories and the resulting "culture of fear" (Constable and Valenzuela, 1991, ch. 6) reenforced the rights of employers over workers at the same time as they linked them with the state. Of course, not *all* capitalists benefitted; small, domestically-oriented firms (part of the old, import-substitution coalition) were severely damaged through the removal of tariff and exchange-rate protection. The chief beneficiaries of the regime's policies were initially the large firms and the military.

The concentration of wealth produced is well known, and described in Oppenheim (1993, ch. 6). Edwards and Edwards (1987, pp. 167–168) give Gini coefficients that show significantly increased inequality over the period of the dictatorship until 1983, although they do quarrel with the significance that can be attached to these numbers. However, they do not dispute the increase in unemployment over the period and indeed provide evidence that this occurred partly as a result of the rationing of jobs in the *grupos* (large firms).

---

[8] Dornbusch and Park (1987, p. 391).

[9] For details, see Edwards and Edwards (1987), Oppenheim (1993), or Constable and Valenzuela (1991).

Although I do not have the space here to provide proper details, perhaps enough has been said to suggest that the economic success of "capitalist authoritarian" governments is not difficult to explain. It is not because they do not redistribute income, but because they *do* redistribute income – in particular, by adopting measures that transfer rights over the control of labor from labor to capital. Dictators whose support is based on capital (either domestic or international) have an obvious reason to be future oriented, because the future returns to capital are capitalized into its price, and an increased prospect of economic growth that raises those returns increases the wealth of capital owners in the present. Moreover, to the extent that these regimes successfully discipline labor, and attract capital investment, the marginal product of labor is raised, possibly bringing long-run increases in real wages as well [though as of 1990, real wages in Chile, for example, were not much above their 1970 levels (Bresser-Pereira, et al. 1993)]. This is not a complete explanation of the economic success of these countries, because many other elements (especially their export orientation) obviously enter the picture as well. But, insofar as the rent-seeking and redistributive elements of policy are concerned, this explanation strikes me as superior to the idea that their success is due to an absence of redistribution.

References

Amsden, A. 1989. *Asia's Next Giant: South Korea and Late Industrialization*, Oxford University Press, New York.

Axelrod, R. 1984. *The Evolution of Cooperation*, Basic Books, New York.

Bardhan, P. 1990. Symposium on the state and economic development, *Journal of Economic Perspectives*, **4**(3), 3–7.

Becker, G. 1983. A theory of competition among pressure groups for political influence, *Quarterly Journal of Economics*, **98**, 371–400.

Bresser Pereira, L. C., J. M. Maravall, and A. Przeworski. 1993. *Economic Reform in New Democracies: A Social Democratic Approach*, Cambridge University Press, Cambridge.

Buchanan, J. 1975. *The Limits of Liberty*, University of Chicago Press, Chicago.

Constable, P., and A. Valenzuela. 1991. *A Nation of Enemies: Chile Under Pinochet*. W. W. Norton and Co., New York.

Coughlin, P. 1986. Elections and income redistribution, *Public Choice*, **50**, 27–99.

Coughlin, P., D. Mueller, and P. Murrell. 1990. Electoral politics, interest groups and the size of government, *Economic Inquiry*, **28**, 682–705.

Dornbusch, R., and S. Edwards. 1990. The macroeconomics of populism in Latin America, *Journal of Development Economics*, **32**, 247–77.

Dornbusch, R., and Y. S. Park. 1987. Korean growth policy, *Brookings Papers on Economic Activity*, **2**, 389–454.

Edwards, S., and A. C. Edwards. 1987. *Monetarism and Liberalization: The Chilean Experiment*, Ballinger Publishing Co., Cambridge, Mass.

     1992. Markets and democracy: Lessons from Chile, *The World Economy*, **15**, 203–219.

Haggard, S. 1990. *Pathways from the Periphery: The Politics of Growth in the Newly Industrializing Countries*, Cornell University Press, Ithaca, N.Y.

Hawthorn, G. 1993. Liberalization and 'modern liberty': Four southern states, *World Development*, **21**, 1299–1312.

Herbst, J. 1993. *The Politics of Reform in Ghana, 1982–1991*, University of California Press, Berkeley.

Hutchcroft, P. D. 1991. Oligarchs and cronies in the Philippine state: The politics of patrimonial plunder, *World Politics*, **43**(3), 414–450.

Kater, M. 1983. *The Nazi Party: A Social Profile of Members and Leaders, 1919–1945*, Harvard University Press, Cambridge, Mass.

Krueger, A. O. 1974. The political economy of the rent-seeking society, *American Economic Review*, **64**, 291–303.

Meltzer, A. H., and S. F. Richard. 1981. A rational theory of the size of government, *Journal of Political Economy*, **89**, 914–927.

Mueller, D. 1989. *Public Choice II*, Cambridge University Press, New York.

Nordlinger, E. 1977. *Soldiers in Politics: Military Coups and Government*. Prentice-Hall, Englewood Cliffs.

O'Donnell, G. 1993. On the state, democratization and some conceptual problems: A Latin American view with glances at some post-communist countries, *World Development*, **21**, 1355–1369.

Olson, M. 1982. *The Rise and Decline of Nations*, Yale University Press, New Haven, Conn.

  1993. Dictatorship, democracy and development, *American Political Science Review*, **87**, 567–575.

Oppenheim, L. H. 1993. *Politics in Chile: Democracy, Authoritarianism and the Search for Development*, Westview Press, Boulder, Colorado.

Posner, R. A. 1975. The social costs of monopoly and regulation, *Journal of Political Economy*, **83**, 807–27.

Przeworski, A. 1991. *Democracy and the Market: Political and Economic Reforms in Eastern Europe and Latin America*, Cambridge University Press, New York.

Przeworski, A., and F. Limongi. 1993. Political regimes and economic growth, *Journal of Economic Perspectives*, **7**(3), 51–69.

Remmer, K. 1989. *Military Rule in Latin America*, Unwin-Hyman, Boston.

Rodrik, D. 1993. Trade and Industrial Policy Reform in Developing Countries: A Review of Recent Theory and Evidence, *Working Paper #4417*. National Bureau of Economic Research (NBER), Cambridge, Mass.

Stigler, G. 1970. Director's law of public income redistribution, *Journal of Law and Economics*, **13**, 1–10.

Tullock, G. 1967. The welfare cost of tariffs, monopolies, and theft, *Western Economic Journal*, **5**, 224–32.

  1981. *Autocracy*, Martinus Nijihoff, Dordrecht.

Wade, R., 1990. *Governing the Market: Economic Theory and the Role of Government in East Asian Industrialization*, Princeton University Press, Princeton, N.J.

Wintrobe, R. 1990. The tinpot and the totalitarian: An economic theory of dictatorship, *American Political Science Review*, **84**, 849–872.

  1997. *The Political Economy of Dictatorship*, Cambridge University Press, New York, in press.

Wurfel, D. 1988. *Filipino Politics: Development and Decay*, Cornell University Press, Ithaca, N.Y.

CHAPTER 7

Democratic governments, economic growth, and income distribution

Pierre Salmon

Il y avait déjà longtemps que le comte Mosca était de retour à Parme, comme premier ministre, plus puissant que jamais... Les prisons de Parme étaient vides, le comte immensément riche, Ernest V adoré de ses sujets qui comparaient son gouvernment à celui des grands-ducs de Toscane (Stendhal, 1839).

1   Introduction

That more inequality leads to more redistribution in democracies is an implication of Allan Meltzer and Scott Richard's (1981) well-known model.[1] That, in turn, more redistribution leads to less growth is a generally accepted proposition. That "inequality is harmful for growth" (title of Persson and Tabellini, 1994) is thus the predictable result of the introduction of policymaking à la Meltzer and Richard into the theory of growth. The small body of literature in which such an introduction has been attempted includes contributions by Alberto Alesina, Giuseppe Bertola, Roberto Perotti, Thornsten Persson, Dani Rodrik, Gilles Saint-Paul, Guido Tabellini, and Thierry Verdier. Short surveys are provided by Perotti (1992), Persson and Tabellini (1992b), and Verdier (1994). The proposition that inequality of income or wealth, measured at one point in time, has a negative influence on subsequent growth is derived by all these authors with the exception of Saint-Paul and Verdier (1993). Some empirical support for the proposition is displayed in Alesina and Rodrik (1992, 1994) and in Persson and Tabellini (1992a, 1994).

For these two pairs of contributors – and, with qualifications, in some of

In addition to the participants in the 6th Villa Colombella Seminar, especially Francesco Forte and Adam Przeworski, I am grateful to the participants in the Research Seminar of the Department of Political Economy of the Universita of Siena and in the Meetings of the European Public Choice Society for helpful comments on earlier versions of this text or parts of it.

[1]   For a critical discussion of Meltzer and Richard (1981), see, for instance, Mueller (1989), Brosio and Marchese (1993), and Winer and Rutherford (1993).

Alesina and Rodrik (1994)
Perotti (1993)
Persson and Tabellini (1994)
Saint-Paul and Verdier (1993)

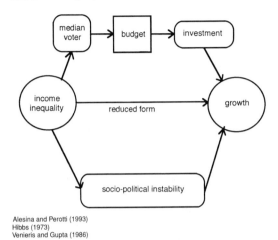

Alesina and Perotti (1993)
Hibbs (1973)
Venieris and Gupta (1986)

Figure 7.1. Models of the relation between inequality, voting, and growth.

the articles of the others (Bertola, 1993; Perotti, 1993) – the causality is the following: Inequality of income or wealth generates, through a political mechanism identical or analogous to the one proposed by Meltzer and Richard (1981), redistributive policies (e.g., taxes and transfers) that are unfavorable to investment (tangible investment and/or investment in human capital), and hence to economic growth (see Figure 7.1). In the simplest models (Persson and Tabellini, 1992a), collective policymaking consists of fixing the rate of a linear income tax and redistributing the proceeds of that tax equally to all individuals. The only issue is the tax rate, voter preferences are single peaked, and the median voter sets the policy according to his or her own cost-benefit calculation. This is modeled as the maximization of a utility function whose form ensures that the income distribution and consequently the identity of the median voter remain the same in the future.[2] The larger the difference between the median income and the average income, the higher the tax rate (i.e., larger

---

[2] There is thus something in the approach discussed here that reminds one of Tocqueville's famous distinction between the effects of equality and of the attempts to reduce inequality. Jon Elster (1991, p. 29) writes: "From a political perspective, the distinction between transitional effects and equilibrium effects is perhaps the central idea in *Democracy in America*. Tocqueville wanted his compatriots to understand the distinction between the often disruptive effects of equalization and the much less dangerous effects of equality." However, in the approach discussed in Section 1, redistributive policies do not, as a rule, produce more equality.

the transfer) that the median voter chooses. The higher the tax rate, the lower the after-tax return of individual investments and thus the level of aggregate investment. The lower the latter, the smaller the rate of growth. In the somewhat more complicated model of Alesina and Rodrik (1994), among other differences, the proceeds of taxes are used for the production of public goods favorable to growth as well as for transfers. But the basic logic remains the same: The net effect of taxes (and underlying that, of inequality) on investment is negative.

As noted, Alesina and Rodrik (1992, 1994) and Persson and Tabellini (1992a, 1994) present empirical work that, they argue, supports the predictions of their models. But whatever confirmation they can claim to find in the data only applies to the reduced-form relation between inequality at one point in time and subsequent growth. To say the least, the regressions do not confirm the intermediary relations that are necessary components of the causal chain spelled out above. Indeed, the findings reported in Perotti (1994) are that a more equal distribution of income leads to *more* (not less) transfers and that more transfers results in *more* (not less) investment.

Both Perotti (1994) and Thomas Piketty (1995) consider that this evidence casts serious doubts on the approach summarized above – especially because the negative relation between inequality and investment or growth can be explained by other factors or mechanisms than those borrowed from Meltzer and Richard.[3]

There is an additional reason not to claim too much for what has been achieved so far.[4] On the basis of empirical work, it is a moot point whether the nature of the political regime plays a role in the relationship. Is democracy an important variable or condition? Or, in spite of the models being inspired by

---

[3] See also Saint-Paul and Verdier (1996). One approach that does not bring us too far astray from the foregoing involves "sociopolitical instability" – a composite variable that is increased by inequality in the distribution of income and that negatively affects the rate of investment. Other approaches focus exclusively on nonpolitical variables or relationships such as demand or capital markets. For the sake of testability, Perotti (1994) interprets these various approaches as alternatives, but it is conceivable that they work together in the real world. As a consequence, even if the reduced-form, negative relation between inequality and growth is considered to be established, it is not compelling with regard to models or explanations that are avowedly partial or *ceteris paribus*. This applies, for example, to the minority position, so to say, of Saint-Paul and Verdier (1993). In their model also, following Meltzer and Richard, the median-income voter sets a tax rate, but the proceeds of the tax are used for public education instead of transfers. Public education is a form of investment and thus favorable to growth. As a consequence, greater income inequality tends to affect growth positively, contrary to what is argued by the other authors. That the data answers otherwise (it seems) would be a serious objection to Saint-Paul and Verdier's story only if it was posited as the whole story. As argued elsewhere (Mingat, Salmon, and Wolfelsperger, 1985; Salmon, 1994), contributions like Saint-Paul and Verdier's should be interpreted as implicit counterarguments (addressed to the suggestion that inequality is always, under democratic decision making, unfavorable to growth).

[4] To be fair, it must be stressed that all this work is relatively recent, with more in process (see references in Perotti, 1994; Verdier 1994; Saint-Paul and Verdier, 1996).

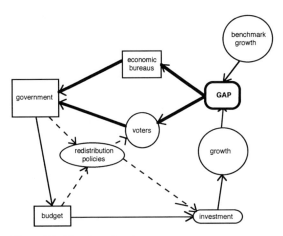

Figure 7.2. The alternative view.

Meltzer and Richard, is the reference to democracy included in the models merely convenient as an expository device? Persson and Tabellini (1992a, 1994), as well as Alesina and Rodrik (1992), find the democratic character of a country to be empirically significant, whereas Alesina and Rodrik (1994) no longer do, and thus argue that the reference to it in their theoretical reasoning should not be interpreted literally.

If it is clear to all that we are still at an early stage of reflection on the relationship between inequality and growth and about how political variables, and especially the democratic nature of the political regime, might play a role in it, this has a pleasant consequence. It allows us to explore new possibilities or lines of research in as informal and unempirical a way as we wish, provided we do not claim too much for what such explorations or speculations may lead to.

In the remainder of this essay I will indulge in such speculation and develop an argument whose starting point is that growth, especially relative growth, often enters directly as an argument in the preference functions of voters. More exactly, I will argue that voters become concerned with economic growth when they perceive it to be, or fear it to become, abnormally low in their country. This may very well lead, depending on the circumstances, to redistributive concerns (among others) being subordinated to the single policy objective of fostering growth. However, in this story, there will be considerable variation across countries. This variation will be related to differences in the sensitivity of public opinion to growth comparisons and in the nature of the political regime. We will in particular consider whether democracy is likely to be a significant variable in the cross-section explanation of growth. Figure 7.2 provides a first view of this alternative hypothesis.

2   From insufficient growth to discontent: Similarity and variation across countries

With the magnitude of growth rates experienced since the beginning of the 19th century in an increasing number of countries, economic growth has become, almost "objectively," of the utmost importance – arguably more important than any other economic or social issue except extreme deprivation or poverty (noneconomic issues such as peace or freedom are another matter). One reason for this "quasi-objective" importance, in a world whose economy is generally growing, is that, for a given country, to experience no growth or only a rate of growth much smaller than that of otherwise similar countries, means falling behind these other countries rapidly – not at all the same situation as if growth were slow or nonexistent everywhere.

A comparison of the first two columns of Table 7.1 shows what growth has done to income per head in a number of countries over a period of time as short as forty-three years. In 1870, the income per head of Spain was quite respectable, close to the income per head of Germany, higher than that of Finland, Norway, or Sweden, and about two thirds of the income per head of the United States, already one of the highest.[5] Forty-three years later, income per head in Spain was about half the income per head of France and Germany and about one-third of the income per head of the United States. Spain was not part of the first world anymore, if I may venture to use this anachronism.[6] By 1979 (see Table 7.1), one can say that Spain had recovered its place in the first world, whereas Portugal, Argentina and Chile – also part of the first world in 1870 – had not.

It is unlikely that the public in Spain realized what was happening. No statistics for rates of growth were available, and economics was not in the news or in the minds of people to the extent that it is now. That this situation has changed profoundly is clear from everyday experience. According to *The Economist* (August 13, 1994, p. 52), in countries such as Malaysia, Singapore, or Indonesia, "the latest GDP figures invariably get banner headlines." In these countries, the article goes on, "like shareholders in a rising market, the locals like to monitor their countries' ascent up the world GDP league table." I do not claim that our locals, in Europe or North America, are similarly obsessed with growth rates. Unemployment or inflation probably get more attention. But differences in growth have cumulative effects (arguably more so than inflation). What happened to the Spanish economy between 1870 and 1913 may have

---

[5] Calculations of this kind are obviously precarious. But the enviable position occupied by Spain around 1870 is not a statistical aberration. As explained by Bradford De Long (1988, p. 1,142), it is confirmed by other indicators (for instance, about 4,000 miles of railroad built by 1877).

[6] I borrow the expression from Carlos Diaz-Alejandro (cited by De Long, p. 1,142), who was referring in fact to what happened to Argentina at a later date.

Table 7.1. *Per capita income estimates in 1975 dollars*

	1870	1913	1979
Argentina	762	1,450	3,119
Chile	519	1,156	2,337
Finland	506	1,053	5,640
France	847	1,658	6,705
Germany (West)	731	1,562	6,789
Norway	665	1,162	6,475
Portugal	637	725	2,845
Spain	728	854	4,246
Sweden	557	1,336	6,594
United States	1,038	2,462	8,205

Source: Selected from Table A4 of De Long (1988, p. 1152). All estimates of 1979 per capita income are taken by De Long from Summers and Heston (1984). For most countries, the estimates for 1870 and for 1913 are calculated from these 1979 estimates and from estimates of annual growth provided by Maddison (1982). The way De Long estimates the income per capita in 1870 and 1913 of Argentina, Chile, Portugal, and Spain is explained in the appendix of his article (pp. 1148–52).

remained unnoticed at the time. I submit that an evolution of much smaller amplitude would not remain so today.[7]

On the basis of the figures of Table 7.1, everybody would agree, I think, that the Spanish economy did badly between 1870 and 1914, but this is an easy case. In most other cases, things are not so clear. I make, nonetheless, the assumption that experts can determine, and even measure "growth performance gaps," thanks to comparisons with what obtains in comparable countries or by more sophisticated means. That such an assumption is unrealistic is clear. But to what degree? An example of the capacity that I have in mind is the interesting article of Steve Dowrick and Duc-Tho Nguyen (1989) from which I derived Table 7.2. The authors start for each period from the OECD average growth rate of per capita GDP and indicate how each country deviates from

---

[7] It should be stressed that, contrary to the assumption made in Meltzer and Richard's model and in the models that borrow their structure from it, the foregoing discussion about what people may be concerned with is based on the assumption that their policy preferences and evaluations are of a "sociotropic" rather than "pocketbook" kind (Lewis-Beck, 1985). According to Martin Paldam (1991, p. 14), "there seems to be a fairly general agreement ... that what people react to is their perception of the general economic conditions, and not their own economic grievances" [the classical reference on this matter is Kinder and Kiewiet (1979)]. The reasons that voters may have to behave as Paldam and others claim they do may involve some altruism. But a high level of uncertainty about the idiosyncratic effects of policies may do just as well.

Pierre Salmon

Table 7.2. *Relative growth rates of per capita GDP (1950–85) Adjusted (and unadjusted) deviations from OECD average*

	1950–60	1960–73	1973–85
OECD average	*3.12*	*3.95*	*1.55*
Canada	− 0.96 (− 1.86)	+ 0.65 (− 0.13)	+ 0.64 (− 0.03)
France	+ 0.48 (+ 0.42)	+ 1.08 (+ 0.68)	+ 0.42 (− 0.08)
Germany	+ 3.15 (+ 3.64)	+ 0.10 (− 0.36)	+ 0.93 (+ 0.36)
Ireland	− 1.95 (− 1.06)	− 0.95 (− 0.21)	− 1.09 (− 0.26)
Italy	+ 1.29 (+ 2.05)	− 0.23 (+ 0.21)	− 0.45 (+ 0.06)
Japan	+ 2.17 (+ 4.14)	+ 3.34 (+ 4.50)	+ 0.98 (+ 1.24)
Switzerland	+ 1.28 (+ 0.39)	− 0.32 (− 1.05)	− 0.54 (− 0.98)
United Kingdom	− 0.41 (− 0.85)	− 1.17 (− 1.42)	− 0.52 (− 0.42)
United States	− 0.26 (− 1.79)	+ 0.02 (− 1.15)	+ 0.61 (− 0.28)

Source: Selected from Table 6 of Dowrick and Nguyen (1989, pp. 1026–27). The numbers in parentheses are the unadjusted deviations. An example of the calculation: For the period 1950–60, the average annual per capita GDP growth in the OECD countries is 3.12 percent; with regard to that, the deviation of the average GDP growth per capita of the United States is equal to −1.79 percent. To that (negative) figure, 0.22 is subtracted for "cyclical bias" and 1.75 is added for "catch-up" (or, rather, the absence thereof). As a result of these corrections, the adjusted deviation is equal to −0.26. For the periods 1960–73 and 1973–85, the same kind of calculation yields, for the United States, an adjusted deviation that is equal to zero and is positive, respectively.

that average (the numbers in parentheses in Table 7.2). If there is a tendency for countries to converge (see Sala-i-Martin, 1994), and thus for countries that have a lower productivity to catch up, countries such as Canada, the United States, or Switzerland, which have a high productivity at the beginning of the period, should not be expected to grow over that period as fast as countries that start with a much lower productivity level, such as Ireland, Italy, or Japan, hence the adjusted deviations presented in Table 7.2. By idealizing somewhat from that example, I will assume that experts can say when the relative performance of a country with regard to economic growth is negative and measure the corresponding gap.

This growth performance gap, deemed "objective," is measured on the horizontal axis of Figure 7.3. I assume now that objective gaps cause discontent among voters and/or in public opinion and that for a given country, the larger the gap, the higher the level of discontent. This is a reduced-form relation, whose strength and shape depend on two sets of underlying forces. A first set, pertaining to information, concerns the way objective gaps translate into perceived gaps. We do not have to specify how this works to predict the outcome:

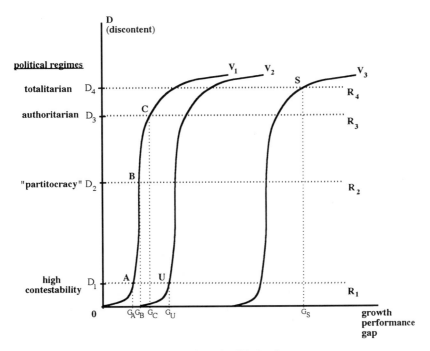

Figure 7.3. Growth gap sensitivity and political regimes.

The larger the objective gap, the more (in a given country) it is perceived by voters and/or in public opinion. The second set relates to how a perceived gap causes discontent to build up. Again, we can safely assume that the outcome is unambiguous. For a given country, the larger the perceived gap, the larger the level of discontent.

In Figure 7.3, where discontent (D) is measured along the vertical axis, the overall (reduced-form) relation for a given country is an S-curve, as illustrated by curve V_1. In the case of this particular curve, the two underlying mechanisms operate with maximum vigor. Some sectors of opinion perceive the performance gap as soon as it appears, and even a small perceived gap creates some discontent. Then, a unitary increase in the performance gap has an increasing effect on the amount of discontent (the curve becomes steeper). Other people, less perceptive, discover the gap as it gets bigger, conversations and the media focus on it to an increasing degree, etc. When discontent caused by underperformance is very widespread, however, unitary increases in underperformance have decreasing effects on discontent. The reasons for this are that most people who could be informed about the existence of a gap have already been informed, that the discontent of informed people is already so high that the gap becoming even more serious does not increase their level of discontent very much, and that a fraction of the population are left more or less unconcerned by the performance gap whatever its level. The process considered here is not a pure diffusion process, but it does include a process of information diffusion as one of its components. Thus it is not surprising that the shape of the curves is of a kind that is typically found when diffusion processes are involved.

Curve V_2 corresponds to a situation in which the mechanisms underlying the reduced form relation are weaker than is the case with curve V_1. This difference may stem from obstacles to assessing the country's growth performance by comparison with what obtains in other countries. The situation of the country is felt to be special in one way or the other; for instance, the economy may be more subject to risks of the kind called idiosyncratic in the tournament literature than to risks common to the country and comparable countries. The difference can also be the result of geographical, linguistic, or other obstacles to information flow from abroad. It can arise from the population being relatively unwilling, for instance for cultural or historical reasons, to engage in comparisons.[8] Finally, the population may not be as concerned with growth as is the case elsewhere. These various factors can interact. Anyhow, at some level of the performance gap, discontent will appear and, if the gap becomes bigger, it will spread to a large part of the population. Thus curve V_2 has the same general shape as curve V_1. I make the obviously simplifying assumption that the only difference between the two is that any given amount of discontent is caused by a performance gap larger in the case of curve V_2 by a fixed amount. This is reflected in Figure 7.3 by curve V_2 being derived from curve V_1 through a straightforward horizontal translation. The same applies to curve V_3, which corresponds to mechanisms even weaker than is the case for curve V_2.

3   From discontent to political or policy change: The role of political regimes

A given level of discontent will not have the same effect

- under a system of majority rule that allows rapid alternation in office of competing political parties and thus in which office-holding is highly "contestable,"
- under a system of proportional representation with strong political parties of the kind observed, for instance, in Italy until recently (called "partitocracy" by many Italians),
- under an undemocratic or authoritarian regime that does, however, tolerate some expression of dissenting opinion,

---

[8] I have discussed all these points more in detail in previous work (Salmon, 1987, 1991).

- and under a totalitarian dictatorship in which no such expression is tolerated.

The effect of discontent on the likelihood of political or policy change may thus serve as an indicator of the nature of the political regime.

In Figure 7.3, the horizontal lines R_j indicate the levels of discontent that create a political crisis and endanger the incumbent politicians or political parties, or even the existing political regimes or systems. Each line reflects the nature of the political system or of a state of the political system. As soon as the level of discontent reaches the relevant line, it is assumed that this is a sufficient condition for political change – or drastic policy change with the same politicians – to take place. If, following Karl Popper (1945, p. 121), we define democracy as a system by which ordinary people can get rid of what they think of as bad government "without bloodshed" and "by the way of general elections," line R_1, labeled "high contestability" in Figure 7.3, corresponds to "maximum" democracy.[9] Line R_2 corresponds to "partitocracy," say, of the kind alleged to have existed in Italy – somewhat less democratic under Popperian definitions. Line R_3 corresponds to relatively mildly undemocratic regimes of the kind observed in many third-world countries. Finally, line R_4 corresponds to totalitarian dictatorships.

4   From insufficient growth to potential political or policy change

At a point in time, each country has two structural attributes, which can be called, for convenience, "growth gap sensitivity" and "nature of political regime." Each country can thus be located at the intersection point of a V_i curve (the first attribute) and a R_j horizontal line (the second). This gives us the maximum objective growth performance gap that can be tolerated in the country.

Let me illustrate this by commenting on some such points in Figure 7.3.

- *Point A* reflects a situation in which office-holding is highly contestable and in which objective gaps cause discontent swiftly. A small objective performance gap (G_A) would cause an amount of discontent D_1, which, although very small, would be sufficient to provoke political change. Thus the government is highly constrained by performance competition.
- *Point B* reflects a situation in which office-holding is not very contestable (the "partitocracy" situation, say), whereas objective gaps cause discontent swiftly. As a result of the first characteristic, only a relatively high level of discontent (D_2) would provoke political change,

---

[9] As is clear from the reference to Popper, democracy here is viewed under a retrospective voting perspective.

but, as a result of the second characteristic, this high level of discontent could be brought about by an objective performance gap (G_B) that is still relatively small (although higher, of course, than in the previous case).

- In case of *point C*, an authoritarian regime could survive a very high amount of discontent (up to D_3), but, as a result of a high sensitivity of the population to growth comparisons, discontent could nonetheless reach its limit with a performance gap (G_C) still relatively modest.
- *Point U* corresponds to a situation in which office holding is extremely contestable but in which the sensitivity of the population to growth comparisons is mediocre. A very small amount of discontent (D_1) would provoke political change but the performance gap (G_U) would have to be relatively important to cause that amount of discontent.
- Finally, *point S* reflects the situation in a totalitarian regime of the worst kind. Very little information from abroad trickles in and the regime could survive a very high level of discontent although for such a level to obtain, the performance gap would have to be considerable (G_S).

Figure 7.3 suggests an hypothesis that I now formulate but on which I do not want to insist too much in this paper. It is that the sensitivity of public opinion to comparisons in growth rates is more important or constraining than the political regime or system (totalitarian dictatorships excepted) for explaining observed growth. This is reflected in the shape of the V_i curves, which suggests that moving along a V_i curve does not change the maximum tolerable performance gap very much, whereas moving from one V_i curve to another has a more significant effect on this gap.

Let me illustrate this by a comparison of two countries, Italy and Britain. In a previous paper (Salmon, 1991), I argued that all Western European continental countries, and in particular, the six founding members of the European Community, have been for a long time and still are in a situation that favors comparisons of performance. In the same paper, I also argued that Britain, for historical reasons (having won the war, starting from a relatively high level, being culturally insulated, etc.) was not until the 1970s in such a situation. This means that, in Figure 7.3, I would put Italy, say, on the V_1 curve, and Britain in the 1960s and 70s, say, on the V_2 curve. On the other hand, Britain has a political, and in particular electoral, system that is considered to make its government highly contestable, whereas Italy has had until recently the, already referred to, so-called "partitocracy" system that made the Italian government much less contestable. This implies putting Britain, say, on a R_1 line and Italy, say, on a R_2 line. If we consider both structural attributes, Italy would thus be in B, and Britain in U. But, then, the maximum performance gap tolerable for Italy (G_B) would be much smaller than it would be for Britain (G_U). And, in fact, as argued in the same paper, the Thatcher revolution came as a consequence of a particularly serious performance gap over an extended period of time (see also Table 7.2). If Italy were to move leftward on the V_1 curve, as now seems plausible as a result of the change in the electoral system, the foregoing discussion implies that the effect of this move on the tolerable performance gap of the country would be limited (from G_B to G_A). But, let me repeat, this hypothesis is even more tentative, if that is possible, than the rest of the paper.

5   Implications: From potential political or policy change to actual policymaking

What are the implications of the foregoing hypothesis on the questions raised in Section 1 about the relationship between democracy, redistribution, and growth? Before trying to spell out these implications, let me formulate two remarks. First, so far I have referred to discontent without being too specific about what this discontent is directed toward. The models discussed in the introduction, like the model of Meltzer and Richard, are "direct democracy" models, in the sense that no government is mentioned and policymaking reflects without bias the preferences of the median voter. Even as an idealization, this kind of approach to democracy is often misleading (Salmon, 1993). Here, however, I must admit that one might wish to use the vocabulary of direct democracy and assume that the median voters, when dissatisfied, are dissatisfied mainly with their past decisions (I use the term "median voter" for convenience). This is related to the line adopted, for instance, by Daniel Cohen (1994) to explain policy reversals in France and elsewhere in the early 1980s. In his very interesting analysis, median voters progressively discover new realities and change their minds. Especially given what was observed in France in 1982–83, I must admit that, in important respects, what counts is the policy reversal itself and the fact that it was supported by a majority of voters, not whether it was operated by the politicians elected in the first place or by their opponents. Although I use the vocabulary of representative democracy and refer to politicians as well as to voters, the possible equivalence just noted should certainly be kept in mind.

Whether voters ascribe underperformance to officeholders or to their own mistaken policy preferences, it causes discontent with current policies and arrangements, which, when reaching or moving near the threshold lines identified in Figure 7.3, creates a compelling incentive for policy change. That is the case (and this is my second remark) provided of course that domestic policies are responsible for economic growth, or are considered as such by voters. More exactly, the logic of the foregoing discussion is that domestic policies are assessed in the light of growth comparisons – which makes sense if part of total growth can be ascribed to an element common to all countries (or to a subset, e.g.,

Western European countries). The average growth rate of GDP per capita of OECD countries fell from about 4 percent over the period 1960–73 to about 1.5 percent over the period 1973–85 (Table 7.2). It was argued by most observers that all countries were affected by a common factor. The foregoing discussion concentrates on the actual or feared underperformance of individual countries vis-à-vis the average (or some benchmark of the kind), not on the evolution of the average (this statement is qualified below).

How difficult is it for a government to remain within the tolerance limit? Much depends on what happens abroad. If we introduce uncertainty as to policy outcomes, and if governments are risk-averse, it may be the case that each one will tend to adopt policies that endeavor to generate a growth rate well above what is needed to avoid excessive discontent. But this means that all policies that are detrimental to growth will tend to be discarded. This includes redistribution of the kind considered by Alesina and Rodrik (1994) or by Persson and Tabellini (1994), though not of the growth-enhancing kind considered by Saint-Paul and Verdier (1993). Thus the first implication of the hypothesis developed in this paper is that, in each country, redistribution will be accepted only if it is favorable to growth or if that country is far enough from its threshold point (determined by the factors analyzed previously) in terms of Figure 7.3. This may explain why transfers are correlated positively with investment and growth, as was found, as we noted above, by Perotti (1994).

A second implication is that, at the international level, several equilibria are likely to be possible. Performance competition may be very intense; we may have a kind of "rate race"; and the consequences on income distribution may be severe. Alternatively, we may be in a situation in which the best-placed countries use their discretion margin in a way that lowers their own economic growth and that, as a side effect, makes life easier for the potentially underperforming countries. Thus an average rate of growth at the international level that is low according to comparisons in time (for instance between 1973 and 1985 as showed in Table 7.2) may be the outcome (unlikely in the particular case) not of a common exogenous factor as suggested above, but of a coordination game that allows all governments, under the leadership of some, to pursue policies inimical to growth in the domain of redistribution most notably. In that case, as predicted in the models discussed at the beginning of this paper, and contrary to the result that I have just recalled, it might be the case that a positive correlation between redistribution (or high taxes) and low growth could be found.

If individuals compare growth rates only within a small set of neighboring countries, the foregoing analysis could lead to multiple equilibria in space rather than in time, so to say. For instance, European countries, under the leadership, say, of Germany might adopt with regard to growth a standard less demanding than that adopted by East Asian countries. As a consequence, more redistribution could be indulged in Europe than in East Asia.

The third implication of the foregoing analysis is more a set of assumptions formulated somewhat differently than a real implication. The way Figure 7.3 has been drawn embodies the assumptions that the degree of democracy has, *ceteris paribus*, a positive influence on growth (more democracy, in the Popperian sense, reduces the tolerable growth gap). It also reflects the assumptions that there is no discontinuity between democracies and mildly undemocratic regimes (the discontinuity being between these regimes and totalitarian dictatorships) and that the degree of democracy may have less influence on growth (via the tolerable growth gap) than does sensitivity to growth performance comparisons.[10] This may help explain some of the hesitation found in the empirical literature about the significance of democracy as an explanatory variable or condition.

6 Concluding remarks

Contrary to Figure 7.1, Figure 7.2 should be read from right to left. The foregoing discussion suggests a relationship between democratic politics, growth, and redistribution that is at least sometimes the opposite of that underlying the models summarized in Section 1. In the modern world, when endangered, growth is too important to be left to the petty calculations of a median voter à la Meltzer and Richard. More generally, redistribution objectives or considerations often seem compelling because the reasoning is developed under the assumption of certainty or perfect information (or of rational expectations), and thus as if we were already on a utility frontier of some sort (Salmon, 1993). In the real world, we are very far from the frontier, there is plenty of scope for Pareto improvements that benefit most people if not everybody and the effects of various policies on income distribution are extremely uncertain. This explains also why redistribution is less important and growth more important than assumed in many analyses.

All this is tentative, of course. Among the many problems I am aware of, let me mention one that seems to me particularly intriguing. By way of introduction, let me note how puzzling, to say the least, is the time dimension implicit in the hypothesis developed in the preceding sections. Typically, politicians care most about their current popularity and the results of the next election. But policies have effects on growth that are delayed and voters cannot be assumed to be competent enough to anticipate these effects. The usual solution of that kind of puzzle is party reputation. I agree that parties may play an important role here.[11] I think, however, that even within a perspective of reputation building or maintaining, an actor unmentioned so far must be given a role. This actor is the bureaucracy, and more precisely, the subset of it referred to in France as

---

[10] Countries such as Malaysia, Singapore, and Indonesia are not democracies but, following the observation of *The Economist* cited in Section 2, they are indeed sensitive to growth comparisons. That they grow fast is what we should expect from the assumptions embodied in Figure 7.3.

[11] The reputation concerns of individual politicians may be also essential (Salmon, 1993).

the *administrations économiques et financières*. Let me conclude with a brief discussion of what could have been, ideally, a major component of this essay.

The rigorous, relatively far-sighted, and not very popular policy adopted by France between 1983 and 1993 was not invented by the president, the prime ministers, or the political parties in power (the Socialist Party most of the time).[12] Nor is it very enlightening for our purpose to observe that it was eventually accepted by the "median voter." It came out progressively, I suggest, from the reflections of that part of the bureaucracy that in France is concerned with economic and budgetary policies (*Budget, Trésor, Banque de France, Direction de la Prévision, INSEE,* etc.). In France, every *Ministre de l'Economie et des Finances*, after a while, expresses views that – it is difficult not to suspect – reflect the views that have come to dominate in these bureaus. Obviously, bureaus are much more able than voters to decide whether a policy is oriented toward long-term objectives. By adopting policies that have such orientation, political officeholders build up their reputation with the bureaus.

Here, what are the motivations of the bureaucrats? Why are politicians interested in this kind of reputation? How does this interact with their concern with public opinion and voters? These questions are difficult to deal with and may be viewed as somewhat unusual from the perspective of the public choice approach to politics. But I think that they will need to be explored for an improved understanding of policymaking in contemporary representative democracies.

References

Alesina, A., and D. Rodrik. 1992. Distribution, political conflict, and economic growth: A simple theory and some empirical evidence, in *Political Economy, Growth, and*

---

[12] The objectives of this policy are interpreted by Patrice Vial (1993, p. 48), an insider in many respects, as follows:

> "While it can be argued that the French experience has developed as a pragmatic construction rather than from a well-defined *ex ante* concept, the ultimate objective has never changed; it has consistently been to restore long-term, and not just short-term competitiveness – and this was understood as the capacity to sustain permanently adequate growth with a balanced current account in the context of a stable exchange rate against the DM."

Let me also quote Vial's analysis of the policy implications:

> "Central to the strategy, therefore, was the idea that it was necessary to promote or enforce structural change and reforms in the basic relations governing, among other things, the price-setting mechanism, wage settlement procedures and the pattern of income distribution. One of the important features differentiating France from Germany in the 1973–82 period has been that wages had consistently increased faster than labour productivity, leading to low margins, high indebtedness and a global impoverishment of the enterprises. To reverse this tendency was considered a priority. Clearly this meant a diminution in the relative price of labour."

Note the reference to permanently adequate growth, comparisons with Germany, the need of antiwage redistribution, all this concerning policies adopted over almost the entire period by a left-wing government.

Business Cycles, A. Cukierman, Z. Hercowitz and L. Leiderman, eds., pp. 23–50, MIT Press, Cambridge, Mass.

1994. Distributive shares and economic growth, *Quarterly Journal of Economics*, **109**(2), 465–90.

Alesina, A., and R. Perotti. 1993. Income distribution, political instability, and investment, National Bureau of Economic Research (NBER), *Working Paper*, 4486, Cambridge, Mass.

Bertola, G. 1993. Factor shares and savings in endogenous growth, *American Economic Review*, **83**(5), 1184–98.

Brosio, G., and C. Marchese. 1993. Voting rights and the demand for public expenditure: An analysis of the redistributive impact of universal suffrage, in *Preferences and Democracy*, A. Breton, G. Galeotti, P. Salmon, and R. Wintrobe, eds., pp. 329–49, Kluwer, Dordrecht, Netherlands.

Cohen, D. 1994. *Les infortunes de la prospérité*, Julliard, Paris. (English translation, *The Misfortunes of Prosperity*, MIT Press, Cambridge, Mass., 1995.)

De Long, J. B. 1988. Productivity growth, convergence, and welfare: Comment, *American Economic Review*, **78**(5), 1138–54.

Dowrick, S., and D.-T. Nguyen. 1989. OECD comparative economic growth 1950–85: Catch-up and convergence, *American Economic Review*, **79**(5), 1010–30.

Elster, J. 1991. Patterns of causal analysis in Tocqueville's 'Democracy in America', *Rationality and Society*, **3**(3), 277–97.

Hibbs, D. 1973. *Mass Political Violence: A Cross-National Causal Analysis*. Wiley, New York.

Kinder, D. R., and D. R. Kiewiet. 1979. Economic discontent and political behavior: The role of personal grievances and collective economic judgments in congressional voting, *American Journal of Political Science*, **23**, 495–527.

Lewis-Beck, M. S. 1985. Economics and electoral behavior in France, in *Political Economy in Western Democracies*, N. J. Vig and S. E. Schier, eds., pp. 284–303, Holmes and Meier, New York.

Maddison, A. 1982. *Phases of Capitalist Development*, Oxford University Press, Oxford.

Meltzer, A. H., and S. F. Richard. 1981. A rational theory of the size of government, *Journal of Political Economy*, **89**(5), 914–27.

Mingat, A., P. Salmon, and A. Wolfelsperger. 1985. *Méthodologie Économique*, Presses Universitaires de France, Paris.

Mueller, D. C. 1989. *Public Choice II: A Revised Edition of 'Public Choice'*, Cambridge University Press, Cambridge.

Paldam, M. 1991. How robust is the vote function? A study of seventeen nations over four decades, in *Economics and Politics: The Calculus of Support*, H. Norpoth, M. S. Lewis-Beck and J.-D. Lafay, eds., pp. 9–31, The University of Michigan Press, Ann Arbor, Mich.

Perotti, R. 1992. Income distribution, politics, and growth, *American Economic Review*, **82**(2), 311–16.

1993. Political equilibrium, income distribution, and growth, *Review of Economic Studies*, **60**(4), 755–76.

1994. Income distribution and investment, *European Economic Review*, **38**, 827–35.

Persson, T., and G. Tabellini. 1992a. Growth, distribution, and politics, in *Political Economy, Growth, and Business Cycles*, A. Cukierman, Z. Hercowitz and L. Leiderman, eds., pp. 3–22, MIT Press, Cambridge, Mass.

1992b. Growth, distribution, and politics, *European Economic Review*, **36**, 593–602.

1994. Is inequality harmful for growth? *American Economic Review*, **84**(3), 600–21.

Piketty, T. 1995. Inégalités et redistribution: Développements théoriques récents, *Revue d'Economie Politique*, **104**(6), 769–800.

Popper, K. R. 1945. *The Open Society and its Enemies. Vol. 1: Plato*. 5th ed., Routledge and Kegan Paul, London.

Saint-Paul, G., and T. Verdier. 1993. Education, democracy and growth, *Journal of Development Economics*, **42**(2), 399–407.

1996. Inequality, redistribution and growth: A challenge to the conventional political economy approach, *European Economic Review*, **40**(3–5), 719–28.

Sala-i-Martin, X. 1994. Cross-sectional regressions and the empirics of economic growth, *European Economic Review*, **38**, 739–47.

Salmon, P. 1987. Decentralisation as an incentive scheme, *Oxford Review of Economic Policy*, **3**(2), 24–43.

1991. Checks and balances and international openness, in *The Competitive State*, Albert Breton, Gianluigi Galeotti, Pierre Salmon and Ronald Wintrobe, eds., pp. 169–84, Kluwer, Dordrecht, Netherlands.

1993. Unpopular policies and the theory of representative democracy, in *Preferences and Democracy*, Albert Breton, Gianluigi Galeotti, Pierre Salmon and Ronald Wintrobe, eds., pp. 13–39, Kluwer, Dordrecht, Netherlands.

1994. Outrageous arguments in economics and public choice, *European Journal of Political Economy*, **10**(3), 409–26.

Stendhal, 1839. *La Chartreuse de Parme*, Edited by Henri Martineau, Gallimard, Paris, 1952.

Summers, R., and A. Heston. 1984. Improved international comparisons of real product and its composition 1950–1980, *Review of Income and Wealth*, **30**, 207–62.

Verdier, T. 1994. Models of political economy of growth: A short survey, *European Economic Review*, **38**, 757–63.

Venieris, Y. P., and D. K. Gupta. 1986. Income distribution and sociopolitical instability as determinants of savings: A cross-sectional model, *Journal of Political Economy*, **94**(4), 873–83.

Vial, P. 1993. Discussion of Olivier Blanchard and Pierre-Alain Muet's 'Competitiveness through disinflation: An assessment of the French macroeconomic strategy, *Economic Policy*, (16), 46–51.

Winer, S. L., and T. Rutherford. 1993. Coercive redistribution and the franchise: A preliminary investigation using computable general equilibrium modelling, in *Preferences and Democracy*, A. Breton, G. Galeotti, P. Salmon, and R. Wintrobe, eds., pp. 351–75, Kluwer, Dordrecht, Netherlands.

PART III

Democratic deficiencies and possible improvements

CHAPTER 8

Democracy and the public machinery: The case of the headless Leviathan

Gianluigi Galeotti

1   Introduction

The quest for control of the public machinery has accompanied the entire history of political life, insofar as "the utility function of the agents is not identical with that of the ruler" (North, 1981, p. 25). Today, when we contrast the ramification of public action with the effectiveness of parliamentary control, it is easy to see that the quest is still going on, and if anything is more impelling. Should we conclude that the growth of the welfare state and the widening of democracy has brought about the dethronement of the voter? And who has gained effective power? The notion of bureaucratic capture is one answer, though it is difficult to assign the roles of captor and captive when the rules of the bureaucratic game are concocted inside the political game. Why should representative bodies accept to be dispossessed if they can enact new rules, deny money, and redress the balance of power at any time? Mathew McCubbins and Thomas Schwartz (1984) suggested that the control of the elected assemblies materializes through either "fire-alarm" or "police-patrolling" devices, the former being the case of the U.S. Congress called to act when needed, the latter of the more systematic control exerted by parliaments. Both systems, however, seem to face similar problems, and it is not easy to assess whether that metaphor effectively expresses real differences or generalizes scattered pieces of evidence. In either case, the intriguing question is to ask why the controls and the features of bureaucracies should be different under different democratic systems.

Albert Breton (1996) suggested recently that a permanent and nonpartisan bureaucracy is the institution that helps to solve the legislative drift (fluctuations in the choices of the decision makers) in a parliamentary system, just as standing committees do in congressional governments (Weingast and Marshall,

The author is grateful to two anonymous referees for their comments and to Ron Wintrobe for the discussions that helped shape the essay.

163

1988). The ultimate logic of his explanation, however, appeals to the overall degree of competitiveness of different political systems. And that seems to be the key variable that helps explain the working of the bureaucratic machine. More precisely, all modern democracies seem to share the common feature of complex administrative procedures – bureaucratic rules, a mix of privileges and restrictions – aimed at reducing monitoring costs and at providing structured incentives. Diversity comes later on, when the competitiveness of the system molds positions and powers of political and bureaucratic nature. In this essay we discuss a polar case where a too-close legislative interaction with the public machinery combines with insufficient political competition to generate a circle of power prone to paralyzing short circuits.

Section 2 recalls the traditional debate about who dominates the process of democratic decision making and addresses the question of why a parliamentary system should lead to different bureaucratic institutions. Section 3 discusses the demand and supply sides of the provision of bureaucratic rules and the role played by political competition. Section 4 presents a number of traits of the Italian experience characterized by lack of political competition, the passivity of the senior bureaucracy, and an extreme complexity of laws and regulations. The proposition illustrated should, however, convey a broader message.

2   The unsettled geometry of power

Control of the public machinery, an issue as old as modern democracies, has received a new emphasis in recent years, because the growth of the public sector has revealed the limits of the traditional equilibria of power. During the seventies a wave of reforms swept many countries with the purpose of reinforcing both accounting and political monitoring (Hellstern, 1986). At the same time, scholars' reflections addressed the issue of who ultimately dominates the design and the implementation of public action.

Firstly, the information and agenda-setting power enjoyed by public bureaucrats has been stressed, with regard to the costs of production of public services. William Niskanen's (1971) book is a conventional reference, though later reflections diluted his propositions to the benefit of a more realistic emphasis on the *ex ante* and *ex post* costs of planning, auditing, and monitoring of bureaucrats. At the same time, the Chicago reflection on capture by interest groups put forward a warning message of important but – it should be said – of a not all-encompassing nature. Later on, politics – a neglected, but still present vertex of power – regained lost ground when it was stressed that the legislature (essentially the U.S. Congress) effectively had the last word, through a number of instruments (oversight, new statutes, budgets, appointments) that allowed the control of its own creatures and of the bureaucracy at large (Weingast, 1984; Kiewiet and McCubbins, 1991). Lastly, the triangle became a pentagon when

Terry Moe (1990) and John Ferejohn and Charles Shipan (1990) recalled the role played by the president and by the courts, and that led to the mixed result that the outcomes of statutory policymaking are not always more attractive to Congress than the results of agency policymaking (Steunenberg, 1992).

The substance of this brief recollection can be read in terms of a struggle "among multiple principals for the control of the bureaucracy, with the main determinants being the extent to which the legislative and executive bodies are aligned in their interests, who is politically more powerful, whether they have different political horizons, and to what extent political parties control their representatives" (Spiller and Urbiztondo, 1994). And that struggle has a long history, showing what could be called the "the onlooker gets the better of a fight" effect. At first parliaments granted rights and independence to public employees to attract them and to get them out of the influence of the king's government (Cassese and Pellew, 1987). Later on, a further push in the same direction came out of the workings of party competition, essentially a system of separation of powers along a time dimension. In each instance, those in substantial power try to protect their innovations from any risk of change, and formal structures appear as the best protective devices for insulating public bodies from the legislative drift.[1] Indeed, that was the humus where the Weberian notion of a politically neutral bureaucracy blossomed, and the legal rhetoric stressed its relevance for fairness and due process of law that would axiomatically substantiate its staying on target.

The outcome of those old and new political struggles between multiple principals was that public employees gained the following liberties and privileges: political neutrality, job tenure, promotion by seniority, and articulated sets of law-protected prerogatives. The other side of the coin is represented by a growing institutional complexity, with its well-known consequences: As public bureaus are encumbered by formal constraints, attention shifts from output to formal accomplishment, self-administration becomes paramount, functions have to adapt to structures, etc. In Coasian terms, this complexity should represent an unavoidable brake to the growth of the public sector.

The real issue, however, is to discuss who gets the most benefits out of that complexity: If administrative procedures and detailed legislation are instruments of control, who is controlling whom? If those procedures are means of enforcing bureaucratic compliance, why should bureaucrats accept to be hyperconstrained? Conversely, if that complexity supplies the bureaucrats with a protective shield, why should legislators indulge in it? The horns of the dilemma can be better clarified if we pause to consider the demand and supply forces that are behind the provision of administrative legislation, that is, why there

---

[1] Only Jonathan Macey (1992) finds in elections a damping factor that alleviates the legislative drift (coalition drift in American terms).

is a strong bureaucratic demand for more legislation and why government and parliament accept willingly to supply it.

3   Bureaucratic demand and political supply of rules

A good deal of administrative legislation is set in motion, directly or indirectly, by the bureaucracy itself. To some extent that is not surprising, as bureaucrats should be the experts in how to amend and improve the working of the public machinery. But bureaucratic demand is much stronger than that, and the analysis calls in more structural and subtler phenomena than just a struggle fought in the conventional terms of fund appropriation.

First of all, the definition "in excruciating detail .. [of] decision criteria, timetables, internal procedures, personnel rules" (Moe, 1990) does not necessarily tie bureaucrats' hands. There is a stage when the number of administrative rules provides unsuspected occasions for discretionary behavior, not only because of the costs of *ex post* monitoring required to make those rules credible. Rules provide subordinates with information by setting standards that partition actions into permitted and forbidden ones. It pays to conform to the standard even if there are many imperfections in its application: In a world of formal prescriptions, it is not the subordinate who has to justify the best course of available actions undertaken, but it is the supervisor who has to prove that the subordinate has violated any of the prescribed rules. For that reason, a risk-averse employee prefers to be judged not on his eventual performance, but on his observance of the rules. In other terms, the procedural formalities move the administrative exchange from the world of contracts to the world of torts. In a previous paper (Galeotti, 1988) I recalled how rules and formal constraints provide a set of information for what is expected of employees that makes their decision environment less uncertain and *therefore* makes their reactions more unpredictable. And the empirical evidence shows that the proposition is almost the same in different political environments: When the Italian scholar Sabino Cassese (1993) remarks that in presence of many rules, bureaucrats are able to choose which rule to apply, he is substantially echoing the American refrain "There is always a way to get around the rule: look for it."

Two specific reasons[2] have been put forward by Cassese (1993) to explain why bureaucrats favor embedding in law a detailed regulation of their own work: The search for immunity and the management of internal conflicts. Bureaucrats want to be told in detail what to do – and how to do it – in order to protect themselves against charges of inappropriate use of their power, which could

---

[2] Apart from the consideration that formal legislation shields bureaucrats from the whims of future governments, while allowing them to get the best they can at the propitious moment.

come from politicians, superiors, auditors, and judges.[3] Moreover, the dilution of responsibility linked to the fragmentation of capacities implies that each office is in control of a limited piece of an entire procedure. That fact implies that not only does it become more difficult to trace back the responsibility for poor performance, but also that there is a sharing of power that allows each office to hamper and limit the work of other bureaus. The ensuing conflicts provide the second reason for asking for legislative intervention, seen as an offensive weapon to weaken the resistance and the opposition of other bureaucrats. Indeed, according to some critics, internal feuds are the main daily occupation of many bureaucrats, particularly when principals are passive.

As detailed norms are enacted, more norms are required to correct, amend, adapt, limit, update – and circumvent! – the original ones. Formalization and conflicts can beget a self-feeding process of more formalization and conflicts only when politicians give in to bureaucrats' demands. Why would they? It has been suggested that politicians can be victims of a sort of illusion: Being asked to act, they think they can keep the administration under control with more, and more specific, regulations.[4] Though an illusory component cannot be excluded (see below), other reasons are needed to explain its persistence in the face of repeated and blatant ineffectiveness.

Most new legislation tends to complement existing legislation, and even the few attempts at a more systematic approach eventually boil down to a piecemeal approach whose results are affected by many minor factors under the control of the bureaucracy. The reasons are manifold. Firstly, it is difficult to modify anything without the expertise of the same bureaucrats, whose advice is inevitably biased toward their own above-mentioned parochial targets. Secondly, it is difficult to undertake radical and daring reforms that are perceived as a threat by the bureaucracy, and that is true even for strong governments.[5] Thirdly, minor reforms and fractional initiatives provide some political advantage in themselves – by showing that the government is acting – particularly in terms of patronage, in that changes are often accompanied by promotions and immediate benefits for bureaucrats.

Fourthly, bureaucrats represent an important electoral constituency. This general remark has been made specific by Johnson and Libecap (1989, pp. 57–58). Their interpretation combines politicians' fear of the opportunistic behavior

---

[3] In the recent Italian cases of embezzlement, relatively few bureaucrats have undergone judicial inquiry.

[4] McCubbins, Noll, and Weingast (1987) submit that politicians [should] prefer flexible procedural instruments to more substantive ones, in order to control the evolution of policymaking and the bureaucratic drift in an indirect way.

[5] In Italy it is said that Mussolini himself did not back a reform plan of the public administration because he was afraid of the negative reactions of the bureaucracy.

on the part of supervisors (top- and middle-rank bureaucrats) with the lower ranks' demand for greater job protection and easier promotions up the hierarchy. In what appears an asymmetric reaction, the legislature enacts regulations that make the costs very high "to supervisors for disciplining poor performance by subordinates through dismissal or the denial of salary increase and promotions." At the same time, however, supervisors "are rewarded in part on the performance of their subordinates. Thus, the incentive remains for them to find ways to motivate their workers. Given the protection enjoyed by the employees, the range of feasible actions available to supervisors is limited principally to overgrading to increase the salaries of subordinates."

The above analysis refers to the U.S. experience, but it is general enough to be valid for other systems, as the reader can easily check in terms of his own national experience. Granted those pressures on the demand and supply side, complexity of administrative procedures comes to be a feature common to almost all modern polities. Though our initial question – who is controlling whom? – remains substantially unanswered, let us turn to the problem of whether there is any difference between congressional and parliamentary systems.

4   Competitive governments and competitive bureaucracies

To a number of American scholars, the absence of the contrast between the president and the congress seems to confer to parliamentary regimes the status of a quasi-Eden of simplicity and order. According to Moe (1990, p. 240), parliamentary systems are less bureaucratic, "less encumbered by formal restrictions, more informal and discretionary, free of the burdensome layering of executive and legislative constraints." And all that because "whichever party gains a majority of seats in Parliament gets to form a government and, through cohesive voting on policy issues, is in a position to pass its own program at will." Rather paradoxically, it would be the lack of competition – the concentration of power occurring when the executive and the legislature are controlled by the majority party – that generates agencies that are provided with "lots of discretion, built to do their jobs well, and coordinated within a coherent system of democratic control" (Moe and Caldwell, 1994, p. 193). And in the same vein, James Wilson (1989) and Seymour Martin Lipset (1994) underline the superiority of the parliamentary systems in keeping bureaucracy under control.

Many people living under parliamentary bureaucracies would reverse the case and not only in anecdotal terms.[6] Apart from empirical evidence (always

---

[6] When the legislative and the executive vertices collapse into one – if that is a fact – one level of control is blurred. The cohesion of the incumbents works against a careful scrutiny of the government, and the opposition party does not perform much better, being more interested in putting forward broad political alternatives than in monitoring a bureaucracy that sooner or later is going to be under its control.

difficult to build up in the absence of interpretative models), is there any genetic or functional difference between those two systems? The question has been squarely faced by Breton (1996), who suggests that a permanent, nonpartisan, senior bureaucracy is the institution that helps reduce the risk that future legislators will change the balance of protected interests (the legislative drift). In exchange for preserving extant equilibria and enforcing the equilibrium allocations, senior bureaucrats have a word in the eventual choices agreed upon in the political and budgetary decision making of parliamentary governments. When today's legislators give up some of their present power in order to safeguard in the future most of what has been achieved, politicians and (top) bureaucrats become indispensable to each other. Does that imply a more sluggish or more energetic bureaucracy?

To test the implication in terms of institutional design and the working of the public machinery would require a systematic comparative analysis, especially in terms of what occurs under parliamentary systems, which are varied and many.[7] Lacking such evidence, let us move forward with the help of Breton's analysis where the enforcement function directly concerns top bureaucrats only, "arbitrarily defined to include those bureaucrats who have legitimate access to cabinet documents" (Breton, 1996, p. 110). To test its effective impact down the sequential incentive structure and therefore upon the working of the entire bureaucratic machine is another matter, one that involves consideration of the competitive pressure on the government *and* on those senior bureaucrats. The relative impact of that pressure identifies the trade-off between the bureaucratic and the legislative drift, a trade-off that does not necessarily imply a zero-sum game: One side's loss is not necessarily equal to other side's gain as long as the institutional setting allows noncompetitive political/bureaucratic returns.

When the competitive whip on both the government and the bureaucracy is vigorous, the asymmetric result underlined by Johnson and Libecap (1989) should not apply. In such a world, the existence of strong links between government and senior bureaucracy should dissipate any fear of the latter's opportunistic behavior, thus reducing the need "to provide protection to workers at the behest of white-collar unions." If we accept that conclusion, two consequences follow. First, the contrast between different regimes has to be seen not so much in terms of congressional versus parliamentary systems as in terms of the strength of the competitive goad endured by each system. Second, weak competition on both the political and the bureaucratic side does not reduce but makes stronger the demand and the supply of bureaucratic rules. In this way we get closer to the headless Leviathan's world.

---

[7] Let us only contrast the richness of the French administrative history to other leaner traditions (remember the neat statement attributed to Albert Dicey: "In England we know nothing of administrative law; and we wish to know nothing").

5   Unaccountability and collusion

Awaiting more comparative evidence about the features of the civil service blossoming under the parliamentary systems, in this section we consider the Italian variant of a parliamentary system, a variant characterized by tenuous political competition, passivity of the senior bureaucrats that boils down to lack of accountability, and a legal complexity that makes it difficult to understand who, if anyone, runs the show. We illustrate those points in sequence.

It is outside the scope of this essay to discuss the reasons why the Italian politics has not been adequately competitive so far. We refer the reader to a previous work (Galeotti, 1994) where it is shown that the presence of solid party organizations induces a reunification of the fragmented political power that has evolved with the modern democratic state.

As for the second point, it has been said that since Italian unification a tacit pact has been agreed upon between senior bureaucrats and politicians, with the former giving up their power in exchange for a quiet life and promotion by seniority.[8] It is difficult to say if this is only the legacy of the previous tradition of absolute government. However, a number of facts are consistent with either interpretation. Senior bureaucrats fail to perform their role in monitoring and addressing their subordinates' behavior, nor are they rewarded for the performance of their subordinates. If Breton is right in emphasizing the stabilizing function of senior bureaucrats, in the Italian case this function must be seen in the context of the essentially negative nature of their power.

It is true that the highest promotions depend on a formal decision by the Cabinet, a decision that can respect seniority only up to a point, as inevitably a comparative choice will have to be made between candidates who belong to the same age range. Why, at that level, is competition not fought out in terms of personal merits and personal achievements in running the machinery? Why do all candidates tend to appear equal, with no special merit deriving from their past performance? The answer lies in the observation that the working of internal competition is not in terms of gaining merit, but in terms of avoiding demerit. To account for this, we have to make clear that no law establishes that careers are dictated by seniority. Formally, they should be based on merit, assessed over the entire career by the superiors through a system of internal contests, formally regulated (although easily sidestepped in practice). The real implication of the formal rule, is that a career can only be stopped by demerit. And in order to avoid demerit, the rational strategy is to conform to the standard of accepted behavior: "live and let live." As soon as anybody does anything special (taking initiatives, improving the output, doing his or her best), peers are ready to cut

---

[8] Cassese and Pellew (1987) observe that the growth of public bureaucracy as an autonomous center of power implies its independence from other powers in terms of recruitment controlled by the bureaucracy itself.

the ground from under his or her feet. By "doing" you run the risk of demerit, by "not doing" it is very hard to be stopped in your career (and the Administrative Courts are there to enforce that tacit rule: see below).

It is this perverse working of competition that explains the lack of bureaucratic leadership and the presence of strong horizontal ties (de facto encouraged all through the bureaucratic career) that ultimately amount to collusion. Collusion and inaction are closely intertwined, in a combination that is the quintessence of a headless Leviathan. The newspapers report blatant forms of inefficiency of the public bureaucracy almost daily. Take the case of tax controls. One of the reasons why tax evasion is widespread is because tax officers are not overzealous in the application of their powers. In an attempt to get the best out of tax inspectors, the government tried to subordinate their wage increase to the realization of a minimum number of tax controls to be reached by each of them. After a while, the inspectors' tendency to concentrate their activity on the easiest cases (those, by the way, where tax evasion could be least expected) in order to reach the prescribed quota with a minimum of effort was reported. But this could have happened only with the tacit approval of the supervisors.

The last feature concerns the legal complexity nurtured by a traditional legalistic approach framed within a universe of more than 100,000 laws in force.[9] A sign of the "vivacity" of legislative and administrative production is provided by the fact that the *Gazzetta Ufficiale* (the equivalent of the *U.S. Federal Register*) can be bought daily at most newspaper stands.[10] Provided with that scenery, it is not difficult to imagine how Italian public administration is highly constrained and formalized. As a cause and consequence of that complexity, a large number of actors have to be considered in order to understand the working of public administration. Besides junior and senior bureaucrats and their strong unions, the Internal Auditing Office, the General Auditing Office and the Administrative Courts deserve attention and help in the understanding of a number of features. Firstly, the need for coordination inside the complex formal structure requires the constant creation of new bodies for that specific function in a labyrinth of capacities that few people know and can master. The resulting structure resembles a system of Chinese boxes, in which the last word – in terms of internal power – stays with the Internal Auditors who control the purse

---

[9] The related figures are 7,325 for France and 5,587 for Germany (Cassese, 1993). In the Italian case, the difficulty of counting is due to the fact that few laws are formally abrogated. Old laws are normally amended, so that there are always some clauses left over, and even experts often debate which clauses are actually in force. The historical roots of this overlegislation cannot be addressed here. Let us only mention how laws and legal devices have been a traditional battleground of social life. The struggle for power inside the elite has been always fought in terms of legal subtleties and monopolized by experts expressing different interests.

[10] On matters related solely to the budget there are 1,850 laws, 233 of which have been introduced between 1990 and 1993.

strings and who are able to delay or speed up any action in which payments are involved. Here again the power has more of a negative than positive nature. To know what to get, and how to get it, requires the help of a number of bureaucrats who therefore become the primary, though inconspicuous, targets for pressure of different kinds.

Second, a feature of the Italian bureaucratic game is its litigiousness, which absorbs enormous resources for internal disputes and legal conflicts. Every year, the Administrative Courts are flooded by about 100,000 appeals and claims (with a backlog of 800,000 cases pending). In many areas, judges – often of bureaucratic extraction – are there to protect the bureaucrats from any dangerous innovation. Once again, this judicial review – though insufficient for assuring positive performance – works better in delaying or preventing effective changes. In 1986, the government linked an increase of public wages to improvements in individual performance. Following long negotiations with the unions, the government agreed to grant the increase on a per capita basis, qualified simply by the employees' effective presence at work. This incentive to encourage a mere physical presence was soon dispensed with, when the Administrative Courts ruled that those absent from work for "legitimate reasons" had to get their share as well. Later on, in order to avoid that trap, a new proposal limited that distribution to twenty-five percent of the public employees in order to compel some ranking in terms of performance. After long discussion, the percentage was increased to a less credible value of fifty percent, with the implicit understanding (senior bureaucrat involved, necessarily) to grant it to everybody every second year.

Thirdly, as public bureaus are protected by formal constraints, attention is shifted from the output to the correctness of the inputs. Controls and checks tend to be mainly formal, as the attention of each bureau and of the entire bureaucratic machine is concentrated on the process. Self-administration becomes paramount and the connection between functions and structures becomes so feeble that the former increasingly have to adapt to the latter. In order to survive in such a complex and formalistic world, the administration itself cannot fulfill all the regulations it has had passed (the worst threat is "working to rule") and so has to resort to practical rules that get around the law. The threat of legal conflicts thus becomes endemic, though to prevent countermoves nobody must get hurt, and gains in terms of result can be achieved by buying consent: the realm of institutional collusion.

Finally, in this formal setting, the bureaucrats are indeed always able to get what they require. When facing substantive constraints, the bureaucracy could find its way out through a more convenient procedure, as is the case with fiscal controls discussed above. Conversely, when facing procedural constraints, the bureaucrats can find a convenient way out in terms of substantial outcomes, as in the previous case of economic incentives. The reason why we do not face a case of effective bureaucratic capture is that the Italian bureaucracy is more able to stop processes (power of delay, inaction, noncooperation) rather than to get them moving. A point that we stress again in order to underline the lack of lines of vertical leadership, which combines with strong collusive ties to twist formal rules to a routine that becomes impermeable to what the procedures are supposed to achieve.

Faced with that bureaucratic setting, Italian politics has for many years been able only to carve its own niches of power with an apparent activism that to many observes appeared again to be a lack of effective leadership.[11] And the production of new rules attempting to chain the administration turns against the same legislature and begets a world of anonymous and pluralistic exploitation that we include under the label of a headless, though effective, Leviathan.

6 Concluding remarks

We started by discussing the gap between statutory policy planning and institutional policymaking, a theme analyzed from different angles in a literature that has in turn emphasized the monopoly of the bureaucracy, the capture by lobbies and regulated groups, the power of the courts, and the eventual resurrection of the legislature. Here, the question of whether the public bureaucracy retains more power under a congressional system or under some version of parliamentarism has to be interpreted in terms of different combinations of political/bureaucratic competition (and the ample variety of models that falls under the aegis of parliamentary democracy should provide the empirical evidence necessary to test the hypothesis).

McCubbins et al. (1987) presented administrative procedures as a means of reducing the bureaucratic drift. Breton (1996) submitted that a permanent senior bureaucracy can reduce the legislative drift within a model in which pervasive competition prevents all corporate actors from exploiting their power. We discussed a special version of the bureaucratic drift in which bureaucrats are able to win only negative battles, namely, to stop other subjects' initiatives, rather than to achieve positive goals. In a sense, public bureaucracy comes to assume an amoebaelike behavior, ready both to adjust itself to any surroundings and to phagocytize any innovation and change. The environment that makes such a result possible is made of a complexity of rules combined with weak institutional competition and a passive senior bureaucracy. When public bureaus are encumbered by protective formal constraints, and controls and checks are only formal, a point can be reached in which the eventual output and the interests

---

[11] Consider the titles of a number of research works: *Italy: A Republic Without a Government* (by Allum Percy, Weidenfeld and Nicholson, London, 1973), *Surviving Without Governing* (by Giuseppe Palma, University of California Press, Berkeley, 1977), *Does a Government Exist in Italy?* (by Sabino Cassese, Officina Edizioni, Roma, 1980).

of the citizens become irrelevant: Rules become ends in themselves in a sort of institutional narcissism.

We considered a number of features of the Italian civil service that support this interpretation. What comes to be a prototypal case presents peculiarities in terms of the capacity both of the legislature to induce bureaucratic compliance, and of the bureaucracy to impose its own solutions. The tentative conclusion is that in such a world there is no prevailing power, but rather a gray area where formal responsibilities do not match the effective decision power, and the capacity to make decisions is scattered within unstable coalitions of a mixed (bureaucratic and political) nature. And there the notion of the headless Leviathan applies, where the eventual outcome is neither forced by bureaucrats – they need legislation for any change – nor by the politicians, who can only be stopped by noncooperation and therefore prefer to let sleeping dogs lie.

References

Breton, A. 1996. *Competitive Governments*, Cambridge University Press, Cambridge.

Cassese, S. 1993. *Rapporto sulle Condizioni delle Pubbliche Amministrazioni*, Presidenza del Consiglio dei Ministri: Dipartimento per la Funzione Pubblica, Roma.

Cassese, S., and J. Pellew. 1987. Il sistema del merito nel reclutamento della burocrazia come problema storico, *Rivista Trimestrale di Diritto Pubblico*, **36**: 756–770.

Ferejohn, J., and C. Shipan. 1990. Congressional influence on bureaucracy, *Journal of Law, Economics and Organization*, **6**, 1–20.

Galeotti, G. 1988. Rules and behaviors in markets and bureaucracy, *European Journal of Political Economy*, **4**, extra issue, 213–228.

1994. On proportional non-representation, *Public Choice*, **80**, 359–370.

Hellstern, G.-M. 1986. Unwilling to bark, not able to bite? Theories and realities of parliamentary control, in *Guidance, Control and Evaluation in the Public Sector*, F. Kaufmann, G. Majone and V. Ostrom, eds., pp. 691–718, W. de Gruyter, New York.

Johnson, R. N., and G. D. Libecap. 1989. Bureaucratic rules, supervisor behavior, and the effect on salaries in the federal government, *Journal of Law, Economics, and Organization*, **5**, 53–82.

Kiewiet, R., and M. McCubbins, 1991. *The Logic of Delegation: Congressional Parties and the Appropriations Process*, The University of Chicago Press, Chicago.

Lipset, S. M. 1994. Condizioni per la democrazia: una rilettura, *Biblioteca della Libertà*, **29**, 1–40.

Macey, J. R. 1992. Organizational design and political control of administrative agencies, *Journal of Law, Economics and Organization*, **8**, 93–110.

McCubbins, M. D., and T. Schwartz, 1984. Congressional oversight overlooked: Police patrols versus fire alarms, *American Journal of Political Science*, **28**, 165–179.

McCubbins, M. D., R. G. Noll, and B. R. Weingast, 1987. Administrative procedures as instruments of political control, *Journal of Law, Economics and Organization*, **3**, 243–277.

Moe, T. M. 1990. Political institutions: The neglected side of the story, *Journal of Law, Economics and Organization*, **6**, special issue, 213–261.

Moe, T. M., and M. Caldwell. 1994. The institutional foundations of democratic government: A comparison of presidential and parliamentary systems, *Journal of Institutional and Theoretical Economics*, **150**, 171–95.

Niskanen, N. A., Jr. 1971. *Bureaucracy and Representative Government*. Aldine-Atherton, Chicago.

North, D. 1981. *Structure and Change in Economic History*, Norton, New York.

Spiller, P. T., and S. Urbiztondo. 1994. Political appointees vs. career civil servants: A multiple principals theory of political bureaucracies, *European Journal of Political Economy*, **10**, 465–497.

Steunenberg, B. 1992. Congress, bureaucracy, and regulatory policymaking, *Journal of Law, Economics and Organization*, **8**, 673–694.

Weingast, B. E. 1984. The congressional-bureaucratic system, *Public Choice*, **44**, 147–192.

Weingast, B. E., and W. J. Marshall. 1988. The industrial organization of congress; or Why legislatures, like firms, are not organized as markets, *Journal of Political Economy*, **96**, 132–163.

Wilson, J. Q. 1989. *Bureaucracy*, Basic Books, New York.

CHAPTER 9

Democracy and empowerment

Albert Breton and Margot Breton

1   Introduction

We assume that the reality that is captured by the word *democracy* embodies mechanisms similar, though not identical, to those contained in the reality that is identified as the *market*; we further assume that democracy can be correctly analyzed and understood with the tools and methodology of conventional neo-classical economic theory which were crafted to analyze and understand markets. Given these two assumptions, no less than four analytical building blocks must be assembled to model democratic politics. The first building block must focus on the factors that give form to the demand side of politics; a second must concentrate on the variables that shape and determine supply; a third must be concerned with the forces that work to bring about a reconciliation of supply and demand – an equilibrating mechanism also capable of tracking how democracies adjust when they are subjected to external disturbances; – and a fourth must pay attention to the various devices (legal, cultural, social, political, and constitutional) that serve to enforce equilibrium outcomes.

Before proceeding with our discussion, we make two points regarding the above assumptions. First, democratic politics, like market calisthenics, can be more or less competitive and therefore more or less *responsive* to the preferences of citizens – to the demand side of politics.[1] The degree of competition which, at any moment, distinguishes a democracy is the product, again as in

The authors would like to thank seminar participants for useful comments. The first author would also like to thank the Lynde and Harry Bradley Foundation for its financial assistance.
[1] In conventional neoclassical theory, monopolists (and oligopolists) are conceived as being responsive to the preferences of consumers. That view is required by the assumption that monopolists maximize utility functions whose only arguments are profits. It has, however, been recognized for a long time (Hicks, 1935, p. 369) that "the best of all monopoly profits is a quiet life" which, of course, means that monopolists are *not* fully responsive to consumers: they maximize utility functions defined over more variables than profits.

markets, of structural and behavioral attributes of the organization of supply *and* of demand. Though scholars, like other individuals in free societies, can choose the definitions they think are most productive, the foregoing suggests that definitions of democracy and of democratic politics that are based, let us say, on certain components of the demand side alone leave out of the picture much that is relevant to a comprehension of politics. For example, Anthony Downs (1957, pp. 23–24) and a good part of the public choice movement, following Joseph Schumpeter's (1942) conception of politics, either explicitly or implicitly assume that a political system is democratic if there are periodic elections in which two or more parties compete to capture the apparatus of government. If we follow Downs one step farther and assume that the supply side is monolithic,[2] though subject to periodic replacement by an equally monolithic counterpart, the resulting system may be called democratic, but it will be less so, we suggest, than another in which the supply side is made up of a multiplicity of centers of power that compete with each other to respond to demand, which vie with each other to 'represent,' to 'speak for' and/or to 'cater to' the preferences signaled by the demand side.[3]

For most of the discussion that follows, we suppose that the supply side is competitive, though imperfectly so. This is consistent with the view that real world governmental systems, not unlike real world market systems, are never perfectly competitive. To understand the nature of these propositions, we model the process of empowerment as composed of eight steps. (As we explain in Section 3, it is not necessary for all groups that pass from a state of disempowerment to one of empowerment to go through all of the eight steps; our decision to decompose the process into eight steps was governed exclusively by a desire to formalize it). Three of these steps – Steps 4, 5, and 6 – describe the nature and character of the 'imperfections' in the governmental centers of power's responsiveness to the demands of the groups that are becoming empowered and, hence, in the competition that regulates the centers' behavior. As will become apparent, the imperfections, as is often also the case in markets, are to a large extent information problems.

The second point regarding our assumptions is that the analytical focus of an economic approach to politics, like the focus of economics, is the demand and supply of goods and services. This proposition loses all its shock value once it

---

[2] Downs's (implicit) presupposition that the supply side is monolithic comes from his assumption that political parties are coalitions of "individuals who have certain ends in common and cooperate with each other to achieve them" (1957, p. 24); once elected they are therefore (temporary) monoliths or monopolists. Schumpeter (1942) and Brennan and Buchanan (1980), among many others, rely on different assumptions, but these assumptions also lead them to presuppose that supply is monolithic.

[3] For a description of the organization of governmental supply under competition and of the properties of the equilibrium to which that organization leads, see A. Breton (1996).

is recognized that citizens demand and governmental systems supply not only goods and services like roads, schooling, street lighting, national defense, and police protection, but also goods and services like censorship, war, nationalism, isolationism, jingoism, unemployment, price stability, income redistribution,[4] abortion clinics, and drug control programs, to name but a few of the almost infinite variety of goods and services demanded by citizens and supplied by governments.

As already noted, the essay focuses on one component or dimension of the demand side of politics. In democracies, a necessary component of demand is periodic elections, but it must be stressed that they are *only one* dimension. Demand, in other words, is not only revealed every nth year, but, we suggest, is revealed more or less uninterruptedly. Preferences and demand are, indeed, revealed by polls and surveys, by letters to the editors of newspapers, by lobbying, by "appearing" before committees of inquiry (congressional and parliamentary committees, royal commissions, and other similar ad hoc or standing bodies), by communicating with one's elected representatives or with their constituency offices, and by many other means in a more or less continuous flow.

Those who assume that the only vehicle for the revelation of preferences and demand is the ballot-box are easily led to the view that democratic rule is majority rule. Observation of the most casual variety reveals that many minorities are well represented in the political process. We call these minorities *empowered minorities* and pay no further attention to them in what follows.[5] Instead, we focus on *disempowered minorities* and examine how some minorities become

---

[4] In some models of politics (for example, Meltzer and Richard, 1981; Becker, 1983) it is assumed that politics is exclusively about income redistribution. In that view, the building of a bridge, the management of the TGV (Train à Grande Vitesse), and the provision of public education are no more than 'pretexts' to tax some groups and subsidize others. In other models of politics, income redistribution is assumed to be governed by an ethical imperative derived from some a priori 'theory' or 'model' of justice. We hold to the view that in democracies the income redistribution that takes place is a reflection of the preferences of citizens – preferences which may, of course, be molded by some a priori 'theory' of justice. Redistribution must then be seen as motivated by altruism, as in Hochman (1996), by a desire to reduce the cost of securing property rights, as in Eaton and White (1991), by the ability of governments to enforce intergenerational contracts between parents and children when these contracts are obligatorily incomplete, as in Becker and Murphy (1988), and/or by some other preference-based 'motivation'. For an elaboration of this view, see A. Breton (1996).

[5] In Canada, the 150 largest business corporations have created their own lobby, with a permanent secretariat, to represent their interests. The lobby is known as the Business Council on National Issues (BCNI). Between 1984 and 1993, when the Progressive Conservative party formed the Government, it seemed to some parliamentary journalists that the high degree of congruence between the agenda of the government and that of the BCNI could only be explained by the physical presence of BCNI personnel in the bosom of the government. The speculation was denied by both parties. However, it does suggest that a very small minority group like the BCNI can have great influence on the type of goods and services supplied by governments.

empowered in democracies. The point can be put differently. Democracy has often been seen as an institution through which "the people" become empowered, that is, come to have a degree of control over the apparatus of state and therefore over matters that affect their lives. If this is obviously true for some groups of individuals, it is not true for all groups. In Section 2, we identify the disempowered. Then, in Section 3, we describe a mechanism, an important component of the demand side of democratic politics, through which some disempowered groups become empowered and are then capable of revealing their preferences and of signaling their demands in the democratic process. In Section 4, we illustrate the analysis developed in Sections 2 and 3 with examples of two disempowered groups. Section 5 is devoted to a problem that arises whenever the tools and methodology of neoclassical economics are applied to politics, namely, what assumptions should be made regarding the preferences of citizens, and Section 6 offers some brief comments about the effect of newly empowered groups on the status of previously empowered groups. Section 7 concludes the paper.

2   Who are the disempowered?

The disempowered are not, any more than many other people in society, devoid of personal, moral, or spiritual *strengths* or lacking in *personal resources* such as support networks of families and/or friends. They are people who endure particular situations of oppression and have internalized how others, more powerful, have defined these situations, as strictly personal problems capable only of *personal* solutions and not as situations that possess intrinsic political dimensions amenable to genuine *political* solutions. In other words the disempowered are *not* politically aware: (a) they do not perceive themselves as 'political beings', as individuals who have the right to participate and to choose how to participate on the political scene (inside or outside the apparatus of government); (b) they are not alert to the fact that the situations they experience personally are influenced by and related to socioeconomic and political force – they are not conscious of the interconnections between issues, hence their tendency to define problems in personal terms without reference to the socioeconomic, cultural, and political linkages that circumscribe the environment in which these problems fester; (c) they are not aware of being part of, or of belonging to a minority that encounters the same problems and, as a consequence, do not experience their situations as a function of their minority status in society (see Breton, 1994a).

As we have already suggested, to be disempowered is not to be part of a minority, but to be part of a *politically voiceless minority*. It is, at the most basic level, to be unaware that one has things to say, the right to say those things, and a voice to propagate them in the public arena. The essence of disempowerment is to be voiceless or silenced. Even people who come to recognize that they have a voice and that they have the right to use it will remain disempowered if they do not know how to use or are prevented from using their voice in such a way as to be heard and to make their preferences and demands known, just like empowered minorities do.

The disempowered begin to acquire power when *they define* their situations in political terms, when *they decide* how they will deal with their situations, and when *they act* on their decisions. To become empowered does not mean that all actions are successful, but that there is a positive probability, a fighting chance, that actions will be successful.

As has been documented,[6] the disempowered are to be found among the elderly and the low-income elderly (Cox, 1988; Wells and Taylor, 1991), the homeless (Breton, 1988; Lee, 1991; Sacks, 1991), the mentally disabled (Anthony and Blanch, 1989; Chamberlain, 1984), the chronically and severely mentally disabled (Mowbray, Wellwood, and Chamberlain, 1988; Salem, Seidman, and Rappaport, 1988), native peoples (O' Sullivan, Waugh, and Espeland, 1984), poor women, including single mothers (Cosse and Home, 1992; Cox, 1991; Parsons, 1991; Travers, 1995), children in state custody (Hegar and Hunzeker, 1988), various immigrant groups (Gutierrez and Ortega, 1991; Hirayama and Cetingok, 1988), refugees (Duke, 1992), women who have experienced abuse (Gagné, 1993), the physically disabled (Wagner, 1992), disadvantaged youth (Keenan and Pinkerton, 1991; Parsons, 1988), and people of color (Gutierrez, 1990; Mandell and Postel, 1992; Solomon, 1976).

3   An empowerment mechanism

The passage from disempowerment to empowerment has been observed, documented, and conceptualized (see, for example, Boff and Boff, 1986; Breton, 1989, 1994b; Gutierrez, 1973; Hegar, 1989; Rappaport, 1984; Rappaport, Swift, and Hess, 1984) and can be portrayed as a series of *steps* that describe a mechanism or process of empowerment. We insist that those who make the passage will not, as a rule, recognize and experience their progress toward empowerment as neat and well-delineated steps. Furthermore, in some instances the steps will overlap or run together and in others some steps will be skipped. The passage will therefore not be identical for every individual or group achieving empowerment (see also Rappaport, 1985, on this point). At a level of abstraction different from the one that governs Table 9.1 and the following discussion, the passage from disempowerment to empowerment can be collapsed into three essential steps: the first involves changing one's views of self and the world; the second involves taking action to change one's situation; and the third involves provok-

---

[6] The references we provide are only a sample of what exists.

ing a political response that ensures the desired change in the situation. The stylized process or mechanism we present in Table 9.1 and that we explicate in this section abstracts from a multiplicity of details that vary from case to case – and are therefore important in field work and in the analysis of particular cases – but need not be incorporated in what is, in effect, a model of empowerment.

Typically, at the beginning of the process of empowerment, the disempowered do not identify themselves as disempowered: would they do so, they would already be thinking in terms of power and assessing the possibility of becoming empowered. Before they begin to think that way, they have to define their situation as being more than an individual or personal problem. This is why the first step in the process of empowerment involves one or more *activists* bringing together, in a mutual-aid or self-help group or organization, people who share a particular situation of disempowerment. These activists, militants or radicals to a certain degree, are aware of the social and political dimensions of the situation and are concerned with, and knowledgeable about, the plight of the people in that particular situation. Their knowledge may involve firsthand experience of the situation, as when former inmates of psychiatric institutions or members of their immediate families spur the creation of self-help and advocacy groups such as those under the National Alliance for the Mentally Ill (NAMI) in the United States (Anthony and Blanch, 1989; Zinman, 1986) or GROW[7] in Australia, which was founded by a group of ex-patients led by a priest recovering from mental breakdown (Salem et al., 1988). Or the knowledge may be 'second hand' and derived from the experiences of professionals who deal with a given situation on a daily basis, as when social workers instigate the formation of mutual-aid groups for women who have experienced abuse (Gagné, 1993).

It is important to emphasize that activists bring the disempowered together in *groups*, because in groups there is a better chance of addressing the inseparability of private troubles and public issues, for even though themes may surface as private troubles, these private troubles soon become shared troubles, which provides the ground for (though does not guarantee) the analysis of the structural sources of these troubles. As John Longres and Eileen McLeod (1980, p. 273) state: "It is only there [in groups] that the full implications of the effects of social status may become apparent. In working with individuals and families separately, the weight is too strongly distributed in favor of individual uniqueness and private troubles."

The process of conscientization or consciousness-raising that develops in groups is the second step in the empowerment mechanism. It involves two major, closely related but distinct, cognitive shifts: one entails "forging a new identity" (Zinman, 1986), the other entails perceiving the interconnectedness of personal situations and the accompanying socioeconomic, cultural, and political

---

[7] Unlike NAMI, GROW is not an acronym; it means what it says.

Table 9.1. *A stylized mechanism of empowerment*

STEP 1	GROUP FORMATION	A group is formed by one or more **activists** (militants or radicals) concerned about the situation of certain persons. These activists will often have personally experienced the situation that motivates their action.
STEP 2	a) CONSCIENTIZATION	Group members **narrate** life stories, events and episodes and discover that they are not alone experiencing a given situation. They thus discover that the situation cannot be totally of their making.
	b) ACQUISITION OF A VOICE	Group members **reflect** and come to **understand** the socioeconomic, cultural, and political roots and causes of their situation.
STEP 3	ACTION	Group members **voice** their concerns to the community and to politicians through some type of action: demonstrations, rallies, marches, talks, interviews, seminars, articles, books, and other media channels.
STEP 4	PUBLIC INDIFFERENCE	Because of the use of conflicting paradigms, the public is baffled and unable to understand. The group members' voice is **unheard.**
STEP 5	RADICALIZATION	To be heard, group members **form coalitions** with other groups and **engage in strategies and tactics** which, because they are designed to elicit attention, are often provocative, annoying, and even irritating.
STEP 6	POLITICAL RESPONSE	One or more political entrepreneurs and/or governmental centers of power **open up** and **respond** in a minimal way to the voices of the disempowered.
STEP 7	FOCUSED PRESSURE	Group members begin to lobby in an organized fashion and to formulate precise **demands** for legislation, policies, and/or services. The disempowered are becoming an **empowered minority.**
STEP 8	BUREAUCRATIZATION	Group members organize as permanent lobbies with secretariats to watch over the group's interests. They are now part of the process of democratic politics.

dimensions. This process starts as soon as the members of groups begin narrating their individual stories, for as they do so, they become aware of some common 'threads' in their stories; they recognize the similar *patterns* of discrimination or exploitation, the similar 'external' factors that characterize all their individual and personal stories. They see that others, 'in the same boat,' are not to blame for similar situations, and if others are not to blame, they are not to blame either. Thus they begin to rid themselves of the negative self-images they had internalized and to free themselves from the various labels that had been ascribed to them: they begin to perceive themselves and their situation in a new light. This process of surmounting internal blockages is usually a slow one and, as a consequence, Step 2 can last a long time.[8]

In the process of narrating their stories, the members of groups also begin to realize that they have something to say and that each member is the only one who can tell her/his story, even though all the stories resemble one another. They begin to "name the world" (Freire, 1993) – they realize they have a voice. As they discover that they have a voice, they discover that they have the right to speak up and to 'have a say.' Empowerment, in the sense that it involves consciousness-raising, is a process of liberation from voicelessness or from silence. With the awareness of the right to 'have a say,' comes the realization that they have the right to participate in the decisions that affect their lives. Both rights involve self-advocacy, or the power to represent oneself or one's group (Breton, 1994a).

This brings us to Step 3, in which group members do something. Up to this point, they have *reflected* on their situation, and this reflection has produced a 'cognitive restructuring,' a change in their modes of thinking that has altered their subjective reality (their view of themselves and the world): This will often make them *feel* better about themselves and even *feel* more powerful. However, reflection does not produce any change in the objective reality of their particular situation of disempowerment. For change to have a chance of taking place, reflection must be followed by some kind of political action. Groups that stop at Step 2 may have therapeutic value, but they do not reach political empowerment – many of the early consciousness-raising women's groups never went beyond raising awareness and self-esteem, despite their implicit goal of social change (see Home, 1981). Moreover, now that the notion of empowerment has become ubiquitous, it is often misused and abused by individual or group counselors or therapists who, by creating the illusion of power, exacerbate disempowering situations. Studies show, for example, that when divorcing couples agree to what is commonly called an 'empowerment mediation approach' to custody problems

---

[8] In a way, conscientization is a lifelong process, as Segundo (1976, p. 210) argues "the more 'consciousness' one acquires, the more difficult it becomes to translate its growing demands into the complex and objectified social reality around one."

versus a judicial or litigation approach, the women may 'feel' empowered because they are encouraged to be assertive, because the mediation counselor listens to them and makes their husbands listen to them, etc. In the end, however, women give up more, in terms of their own custody preferences, than those who go through the judicial process: this explains why men overwhelmingly prefer mediation versus a judicial process – their disproportionately powerful status tends to be better protected in the more intimate situation of mediation (Astor, 1991; Crean, 1988; Kelly and Duryee, 1992; Neuman, 1992; Regehr, 1994; Rifkin, 1984; Shaffer, 1988), even though the court system frequently discriminates against women (Lerman, 1984).

In empowerment groups, the conscientization or consciousness-raising is seen not only as a personal process of cognitive restructuring but as a politicization process and a liberation process that create a demand for sociopolitical restructuring: Step 3 follows this demand with action. The group members attempt to change their situation by using their newfound voices and seizing opportunities and/or confronting barriers in their socioeconomic, political, and cultural environment. Depending on the sophistication, skills, abilities, and other resources of the members, these attempts will include, for example, taking part in demonstrations, rallies, or marches; giving interviews to newspaper, radio, and/or television reporters; participating in town hall meetings; talking to politicians; leading seminars; and writing letters to the editors, articles, or books. As more groups engage in these activities, they begin to develop an intergroup solidarity – expectations of being heard grow.

However, when a previously silent and disempowered minority first attempts to make itself heard, it is in effect proposing a new paradigm, and, as is to be expected, the public's initial reactions are bafflement, inability to understand, indifference, or in many cases, downright hostility. The groups' voice thus remains unheard, and expectations are dashed. This is characteristic of Step 4, though it is important to recognize that as more and more conscientized groups voice their concern about a given situation of oppression, they slowly produce a significant shift in the hitherto dominant paradigm, and the public's response becomes more favorable. Thus, for example, when, some fifteen years ago, groups of women who experienced abuse (and their advocates) began to demand protection in the form of safe houses, that is, hostels, the response was minimal. At present, however, when a group of women who have experienced abuse become conscientized and demand a hostel in their area, if none exists, it is somewhat easier for them to obtain one, because there are growing numbers of citizens who no longer accept domestic violence as a purely personal or private matter, but acknowledge its political dimensions and see those as amenable to political solutions. In a real way, Step 4 describes the beginning of a process of conscientization *of the public and of politicians* – a process that continues through Steps 5 and 6. Only if the public and the governing apparatus become conscientized – substitute an old for a new paradigm or alter their information structures – will the governmental system become responsive.

In Step 5, group members evaluate the public's reactions to their demands and reflect again on their situation. Through this movement from reflection to action back to reflection, through this 'praxis,' members acquire an increasingly critical consciousness of the workings of power, which contrasts with their initial naive consciousness of the interconnectedness of issues (Freire, 1993). This increased consciousness leads to increased expectations of being heard and having their requests attended to seriously. Thus, in this step, group members start designing and adopting strategies that will elicit attention and that will 'force' the community and the politicians to listen and to hear them: they become radicalized. These attention-getting strategies will often be provocative, annoying, and possibly irritating, at least to some people, as when groups threaten to pitch tents on a town common or do so on a courthouse lawn (see Section 4). But many do eventually succeed, which introduces Step 6.

In this sixth step, the voices of the disempowered become more difficult to ignore, and one or more political entrepreneurs and/or governmental centers of power open up and respond, even though the response may be minimal (which, as mentioned above, is usual during the initial phase of paradigm shifts). Sensing an opening, group members, in Step 7, begin to lobby in an organized fashion and to formulate precise demands for legislation, policies, and services. The disempowered minority is becoming an empowered minority. In a movement toward consolidating their gains, group members, in Step 8, organize as permanent lobbies. They become bureaucratized, creating secretariats or other organizational systems to watch over their interests. They are now part of the process of democratic politics.

4   Two illustrations

The empowerment mechanism we have just described, though possibly intuitively discerned by all observant social scientists, is for most still largely unfamiliar. For that reason, we present two illustrations. The literature offers many more, though not necessarily with the same orderliness of steps as given in Table 9.1: As we have already indicated, these stylized steps were provided to formalize the mechanism. The first illustration relates to homeless men and women and the second to women on welfare. We sketch each in turn.

Homeless men and women

The first illustration is taken from Jerome Sacks (1991); it reviews work with a group of homeless men and women in a rural town of 18,000 inhabitants in New England (USA). Responding to a thirty-two percent increase over the previous year in requests for emergency shelter, the Northeastern Housing Organization (NHO), a grass roots membership organization made up of tenants, homeowners, and housing advocates, acting as an 'empowered minority,' put forth a rent control bylaw before the town council, which eventually voted to put the bylaw up for a referendum. During the campaign, NHO consolidated its leadership in a six-person steering committee, its mailing list grew to over 150, "and consciousness about the need for affordable housing and homelessness was raised in the town" (Sacks, 1991, p. 190). The bylaw was defeated almost 2 to 1, but "it was the largest turnout in a bielection in the town's history, and made NHO a force to be taken seriously." After licking its wounds and resting during the summer, the core group of NHO, meeting in the fall, discussed how they could work with and organize low-income people. As some of them had themselves been homeless, and as the local newspaper was reporting that people were living in tents in the woods while funds for a year-round emergency shelter had been denied, the decision was made to try to organize a group for homeless people. The task was left to three NHO activists who would become the group leaders: a formerly homeless woman, a paraprofessional who had worked for a food and clothing distribution service in the town, and a professional social worker with experience in single room occupancy hotels (SROs) in New York.

Members for the group were recruited at the community-meals program run in one of the local churches. At their first meeting, there were two homeless men; a week later, three men and two women showed up; and by the fourth week, there were fifteen men and women. As they joined the group, "each told his/her story" (Sacks, 1991, p. 193); eventually, they started to reflect about what they might try doing for themselves, for example, writing a newsletter and inviting members of the Homeless Alliance (the planning organization for agencies working with the homeless) to come and meet with them. "They also asked if they could participate in Homeless Alliance meetings. Homeless people were never consulted by the Homeless Alliance" (p. 195). They were acquiring a voice and were eager to use it.

At the end of each meeting, the group leaders would drive the homeless to "the edge of a secluded woods where they disappeared" (p. 193) – by the second week, it was snowing and the weather had dropped to 30°F (or −1°C). The leaders, acutely aware that they were going home to their warm houses, were angry at local politicians, who had talked about opening Town Hall for emergency shelter and then reneged. At the NHO November meeting, which took place after the second meeting of the homeless group, they suggested that an 'act of witness' be held in front of Town Hall to force the opening of a town building immediately, even though the emergency shelter was due to open two weeks later. The press was called, and: "That night, in 20 degrees Fahrenheit weather six of us stood, from 9-10 p.m. in front of Town Hall" (p. 195). The leaders were becoming radicalized, but the response from town officials, local social service agencies, and many ordinary citizens was definitively negative.

The homeless group continued to meet weekly throughout the winter. They reflected on why it was that they so often verbally attacked each other or defended the professional elite. Eventually, after the leaders had challenged them to question their negative self-images, "the discussion that took place raised both political and psychological consciousness as they recognized how they acted out their frustrations and anger on each other and themselves rather than directing it at those who deserved it. They began to recognize that their energies could be used collectively to help one another" (p. 198).

This reflection prepared them to take action when faced with the closing of the emergency shelter on May 1. In previous years, the homeless would move back to the woods for late spring, summer, and early fall, or go to another town that had a year-round shelter, sleep in doorways or a dumpster, or try to move in with someone. "This year the group asked that [the social worker] pose the issue of where they would go to the Homeless Alliance and suggest that, if a town building or other suitable dwelling was not found, they were prepared to set up tents and sleep on the town common" (p. 200). Resistance was "great" from the politicians and part of the social services community, which called an 'emergency meeting' to berate the social worker personally (p. 200). However, money "magically" appeared to house the homeless in motels that week; the 'tent-in' was scaled down to a 12:00–9:00 p.m. vigil, organized almost completely by group members, who were joined in the vigil by other homeless and poor people from the town.

The political response also involved the town fathers' decision to have the Town Hall used as a shelter from 8:00 p.m. to 7:00 a.m. until a more permanent place could be set up in one of the local agencies. The successful 'focused pressure' exerted by the homeless people of that small town, combined with their radical attention-getting tactics, signaled that they were becoming an 'empowered minority.' As some of them also became a permanent part of the Homeless Alliance, the official bureaucratic organization that watches over the homeless' interests, the homeless of that town can now be seen as part of the process of democratic politics.

Women on welfare

This second illustration is taken from Enid Opal Cox (1991); it describes and analyzes a group of women receiving public assistance from a county department of social services in the United States.

The group was started by a social worker who knew a number of women from her role as their caseworker. "The overall goal was to engage the women in an on-going self empowerment process" (Cox, 1991, p. 84). At the beginning, after getting acquainted, the women told their stories and shared information about the programs and people that affected their lives (i.e., food stamp regulations, aid to dependent children regulations, caseworkers, school systems, etc.). Then they "set about the task of better understanding the power structure of the Department of Social Services" (p. 84), in effect discovering the interconnectedness between their personal situations and the political environment.

After this initial period of reflection, they began to take action: "they identified resource persons and invited them to meetings to explain the role of County Commissioners, the role of the State Department of Social Services, the rules and regulations of programs, etc." (p. 84). As the group members obtained responses and answers and became more knowledgeable, their activities "became more aggressive – calling County Commissioners, attending meetings [such as Department of Social Services Advisory Council meetings] as a group, organizing others to attend meetings, making official requests for increased resources, and requesting changes in the Department of Social Services became regular conduct. They also organized letter writing and telephone campaigns, circulated petitions, and set up tent housing on the court-house lawn" (p. 85).

The effect of these activities was to obtain some changes in food stamp policy and an increase in the operating hours of a service facility used by the group members: "small gains" (p. 88), but also testimony that the women had become part of the process of democratic politics – had started to become empowered – even though they, as a group, did not develop into a bureaucracy or form an institutional lobby.

5   Empowerment and preferences

Frank Knight (1935) has correctly argued that in an economic system in which the suppliers of goods and services are themselves those who promote and advertise what is produced, it is no longer possible to claim ethical authority for that system. Indeed, only in a system in which it is possible to assume that consumers are sovereign and buy or otherwise obtain their information about goods and services from a 'third party' that is competitively organized can an economic system claim ethical authority.

Economists have devoted a significant volume of resources to arguing that business advertising and other types of promotional activities convey unbiased information about products. The argument, in a nutshell, is that consumers are able to test whether what they are told about products is true or false when consuming them and, as a consequence, false advertising is not efficient and will not be a feature of the economic landscape, at least in the long run. In addition, it is argued that the costly persuasion component of advertising and promotion would lose all its value if the information accompanying it was false.

However, when we move from consideration of economic systems to consideration of political systems, a widespread belief is that citizens, as consumers of governmentally provided goods and services, are unable to test whether the advertising and the promotion that go with the supply is true or false. The prevalent view, it is fair to say, is that in the political arena the very same people who, in the marketplace, make rational choices based on stable preferences, become absolute flakes upon entering the political arena.

Joseph Schumpeter (1942), in his essentially vituperative attack on "the classical doctrine of democracy" is, if not the father of that conception of the citizen, at least one of its most articulate champions. For Schumpeter (1942, pp. 260–1), citizens "prove themselves bad judges of their own long-run interests, for it is only the short-run promise that tells politically and only short-run rationality that asserts itself effectively." Later (p. 262) he adds: "Thus the typical citizen drops down to a lower level of mental performance as soon as he enters the political field," and finally[9] (p. 263) he asserts that "the will of the people is the product and not the motive power of the political process."

In more serene language, the same view is expressed by Gary Becker (1983, p. 392, italics and quotation marks as in the original) when he asserts that "*voter preferences* are frequently not a crucial *independent* force in political behavior. These "preferences" can be manipulated and created through information and misinformation provided by interested pressure groups,[10] who raise their political influence partly by changing the revealed "preferences" of enough voters and politicians." In the paragraph that follows this quotation, Becker makes clear that when the same people he has been writing about enter the marketplace they are not the weather vanes that they are assumed to be in the political arena.

The point we wish to emphasize is that if the empowerment mechanism we have described in Section 3 and illustrated in Section 4 captures an important component of real world democratic politics, then the view of citizens as schizophrenic entities is simply false. It is false *in general* because if it is false for those who are initially disempowered and who, through the expenditure of a considerable volume of resources, make the passage to empowerment, it must be false for those who are initially in a more favorable position. Recall that the empowerment mechanism we have modeled is one that describes a process of liberation from negative images, which elites and experts – economists,

---

[9] The word 'finally' applies only to our paper, as any reader of Schumpeter's well-known and important book can verify for herself or himself.

[10] In Becker's model, governments, if they are assumed to exist, are simply the perfectly compliant agents of pressure groups, whose actions alone determine all political outcomes. If one assumes that autonomous governments exist, it is then legitimate to substitute 'government' for 'interested pressure groups' in Becker's text.

political scientists, and social workers – fabricate and then push onto people as an addictive substance, an "opium of the people." The process of empowerment, in other words, is one that leads groups of individuals to discover and articulate their true preferences, to take control of the evolution of these preferences – by filtering political advertising messages and mastering political persuasion – and, through political action, to ensure that these preferences are acknowledged and, in part at least, eventually satisfied.

The possibility of passing from a state of disempowerment to one of empowerment without resorting to violence is a virtue of democratic regimes whose supply side is competitive and responsive and therefore confers on democracy the kind of ethical authority that Knight sought for markets. That is so because in responsive democratic governmental systems, to amend one of Schumpeter's most famous dictums, "the will of the people *is* the motive power of the political process, *not* its product." Responsive democracy also has moral authority because, through empowerment mechanisms, it is capable of meeting the preferences of a large number of minorities.[11]

6   Empowerment and free riding

In *The Logic of Collective Action*, Mancur Olson (1965) suggests that groups formed for the purpose of providing themselves with goods and/or services that possess some measure of Samuelsonian (Samuelson, 1954) publicness will tend to be unstable because each member of the group will have an incentive to free ride – that is, each member will seek to enjoy the benefits of the good and/or service provided by the other members of the group, while reneging on the costs. There can be little doubt that Olson's theory has applications in a large variety of circumstances. The question we raise in this section is whether it applies in the case of groups that become empowered in the fashion described above. Put differently, the question we consider is whether special measures are required to prevent the disintegration of groups that empower themselves, as is necessary for conventional Olsonian groups.

It is obvious that the people who come together in groups and, through the steps described in the foregoing sections, become empowered do so to 'acquire' services that possess some degree of Samuelsonian publicness, given that the test of a group's success is the introduction and implementation of particular public policies from which all benefit. The incentive to free ride is therefore present. We must, however, remember that the process of group formation in this case is one that begins with a reinterpretation of a part of the life histories of its members, a new perception of the roots of their plight that they come

---

[11] Democratic governments, however responsive, can never meet the preferences of all minorities, at least if there are some whose preferences call for the demise of all governments.

to understand as one they share in common. This leads to a solidarity among members that acts to stabilize the groups. The process of group formation is, as a consequence, one that would mitigate and possibly eliminate the incentive to free ride.

7   Sundry reflections on empowerment

So far we have not mentioned a question that must be on the minds of our readers: Does the empowerment of a group of persons necessarily entail the disempowerment of one or more other groups? Does the process of empowerment, in other words, work like the process of acquiring (and holding onto) income in Becker's model of political activity and yield outcomes that are zero sum in empowerment and negative sum in resources? This is not an easy question to answer.

In ancient Rome, fathers had the legal power and the recognized right to kill their children when they deemed it appropriate, and in Great Britain, not long ago, husbands had the legal power and the acknowledged right to beat their wives as long as the rod used for the exercise did not exceed the width of an average male's thumb.[12] In many societies today, men may not have the legal power to batter women and parents may not have the right to abuse children, but except for feeble beginnings here and there, neither are there any strong legal prohibitions and effective penalties against women battering and child abuse. In a number of societies not long ago, slavery was legal and some persons were, as a consequence, legally and effectively defined as the chattel of other persons. In some jurisdictions today, it is not clear whether a wife can obtain an abortion if the husband opposes such a decision, even though abortion may otherwise be legal. This short list of examples of inequality in the extent of empowerment could be considerably extended without difficulty. In the cases we have listed and in all the others that readily come to mind, we have to conclude that, at one level of analysis at least, the empowerment of one group leads to the disempowerment of another.

In our societies today, fathers have less power and children have more than they had in ancient Rome. Husbands can no longer rightfully make use of instruments satisfying the rule of thumb to beat and batter their wives and have been somewhat disempowered and wives proportionately empowered. When male partners can only batter their female partners at the risk of real legal punishment, they will have been even more disempowered and women empowered. The abolition of slavery was a first requirement for the empowerment of former slaves, but it meant the disempowerment of erstwhile owners, and so on.

---

[12] The expression 'rule of thumb,' which our dictionary defines as "a method of procedure based on experience and common sense," derives from this practice. Some common sense!

It is possible to argue that a society in which fathers cannot kill their children when they want to, in which men cannot batter women, in which slavery does not exist, etc., is a better society for *all* its members – former child killers and abusers, women batterers, and slave owners included. If we assume that a measure for the degree of equality of empowerment can be defined for a particular society at a precise moment in time,[13] we could reformulate the preceding proposition to say that it is possible to argue that a society that achieves a greater degree of equality in the distribution of socioeconomic, cultural and political empowerment would be a 'better' society for *all* its members.

Although it is possible to make such an argument, that argument will not be accepted by everyone, and it is impossible to formulate it in a way that would make it generally acceptable: That is why the question that opened this section is so difficult to answer. Formulating the argument in generally acceptable terms is impossible mainly because in a fundamental sense it rests on basic 'values' often rooted in life histories and in life experiences. For example, the virtue of equal empowerment of men and women cannot be fully appreciated except by those who have experienced it; the same is true, we believe, for the virtue of equality of empowerment between parents and children, between ethnic, cultural, and linguistic groups, between the heterosexual and homosexual communities, and so on.

We suggest that these differences in values and in life experiences explain why, when disempowered minorities begin to achieve some degree of empowerment, their new status is often resented by those who are already empowered. The resentment, which would disappear after every one experienced the consequences of more equal empowerment, cannot be removed until equality has been attained, which, as we have seen, can take a very long time.

8   Conclusion

We have tried, in the preceding pages, to incorporate a 'model' of political empowerment into a theory of democracy that is built with the help of neoclassical economic concepts and that is respectful of the methodology of that tradition of economic theory. We have assumed that the supply side of the governmental system was competitive and responsive to citizens, but imperfectly so. We have argued that one essential 'step' in the process of empowerment is that the action of the erstwhile disempowered must eventually become productive. This we have also argued cannot happen unless the public and the politicians change the paradigm they use to analyze particular situations of disempowerment. When the change happens, the imperfection in responsiveness is mitigated. A change in information structures makes competition more effective.

---

[13] It is necessary to identify the society and the point in time, because what constitutes the 'best' or 'optimal' degree of equality will change as societies and persons evolve.

We have decomposed the mechanism or process of empowerment and modeled it as being constituted of eight steps, though we have insisted that this was done to make the mechanism as transparent as possible. In applying the model to particular cases, some steps may not be apparent or may run parallel to each other. We have noted that there are at least three essential steps in the process: (a) achieving conscientization, (b) taking action, and (c) provoking a political response.

The incorporation of the model of empowerment into the analysis of the demand side of democratic politics has led us to briefly discuss three questions that have had a long life in 'the' theory of democracy, at least in the theory erected on 'economic' premises: (1) the matter of the existence, stability, and autonomy of the preferences of citizens; (2) the question of the stability of groups that exist to provide themselves with Samuelsonian public goods and/or services; and (3) the matter of the 'value' to all citizens of more equality in the distribution of socioeconomic, cultural, and political power.

References

Anthony, W. A., and A. Blanch. 1989. Research on community support services: What have we learned, *Psychosocial Rehabilitation Journal*, **12**, 55–81.

Astor, H. 1991. *Position paper on mediation*, National Committee on Violence Against Women, Fyshwick, Australia.

Becker, G. S. 1983. A theory of competition among pressure groups for political influence, *Quarterly Journal of Economics*, **98**, 371–400.

Becker, G. S., and K. M. Murphy. 1988. The family and the state, *Journal of Law and Economics*, **31**, 1–18.

Boff, L., and C. Boff. 1986. *Liberation Theology: From Confrontation to Dialogue*, translated by Robert R. Barr, Harper and Row, San Francisco.

Brennan, G., and J. M. Buchanan. 1980. *The Power to Tax. Analytical Foundations of a Fiscal Constitution*, Cambridge University Press, New York.

Breton, A. 1996. *Competitive Governments. An Economic Theory of Politics and Public Finance*, Cambridge University Press, New York.

Breton, M. 1988. The need for mutual-aid groups in a drop-in for homeless women: The sistering case, *Social Work with Groups*, **11**, 47–61.

1989. Liberation theology, group work, and the right of the poor and oppressed to participate in the life of the community, *Social Work with Groups* **12**, 5–18. Reprinted in *Group Work Reaching Out: People, Placess, and Power*, James Garland, ed., Haworth Press, New York, 1992.

1994a. On the meaning of empowerment and empowerment-oriented social work practice, *Social Work with Groups*, **17**, 23–37.

1994b. Relating competence-promotion and empowerment, *Journal of Progressive Human Services*, **5**, 27–44.

Chamberlain, P. J. 1984. Speaking for ourselves: An overview of the ex-psychiatric inmates' movement, *Psychosocial Rehabilitation Journal*, **8**, 56–63.

Cosse, P., and A. Home. 1992. Groupes de Femmes: Outil de Prise en Charge Collective, In *Actes du Colloque Les Journées Simone Paré*, Université Laval, Québec.

Cox, E. O. 1988. Empowerment of the low income elderly through group work, *Social Work with Groups*, **11**, 111–25.

1991. The critical role of social action in empowerment oriented groups, *Social Work with Groups*, **14**, 77–90.

Crean, S. 1988. *In the Name of Fathers*, Amanita Publications, Toronto.

Downs, A. 1957. *An Economic Theory of Democracy*, Harper and Row, New York.

Duke, X. 1992. Latin American women: In pursuit of empowerment, Manuscript.

Eaton, B. C., and W. D. White. 1991. The distribution of wealth and the efficiency of institutions, *Economic Inquiry*, **29**, 336–50.

Freire, P. 1993. *Pedagogy of the Oppressed*, Continuum, New York.

Gagné, E. 1993. Beyond therapy and mutual aid to social action: A group of survivors of sexual abuse make a video. Manuscript

Gutierrez, G. 1973. *A Theology of Liberation*, translated by Sister Caridad Inda and John Eagleson, Orbis Books, Maryknoll, New York.

Gutierrez, L. M. 1990. Working with women of color: An empowerment perspective, *Social Work*, **35**, 149–53.

Gutierrez, L. M., and R. Ortega. 1991. Developing methods to empower latinos: The importance of groups, *Social Work with Groups*, **14**, 23–43.

Hegar, R. L. 1989. Empowerment-based practice with children, *Social Services Review*, **63**, 372–83.

Hegar, R. L., and J. M. Hunzeker. 1988. Moving toward empowerment-based practice in public child welfare, *Social Work*, **33**, 499–502.

Hicks, J. R. 1935. The theory of monopoly, *Econometrica*, **3**: 1–20. Reprinted in *Readings in Price Theory*, George J. Stigler and Kenneth Boulding, eds., Irwin, Homewood, Ill., 1952.

Hirayama, H., and M. Cetingok. 1988. Empowerment: A social work approach for Asian immigrants, *Social Casework*, 69, 41–7.

Hochman, H. M. 1996. Public choice interpretations of distributional preferences, *Constitutional Political Economy*, **7**, 3–20.

Home, A. 1981. Towards a model of change in consciousness-raising groups, *Social Work with Groups*, **4**, 155–68.

Keenan, E., and J. Pinkerton. 1991. Some aspects of empowerment: A case study of work with disadvantaged youth, *Social Work with Groups*, **14**, 109–124.

Kelly, J., and M. Duryee. 1992. Women's and men's views of mediation in voluntary and mandatory settings, *Family and Conciliation Courts Review*, **30**, 34–49.

Knight, F. H. 1935. *The Ethics of Competition*, Allen and Unwin, London.

Lee, J. A. B. 1991. Empowerment through mutual aid groups: A practice grounded conceptual framework, *Groupwork*, **4**, 5–21.

Lerman, L. 1984. Mediation of wife abuse cases: The adverse effect of informal dispute resolution on women, *Harvard Women's Law Journal*, **7**, 57.

Longres, J. F., and E. McLeod. 1980. Consciousness-raising and social work, *Social Casework*, **61**, 267–76.

Mandell, B. R., and P. Postel. 1992. Consumer control of social agencies: Case study of a black mothers' group, *Social Work with Groups*, **15**, 285–99.

Meltzer, A. H., and S. F. Richard. 1981. A rational theory of the size of government, *Journal of Political Economy*, **89**, 914–27.

Mowbray, C. J., R. Wellwood, and P. J. Chamberlain. 1988. Project stay: A consumer-run support service, *Psychosocial Rehabilitation Journal*, **12**, 33-42.

Neuman, D. 1992. How mediation can effectively address the male-female power imbalance in divorce, *Mediation Quarterly*, **9**, 227–39.

Olson, M. Jr. 1965. *The Logic of Collective Action*, Harvard University Press, Cambridge.

O'Sullivan, M. J., N. Waugh, and W. Espeland. 1984. The Fort McDowell Yavapai: From pawns to powerbrokers, in *Studies in Empowerment: Steps Toward Understanding and Action*, J. Rappaport, C. Swift, and R. Hess, eds., Haworth Press, New York.

Parsons, R. J. 1988. Empowerment for role alternatives for low-income minority girls: A group work approach. *Social Work with Groups*, **11**(4), 27–45.

1991. Empowerment as purpose and practice principle in social work, *Social Work with Groups*, **14**, 7–21.

Rappaport, J. 1984. Studies in empowerment: Introduction to the issue, *Prevention in Human Services*, **3**, 1–7.

1985. The power of empowerment language, *Social Policy*, **7**, 4–20.

Rappaport, J., C. Swift, and R. Hess. 1984. *Studies in Empowerment: Steps Towards Understanding and Action*, Haworth Press, New York.

Regehr, C. 1994. The use of empowerment in child custody mediation: A feminist critique, *Mediation Quarterly*, **11**(4), 361–371.

Rifkin, J. 1984. Mediation from a feminist perspective: Promise and problems, *Law and Inequity*, **2**, 21–31.

Sacks, J. 1991. Action and reflection in work with a group of homeless people, *Social Work with Groups*, **14**, 187–202.

Salem, D. A., E. Seidman, and J. Rappaport. 1988. Community treatment of the mentally ill: The promise of mutual-help organizations, *Social Work*, **33**, 403–8.

Samuelson, P. A. 1954. The pure theory of public expenditure, *Review of Economics and Statistics*, **36**, 387–89.

Schumpeter, J. A. 1942. *Capitalism, Socialism and Democracy*, reprint, Harper Brothers, New York, 1950.

Segundo, J. L. 1976. *The Liberation of Theology*, translated by John Drury, Orbis Books, Maryknoll, New York.

Shaffer, M. 1988. Divorce mediation: A feminist perspective, *University of Toronto Law Review*, **46**, 162.

Solomon, B. B. 1976. *Black Empowerment: Social Work in Oppressed Communities*, Columbia University Press, New York.

Travers, A. 1995. Adversity, diversity and empowerment: Feminist group work with women in poverty, in *Group Work Practice in a Troubled Society*, R. Kurland and R. Salmon, eds., Harworth Press, New York.

Wagner, R. A. 1992. Group work with mainstreamed adolescents who are differently-abled physically, in *Working from Strengths: The Essence of Group Work*, D. F. Fike and B. Rittner, eds., Center for Group Work Studies, Miami, Fla.

Wells, L., and L. E. Taylor, 1991. Empowering older people in residential settings, *Adult Residential Care Journal*, **5**, 249–61.

Zinman, S. 1986. Self-help: The wave of the future, *Hospital and Community Psychiatry*, **37**, 213.

CHAPTER 10

Political participation, voting, and economic policy: Three problems of modern democracies

Luigi Campiglio

1   Introduction

Modern societies depend increasingly on participation to achieve economic efficiency, both in the marketplace and in parliament. For example, in many universities, students assign marks to their teachers to help them be more effective; and many firms, public and private, ask customers to fill in forms that rate customer's satisfaction with the service provided. In politics the main form of participation is represented by the act of voting: It is, however, a very incomplete form of participation, and the economic consequences of this limitation need to be acknowledged and better understood. This essay points to three major issues. The first is related to the lack of representation for a significant share of the population, namely children and young people. The second issue regards the economic consequences of the relationship between younger and older voters, as revealed by the multipeak surface of the joint age–income distribution. A simple way to analyze this issue is to refer to the median voter model, exploiting the implied statistical relationship between median and average income. The third issue points to the problem of low political participation as a possible cause of higher violent crime rates, higher law enforcement costs, and a lower quality of life. Possible solutions to the issues raised are simply hinted, because they need to be specific to each country: in particular, the potential benefits of new information technology need to be explored.

2   The incomplete universal suffrage: Are democracies against children?

In all modern democracies the minimum age requirement for casting a ballot is eighteen years: the share of population without the franchise, because they

---

I thank an anonymous referee for his comments, which helped to clarify the content and exposition of this paper.

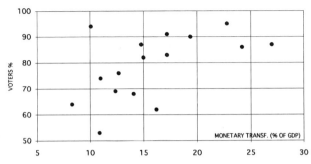

Figure 10.1. Social security transfers and political turnout. (*Source*: OCED (1987): Piven and Cloward (1988)).

are less than eighteen years old, is therefore twenty-six percent in the United States, twenty-four percent in France, twenty-three percent in the United Kingdom, twenty-one percent in Italy, and nineteen percent in Germany. Voting turnout bears a significant relationship to the pattern of public expenditure: In a cross-section comparison, as shown in Figure 10.1 voting turnout is positively related to social security transfers (as a share of GNP), and the percentage of population over sixty-five years old is positively related to the share of collective consumption (Campiglio, 1990).

Elderly voters determine a clear shift in the composition of aggregate demand and public expenditure: By the same token, in a historical perspective, the development of the modern welfare state can be related to the gradual spread of universal suffrage. Franchise was extended to women only in 1928 in the United Kingdom and in 1945 in Italy and France: In most industrialized countries, universal suffrage was achieved between the the two world wars, when the diffusion of social security systems also became more general. It is no accident that after World War II we observe a structural and permanent shift toward more equality in all modern democracies. These indications are further confirmed by Usui (1987), who has studied the adoption of social insurance policies in sixty-three countries in the period 1880–1976. The proportion of old people (defined as over sixty-five) is a significant variable in explaining the first adoption of social insurance policies in a country, and it is a very significant variable in explaining the adoption of an unemployment program. It may seem strange that the proportion of old people does not explain the old-age program, but Usui's results show that this program is mainly determined by the fact that some other programs have already been adopted: Old-age programs seem to be the net result of an "epidemic" diffusion model in which a major factor is the program adopted in the first place. This evidence is further sustained by Wilensky (1976), who claims that in the United States the increase of the elderly as a fraction of the population is the most powerful source for the increase in welfare spending. There is therefore a consistent literature pointing to the crucial role of the (voting) elderly in growing public expenditure, which symmetrically contrasts with the lack of any evidence with reference to the role of (nonvoting) children and youths. However, the fact that one out of four or five citizens has no political voice and electoral weight weakens, by definition, the social force and moral acceptance of universal suffrage. The minimum age requirement has a historical, social, and psychological base: it can nevertheless seriously distort the amount and direction of resource redistribution. In this perspective it is useful to scrutinize a finer distinction of age brackets: in the United States twenty-two percent of the population is less than fifteen years old, fifteen percent is less than ten years old, and eight percent is less than five years old. Children and youth raise fundamental questions of social choice and justice, in both utilitarian and contractualist traditions. Rawls (1971, p. 128) sidesteps the problem when, for the purpose of defining the parties who decide under a veil of ignorance, he asserts that "we may think of the parties as heads of families, and therefore as having a desire to further the welfare of their nearest descendant" with no reference to the possibility that children as parties could also choose under uncertainty. This seems an unfortunate shortcoming because it is among the children that the least advantaged and most unfortunate individuals are more likely to be found: the high infant mortality rates, both in the developed and less-developed countries, are indeed a startling proof. The structural bias against children is implicitly a bias of modern democracies against the family: this is confirmed by the slight but steady decrease of social protection benefits for family and maternity in the major European countries during the 1980s.

The utilitarian tradition is based on the assumption that similar persons share a common and complete pool of information: the exclusion, by assumption, of antisocial preferences allows meaningful interpersonal comparisons to be made. Incomplete information makes the utilitarian calculus more vague, because of the serious problems involved in the choice between *ex ante* and *ex post* utility (Hammond, 1982). Any discussion of the interests of children in terms of utility reveals the existence of a fundamental flaw in modern welfarism because the recognition that education is indispensable to children implies – so to say, by definition – that their lack of information is structural. Moreover, adults are not simply bigger children, which means that a common utility function cannot satisfactorily accommodate the physical characteristics both of the children and of the adults. This does not imply that equivalence scales are not useful but it points to a limit on their social meaning.

An explicit ethical choice, allowing for interpersonal comparison of utility, would assign in the aggregate function weights declining with age to individual utilities (putting upper and lower bounds on the young and the elderly). The existing principle of "one man, one vote" would be replaced with that of one life, one vote. The ethical judgment of equal (or higher) weights for the young implies an imaginative change aimed at giving them a political "voice" within the framework of existing political rules governing democratic societies. At a political level, the children–parents relationship could be seen as an agency relationship, with the children as the principal and the parents as the agents: in this perspective the father and/or the mother could act as representative of their children and vote in their place. Accepting this idea, however, would imply the typical problems of an agency relationship: it cannot be taken for granted that parents will act in the best interest of their children. A more elaborate proposal would consider the younger nonvoters by age groups. Franchise could become an increasing function of age: in the case of small children, the parents, as agents, could exercise their voting rights; whereas teenagers could directly elect their representative, both at local and national levels. Some rules would be useful. For example, representatives should not be older than a given age (e.g., thirty years) and their political agenda should be restricted to the problems of the young. However unusual this proposal may seem, it should be evaluated on its potential benefits, particularly in terms of a better generational allocation of resources or the opportunity for an improvement in civic and political participation.

It is a common complaint that we do not care enough for the future generations when a distant horizon is involved in the decisions. Common examples are the issues of public debt or the environment. To give a political voice to the unborn of the next generation, however, is puzzling because they will have life only if parents decide to have children. Parents may decide not to have children because they are myopic or selfish, but simply, also, because they are uncertain about the future. The existing generation could "optimally" deplete the environment without harming the next generation by deciding to have fewer children and a declining population. Alternatively, the existing generation could optimally accumulate public debt by deciding to have more children and an increasing population. Whereas the debate about the representation of the unborn is inherently controversial, the possibility of giving political voice to the newborn should be undisputed: they do not yet have the right to vote, but they will be the first *existing* generation to suffer the mistakes of their parents.

3   Are young voters altruistic toward older voters or just outvoted?

We have computed the joint distribution of households according to income and age it Italy, and the results put the problem of intergenerational redistribution related to social security and pensions into a new perspective (see Figure 10.2). The results are revealing: The surface of the distribution exhibits many peaks, which can be grouped around two main age groups, the first corresponding to the householder's age group 35–44 with a household income of 20–30 million lira (1993), and the second corresponding to the householder's age group 65–75

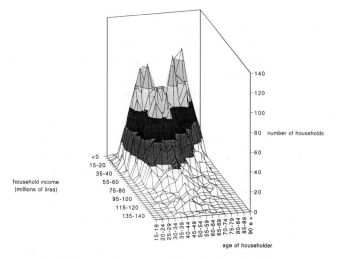

Figure 10.2. Household by income and householder age in Italy. (*Source*: Computation based on Bank of Italy Survey of Households Income and Wealth.)

and with a household income of 10–20 million lira. The age distance between the two main peaks, thirty years, is only four years more than the median age at first marriage and therefore the distance between young and old can also be interpreted as the distance between parents and their children.

The different levels of income and age are an implicit measure of the process of income redistribution, particularly for pensions. Should the young outnumber the old, then parliaments could democratically repudiate the debt implicit in the pensions: There are many ways to repudiate old promises made by parliaments about pensions. It is possible to raise the retirement age or to reduce the ratio of the pension paid with respect to the previous salary: both these methods are part of the pension reform schemes in Italy as well in many other countries. Of course, the process could work in the opposite direction if the old were in the majority. This remark points to a crucial point about the current debate about pension reforms: It is possible to conceive different contractual arrangements, for example, private versus public, in spite of the fact that the economic content of the contract is always the same, namely, the continuous transfer of resources from the young to the old. At each point in time the working young have to transfer resources to the retired old: As the population becomes older the income redistribution from the young to the old will increasingly be the result of the young being outnumbered and this fact calls for a social contract to avoid a generational conflict. With public pensions the state redistributes to the old the taxes currently levied on the young, whereas with private pension schemes the companies redistribute the income deriving from their current investments. The binding force of a private contract is stronger than a promise from parliament: However, a private firm can go bankrupt whereas the state cannot. The main economic power characterizing the state is the power to tax: An overlooked and related power is that of repudiating a previous promise to pay or pay back, and, unfortunately, economic history provides plenty of examples of public repudiation. The instrument of public repudiation is sensitive and delicate because unless it is supported by a quasi-unanimity, it can destroy the moral asset value of the state, namely, the certainty of its promises, of which money is the most obvious example. The point we want to underline is that income redistribution from the young to the old rests inherently on a social contract between parents and children: In fact, a society could decide to transfer the resources directly within the family, as happens in Asian countries where, actually, the burden of the welfare state is also lighter.

This argument also allows us to address the question of the median voter model and a related paradox. The model of the median voter can be considered a crucial link between economics and political science: its importance is stressed in standard textbooks, like Stiglitz's (1988), where it is aptly pointed out that *"if all individuals vote*, the median voter is the individual who has the median income" (our italics). The model of the median voter represents an invaluable shortcut in deriving testable implications of social choice in majority voting: It implies well-known restrictions on preferences that, however, cannot easily be disposed of in empirical testing. The implicit assumption that all individuals do in fact vote is, however, crucial both for the median voter model and, more generally, for social choice theory. Income distribution is usually well approximated by a lognormal distribution, for which mode < median < average: If voters' preferences are single peaked, then the median voter can ask for an income redistribution implemented through an appropriate tax policy under majority rule. The paradox is the following: Why doesn't the majority pursue its self-interest, increasing its income by the percentage implied by the average/median ratio? The previous argument can solve this paradox, which is grounded on an old political debate. As a starting point, we consider the insights of Tocqueville (1835, p. 210), who thought that "public expenses must tend to increase when people rule" because "a democratic government is the only one in which those who vote for a tax can escape the obligation to pay for it." In Tocqueville's view the amount of public expenditures, and therefore the size of government, is inversely related to the degree of inequality: The greater the inequality, the more likely a majority of the poor, who, given universal suffrage, will impose a substantial redistribution. Down's (1957) view, which is that "in a democracy the poor are able to use their votes to obtain transfers from the rest of the society" (pp. 198–201) simply restates Tocqueville's view in different words. A seemingly different and well-known hypothesis about income redistribution in a democracy is the so-called Director's Law, according to which income tends

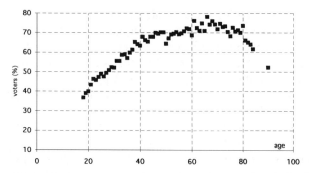

Figure 10.3. Political turnout by age – 1992. (*Source*: U.S. Bureau of Census, Current population report, *Voting and Registration in the Election of November 1992*.)

to be transferred from both high-income and low-income voters to voters who are in the center of the income distribution. Indeed, Tocqueville considered the rule of the middle classes as the most economical for a democracy because "they will not raise extravagant taxes, for there is nothing as disastrous as a heavy levy on a small fortune" (p. 209) and therefore praised their economic role in a modern democracy.

Meltzer and Richard (1981) take up the problem of the size of the government and, following Tocqueville's tradition, make the hypothesis that it depends on the spread of the franchise and the distribution of wealth: Formally, they make the size of the government dependent on the relation of mean income to the income of the decisive voter. The crucial amendment to this explanation is the distinction between voters and nonvoters: In fact, the model of Meltzer and Richard holds only for the subset of voters. In the United States the percentage of voters is positively related to age and income: Therefore nonvoters tend to be concentrated among younger persons and lower income families (see Figure 10.3).

Because the proportion of nonvoters is greater at lower income levels, the shape of the lognormal distribution is modified and shifted toward the normal distribution: As a consequence, the ratio of mean income to the income of median voter decreases, and according to Meltzer and Richard's model so does the tax rate and the size of the government. This is exactly what is borne out by the data: The United States and Japan have a lower turnout and a correspondingly lower share of public expenditure and taxation, whereas Europe has, on average, higher turnout and higher share of public expenditures.

Our framework addresses the issue at two different levels. First, a median income lower than the average can be the result of an implicit social contract; second, each young person can simply prefer a steadily rising income to a falling one and when he is young vote so as to be richer when old. The second argument contradicts the life-cycle hypothesis, but it is strongly supported by the data, if we consider for each age group the average income per recipient and by component. The household income has a peak in the age bracket 50–54, whereas the corresponding income per recipient peaks earlier in the age bracket 45–49: However, the average family size starts to decrease around the age of 50 and the per-component income in the household increases steadily with age, reaching a maximum in the 70–74 age bracket. In terms of welfare it is the income per component in the household that is relevant, rather than the income per recipient: Given a positive relationship between income per component and age, the median vote claiming a redistribution would indeed vote against himself in a matter of few years.

The lognormal distribution of household income therefore reflects collective rational behavior, both for individuals and generational groups: We suggest that the choice of whether to vote or not also reflects rational, or "meaningful," behavior. The so-called voting paradox asserts that the cost of voting is higher than the expected individual benefit and therefore the act of voting has no rational economic basis: It is, however, possible that this argument rests on misleading assumptions and estimates about the cost and benefits of voting. After all, a simple linear regression of turnout on age gives a positive relationship with a strongly significant coefficient: it is no accident that the elderly have the highest turnout and are also the biggest recipients of public expenditure. Existing evidence (Filer and Kenny, 1980) shows that voter turnout increases as the probability of affecting the outcome rises and decreases as the cost of vote rises; reducing the cost of voting by allowing postal vote seems to many an effective way of increasing global turnout. This indeed seems to be the case considering the case of Germany, where it is possible to analyze the role of postal votes over a long sequence of elections since World War II. In Germany, political turnout has traditionally stood at very high levels, ranging from eighty-five to ninety percent until the end of the 1970s. In the 1980s, turnout levels recorded a sharp decline, falling to seventy-eight percent in 1990. The postal vote had been increasing, reaching a peak in 1980, whereas during the 1980s, the postal vote declined simultaneously with the decline in aggregate turnout: In other words, postal vote has not balanced the decline of political participation. Moreover, there is no stable relation, in the elections for the Länder, between postal vote and turnout. It is true, however, that the postal vote, about ten percent of the total, represents a significant proportion of the total vote: The same proportion of postal vote in the United States would crucially modify and improve the political mechanism and as such it should strongly be commended. In the U.S. presidential elections of 1992 the turnout increased, with a major contribution coming from the youngest and the unemployed. The increase in turnout has also been a clear signal for economic policy. We suggest that the problem of persistent European unemployment is further worsened by the lack of a reliable political signal from the voters: The political business cycle can be a source of inefficiency, but it is also the origin of a precious signal for the formulation of economic policy (Campiglio, 1994).

4   Are political participation and peace helpful to welfare and growth?

Economic growth springs from a virtuous coordination led by the "invisible hand": the economy behaves like a self-organizing system, where free individuals keep the system alive simply by pursuing their private interests. In principle, the system coordination could be achieved straightforwardly, simply by commanding the individual to behave in a prescribed manner. After all, this is the way hierarchic organizations, like firms or armies, works. Even in hierarchic organizations, however, commands would be ineffective without the glue of common participation, as Japanese firms exemplify very well: It is no accident that the high growth rates in Japan have been coupled with a low degree of income inequality; higher inequality would have undermined the basis of common participation. Recent literature has contended that, contrary to the conventional view, income inequality and growth are negatively, and not positively, related (Persson and Tabellini, 1994; Alesina and Rodrik, 1992). The theoretical interpretation underlying these new empirical results relies on a model of median voter, without any accommodation for the model's shortcomings, particularly the importance of nonvoters and the possibility of multiple peaks, both empirically documented above. Moreover, it has to be remembered that the median voter model is meaningful only in the context of democracies, because otherwise there is simply no voter of any kind: Persson and Tabellini produce clear empirical evidence of how the positive relation between equality and growth holds only for democratic countries.

We want therefore to suggest a line of interpretation that can fill this theoretical gap and examine more closely the links between economics and politics. We ask whether political participation and peace are helpful in promoting welfare and growth, keeping in mind that peace and political participation are in any case compatible with social conflict over economic resources, but are not compatible with violent behavior. The expected economic consequences of an environment of permanent violence can be summarized as follows: (a) disruption of existing property rights, with an inside shift of the private supply curves; (b) creation of man-made endogenous uncertainty, which can be eliminated only by surrendering to the violence, as in the case of wars and organized crime; (c) waste of private and public expenditure devoted to the purchase of arms and military equipment; and (d) greater economic hardship for the worst off and, as a consequence, greater global inequality. The economic consequences of the violence can be clearly seen in its extreme form in the case of wars between nations or military buildup in less developed countries: If we rank countries in descending order according to the ratio between military spending and GNP, we can observe that countries whose ratio is high form a group that has recorded a steady decrease of percapita GNP over the period 1980–1992. The group selected, which includes the former Soviet Union and some OPEC countries unwilling to reduce arms expenditure in spite of declining oil prices, accounts for about 740 million people and, by western standards, can be classified as nondemocratic countries. In a sample of thirty-seven less developed countries in the early 1980s, no significant direct effect of military expenditure on growth was detected. Military expenditure instead had a clear negative impact on public deficit, trade balance, and private savings (Campiglio, 1982). The internal economic hardship would have been difficult to bear without the force of authoritarian regimes, which hindered the process of economic growth.

Democracies can instead foster economic growth by securing well-defined property rights (Olson, 1993), reducing social endogenous uncertainty, preventing wars unless they correspond to the will of the people, and providing economic protection for the worst off. Unfortunately, democracy, or at least its western version, is not an easy answer because in some countries it is too far away from cultural traditions. Democracy is indeed a complex concept not easy to define. Equality is the common thread that runs through the different conceptions of democracy, even if the notion of equality referred to remains undefined. In the same way, disentangling the relationship between democracy and the economy is complex: Tocqueville (1835), for example, thought that "equality makes not only work itself, but work specifically to gain money, honorable" (p. 551) and that democracy is naturally inclined toward peace, because in democracy "men are the natural enemies of violent commotion"..."Not only do men in democracies feel no natural inclination for revolutions, but they are afraid of them," (p. 636) because "any revolution is more or less a threat to property. Most inhabitants of a democracy have property. And not only have they got property, but they live in the conditions in which men attach most value to property" (p. 636). Most contemporary scholars would still agree with these ideas that imply than an accomplished political and economic democracy is also a peaceful democracy. Violence internal to the country can hinder both democracy and the economy. The subtle link between violence in the street and political participation in parliament is explored by Elias Canetti (1981). Canetti proposes profound insights into the meaning and "essence" of the parliamentary system: He notes that "the modern bipartite system makes use of the psychological structure of armies in battle.... They fight renouncing to kill" (p. 224). About the voting mechanism, he notes that "there is something sacred when the elector casts his ballot; as the sealed ballot boxes containing the ballots are sacred; so is the counting process sacred. The solemnity associated with all these operations derives from the renunciation of death as an instrument of decision. With each single ballot death is, so to speak, swept away" (p. 226).

These insights can be coupled with Tocqueville's views about democracy. He praises the virtues of decentralization and local autonomy, because they provide a necessary link that balances the excessive centralization of the State: Turnout by itself is therefore a partial measure of participation, which is also carried on through many other channels, such as the diffusion of associations. At the same time, Tocqueville raises the problem of atomization and individualism in a democractic society, anticipating many contemporary problems like the risks of envy and hatred of wealthier people. Since Tocqueville, America's social fabric has undergone a profound transformation and some of the civic virtues that made him enthusiastic have weakened. Political turnout in the United States was highest in Tocqueville's day and it was only at the beginning of the twenti- eth century that it declined to lower contemporary levels. However imperfect, voter turnout is therefore one of the measures of democracy, especially when the turnout is low and grass roots democracy is weakened. A low electoral par- ticipation also means, as suggested by Canetti, that parliament can work less efficiently as a clearinghouse for the conflicts and violence of society: When that happens, violence moves back to the streets.

We can summarize our argument by noting that it boils down to the statement that democracy not only has benefits but also has costs: its virtues come with a cost, and pointing to the former while overlooking the latter can lead to serious mistakes. In a broad sense the cost of democracy is the cost of a modern and efficient welfare state: At a low level of participation, the cost of democracy is low while disutility to individuals in terms of violence and social disorder is high. As we move toward an increased political participation, the cost of democracy increases but with the benefit of a lower disutility to individuals caused by social disorder. This interpretation seems to be confirmed at various levels. In the United States, we observe a positive relationship between the percentage of the nonvoting electorate and the frequency of violent crimes across the fifty states (see Figure 10.4). It is significant to note that a similar pattern arises in Italy.

Violent crime rates are positively related with silent violence against chil- dren, measured by the infant mortality rate. Both forms of violence are closely related to the crisis of the family: the percentage of one-parent families is strongly related to both violent crimes and infant mortality as well as to low political participation. An improved democracy in the United States should therefore allow for stronger economic support to families and children because in so doing it would also pave the way for a more just and efficient society. The increase of expenditure would be repaid, at least partially, by more growth, and in any case it would give a better quality of life.

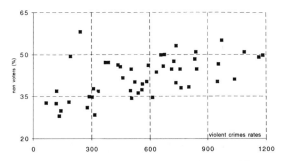

Figure 10.4. Nonvoters and violent crime rates in the fifty states of the United States. (*Source*: Bureau of the Census *Statistical Abstract of the U.S. 1993*, pp. xii–xxii.)

5   Conclusion

We summarize the solutions offered to the three issues raised in this paper. The first issue related to the lack of political representation for children and young people: in fact the old get a proportionally higher share of resources because their needs are politically represented. The lack of political representation of the young distorts resource allocation to their disadvantage in addition to being, of course, contrary to the very nature of democracy. Amendment of this distorsion is required and urgent because there are good reasons to suspect that children and young people can be seriously deprived during the crucial years of their physical and intellectual formation.

The second issue points to the explicit recognition of the ongoing and continuous redistribution of resources from the young to the old, which underlies any conceivable institutional arrangement for pensions and social security. A median income lower than the average seems to be sustained by an implicit social contract and the rational preference of becoming richer when old. The act of voting is strongly and positively related to age and income: A lower turnout by the young and the lower income groups implies a lower tax rate and a smaller government size.

The third issue is whether political participation is beneficial to growth: The answer is that it is, on certain conditions. Recent literature has maintained and empirically tested the existence of a positive relationship between income equality and growth: Its theoretical underpinning is the standard median voter model. We complement this interpretation with a further consideration. Equality is beneficial to growth because it reduces distributional conflicts and brings peace to economic activity. Peace, in turn, is the outcome of a more accomplished democratic society and higher political participation. Democracy has benefits that can be reaped only if its costs are accepted, for example, in the form of an efficient welfare state. Cross-section evidence for the United States supports this point. A low turnout produces savings that may, however, be more than offset by the costs and disutility involved in the existence of a more violent society. The positive relationship between equality and growth can be explained as the positive result induced by more peace and political participation.

References

Alesina, A., and D. Rodrik. 1992. Distribution, political conflict, and economic growth, in *Political Economy, Growth, and Business Cycles*, A. Cukierman, Z. Hercowitz, and L. Leiderman, eds., MIT Press, Cambridge, Mass.

Campiglio, L. 1982. Spese militari e Terzo Mondo in *Spese Militari, Tecnologia e Rapporti Nord-Sud*, Autori Vari, Vita e Pensiero, Università Cattolica, Milan.

    1990. Income distribution, public expenditure and equality, *Labour*, **4**(1).

    1994. La disoccupazione in Europa, *Quaderni dell'Istituto di Politica Economica*, (Working Papers of the Institute of Political Economy), no. 9, Università Cattolica, Milan.

Canetti, E. 1981. *Massa e Potere*, Adelphi, Milan.

Downs, A. 1957. *An Economic Theory of Democracy*, Harper and Row, New York.

Filer, J., and L. Kenny. 1980. Voter turnout and the benefits of voting, *Public Choice*, **35**, 575–585.

Hammond, P. 1982. Utilitarianism, uncertainty, and information, in *Utilitarianism and beyond*, A. Sen and B. William eds., Cambridge University Press, Cambridge.

Meltzer, A. H., and S. F. Richard. 1981. A rational theory of the size of government, *Journal of Political Economy*, **89**(5), 914–27.

OECD (1987). *The Control and Management of Government Expenditure*. OECD, Paris.

Olson, M. 1993. Dictatorship, democracy, and development, *American Political Science Review*, **87**(3), 567–75.

Persson, T., and G. Tabellini. 1994. Is inequality harmful for growth?, *American Economic Review*, **84**(3), 600–21.

Piven, F. F., and R. A. Cloward. 1988. *Why Americans Don't Vote*, Pantheon Books, New York.

Rawls, J. 1971. *A Theory of Justice*, Oxford University Press, Oxford.

Stiglitz, J. 1988. *Economics of the Public Sector*, 2nd ed., W. W. Norton and Company, New York.

Tocqueville, A. de. 1835. *Democracy in America*. Translated by G. Lawrence and edited by J. P. Mayer, Harper and Row Perennial Edition, New York, 1988.

Usui, C. 1987. The Origin and Development of Modern Welfare State: A Study of Social Forces and World Influences on the Adoption of Social Insurance Policies among 63 Countries, 1880–1976, Ph.D. thesis, Stanford University, Stanford, Calif.

Wilensky, H. L. 1976. *The New Corporatism, Centralization and the Welfare State*, Sage Books, Beverly Hills, Calif.

PART IV

Democratic expectations

CHAPTER 11

Components of the democratic ideal

Ian Shapiro

Introduction: Three types of middle ground

Our subject is the meaning of democracy.[1] It is necessarily a complex one, because the term *democracy* means different things to different people. Sometimes it is identified with a particular decision rule, at other times it conjures up the spirit of an age. Often democracy is defined by reference to lists of criteria (such as regular elections, competitive parties, and a universal franchise), yet sometimes it is a comparative idea: the Athenian polis exemplified few characteristics on which most contemporary democrats would insist, but it was relatively democratic by comparison with other ancient Greek city-states. Many people understand democratic government in procedural terms; others insist that it requires substantive – usually egalitarian – distributive arrangements. Sometimes democracy connotes little more than an oppositional ethic, at other times it is taken to require republican self-government, robustly understood.[2]

Given this multitude of meanings, any defense of a particular understanding reasonably begins with an account of why an author proceeds in one way rather than another and who he or she seeks to persuade. My goal here is to sketch a

---

[1] This essay, with the permission of Sage Publications, Inc., draws freely and substantially on my article "Elements of democratic justice," published in *Political Theory*, Vol. 24, No. 4 (November, 1996). It is also reprinted in my collection of essays, *Democracy's Place* (Cornell University Press, 1996), pp. 220–61.

[2] Much of the public choice literature since Arrow has identified democracy with majority rule or unanimity rule somehow defined. For an overview see Mueller (1989, pp. 43–148). The classic account of the democratic spirit of America remains Tocqueville's (1969). For the "defining criteria" approach, see Dahl (1986, pp. 191–225). For the comparative use of the term in the ancient world, see Kitto (1973). On the alleged advantages of substantive over procedural conceptions of democracy, see Beitz (1988), and Ely (1980). On democracy as an oppositional ethic see Moore (1989). On democracy as republican self-government, see the participatory tradition that begins with Rousseau (1972) and finds contemporary expression in such works as Pateman (1970), Barber (1979), and Cohen and Rogers (1983).

view of democracy that stakes out a middle ground in three different debates about democracy. These are the debate between procedural and substantive democrats, the debate between those who defend democracy as an ideal type and those who think of the term as contextually defined, and the debate between those who think of democracy in purely instrumental terms and those who see it as an intrinsically valuable, if not the most valuable, political good. Before getting to the particular view of democracy that I seek to render attractive to protagonists on both sides of these three debates, I begin by characterizing the debates more fully.

For present purposes, the debate between proponents of procedural and substantive democracy can be characterized as a debate between rule-centered and outcome-centered conceptions of democracy. Procedural conceptions of democracy belong to that family of decision rules that Nozick (1974, pp. 28–29, 155–60, 218–24) identifies as *historical*. They specify some procedural condition (unanimity rule in Nozick's case, majority rule in many arguments for democracy) and define an outcome as acceptable so long as the relevant procedure generates it. Substantive conceptions of democracy belong to the class of decision rules that Nozick identifies as *patterned* or *end-state*: they specify distributive outcome or state of affairs (equality, lack of certain types or degrees of inequality, or some other state) by reference to which the results of different decision rules are evaluated for their adequacy or justness.

Just as defenders of end-state arguments defend their claims by reference to the inadequacies of rule-centered views, proponents of substantive conceptions of democracy rest their arguments on objections to pure procedural democracy. Some of these objections focus on the different resources different players bring to the political process, which are often translatable into differential power within it. To this "garbage in, garbage out" rationale for suspicion of pure proceduralism is often added the fate of insular minorities, who can usually be harmed by every decision rule except unanimity rule but who can hold the rest of society to ransom if the latter is adopted. Pure proceduralism is also objected to for its perverse characteristics. Arrow's (1951) general impossibility theorem has spawned a literature that reveals all decision rules to be arbitrary and manipulable in varying degrees and throws into question even the meaning of the term *majority* in most definitions of majority rule. These and related difficulties have led defenders of substantive democracy like Beitz (1988) to argue that no system of procedures can be judged genuinely democratic until we have agreement on a theory of "just legislation," and writers like Ely (1980) to defend the place of an activist supreme court in a democratic constitutional order, to limit and undermine the undemocratic effects of majoritarian legislative procedures.[3]

---

[3] For an accessible review of the technical difficulties of different democratic procedures, see Mueller (1989: 43–148).

The difficulty with arguments for substantive democracy is that they assume that there is some way, independent of what democratic procedures generate, to determine what outcomes are genuinely democratic. In earlier work (Shapiro 1990a, 1994) I have agreed with those who contend that this is not possible. Depending on which of the many available conceptions of justice one is committed to, one will come up with a different account of just democratic legislation. This means that we cannot put off deciding what decision procedures are appropriately judged democratic until we have settled on a theory of just legislation. This is not to say that we should dismiss the criticisms of pure proceduralism advanced by the proponents of substantive democracy. The social world teems with power relations and hierarchies of different kinds that are the arbitrary products of chance and the historical evolution of power relations. These hierarchies operate to impose values, and modes of pursuing them, on people in varying degrees. A democratic theory that fails to respond to this reality is not worthy of the name. My intention here is to develop an account that responds to it without requiring that we first settle the question: What is justice? "More than process, less than substance" would be an appropriate slogan to describe my view, because although I affirm the desirability of some democratic constraints on all of our collective practices, these are conditioning constraints, defined in an open-ended and context-sensitive fashion.

Second, in defending the present account of democracy, I intend to occupy a middle ground in debates between those, like Rawls (1971), who maintain that we do best to begin by thinking in terms of abstract ideals, descending later to the "second-best" world of applications, and those, like Walzer (1983; 1987), who think that we do better to work from the ground up. The contextualists claim that ideal theory is addressed to contrived problems that have no bearing on the actual issues that exercise protagonists in actual political conflicts. Instead, they argue, we should base our political principles on the beliefs and practices that actually prevail in particular cultures so that we can have some hope of developing theories that might appeal to, and influence, those protagonists. Attractive as the contextualist approach is in many respects, it is subject to the criticism that it renders impossible the search for plausible standards of political evaluation.[4] In order to reap the benefits of contextualism without being subject to its weaknesses, the argument presented here is *semi*-contextual in that it varies partly, but only partly, with time and circumstance. Aspects of what democracy might reasonably be thought to require may change over time and vary both across the domains of civil society and from culture to culture. This means that a satisfying elaboration of the argument can only be developed as its injunctions are explored through a variety of contexts.

---

[4] See Shapiro (1990b, pp. 55–90, 207–30).

My central focus here is on the procedural and institutional level of analysis, not on matters concerning higher-order human interests and questions of ultimate justification. In this regard my approach is similar to Rawls's in his "political, not metaphysical" mode, although Rawls (1973, p. 228, 1985) seems to me to press implausibly far the claim that a political conception of justice can be developed independently of controversial philosophical commitments. The account developed here rests on skepticism toward the absolutist epistemologies and ontologies that a Platonist or a classical Marxist might embrace, but this skepticism is political not metaphysical. I take no position on whether or not the accounts are true, only on whether or not it is wise to allow our lives to be governed by their injunctions. This is not the same thing as philosophical neutrality, however, because partisans of such absolutist views are likely to find their political aspirations frustrated by the politics I am advocating in ways that many philosophical fallibilists, pragmatists, empiricists, realists, and philosophical antifoundationalists will not. My claim is that given the impossibility of neutrality among ultimate philosophical commitments, the democratic conception of social justice that I describe is the most appropriate foundational political commitment.

It might be said that, having conceded that neutrality about questions of higher-order interests and ultimate justification is not possible, one is not free to turn to the institutional and procedural level of analysis without first defending the higher-order assumptions on which a given analysis rests. This conclusion seems to me to be unwarranted for two related reasons. It is true, first, that every political theory rests on higher-order assumptions, but it is also true that all such assumptions are controversial. Consequently, if we put off the questions of institutional design until the higher-order questions are settled, we will get to them at the time of the proverbial Godot's arrival. In the meantime, however, life goes on, and we need at least provisional grounds for preferring some institutional arrangements over others. Second, although it is common to think that we should start with general matters because people are more likely to agree on them and then move to more specific and divisive matters – to the details wherein the devil is thought to lurk – exactly the opposite is often true, as Sunstein (1995) has usefully noted. A faculty may be able to reach agreement that a particular person should be granted tenure even though its members could never agree on the reasons why. By extension, in arguing about the merits of different political arrangements, it is often wise to avoid – or at least minimize – attention to controversial questions of higher-order interests and ultimate justification. That is the assumption behind the present discussion.

The third debate in which I seek to stake out a middle ground divides proponents of instrumental conceptions of democracy from those who embrace what might – for want of a better term – be described as satiating conceptions. At one extreme, Schumpeter (1942), Downs (1957), and Buchanan and Tullock (1962) and others have championed an instrumentalist conception of democracy in which time spent participating in collective deliberation and decision making is understood purely as a cost to be minimized, subject to expressing one's preferences or protecting one's interests. In their views, it is rational to invest time in gathering information or participating in decision making only to the extent that this is necessary to protect one's individual interests. At the other extreme, participatory democrats like Pateman (1970) and Barber (1979) see participation as inherently worthwhile for its effects both on the quality of collective decisions and on the participating agents.

In my view, the participatory critics of instrumentalism are partly right. Although participation can be valuable, it can also be tedious and self-defeating – as Oscar Wilde's quip about socialism taking up too many evenings makes clear. It would be going too far to say that we need democracy in the same way that we need garbage cans; this would suggest a purely instrumental view that I do not mean to embrace. Instead, my claim will be that essential as democracy is to a tolerable existence, expecting much in the way of spiritual enrichment or edification from it is wrongheaded. This is not intended as a denial of the value of democratic participation or even of the claim that such participation will often have beneficial effects on participants, although the evidence on this question is mixed.[5] My claim is intended to emphasize that democracy should be our servant and not our master; to the extent that the reverse becomes true, democracy will impoverish our lives, not enrich them.

Democracy as I defend it is a *subordinate* good. By this I mean that although democracy is necessary for ordering social relations well, we should resist every suggestion that it is sufficient, that it is the highest human good, that it is the only human good, or that it should dominate the activities in which we engage. Democracy operates best when it sets the terms for our civil interactions without thereby determing their course. Our lives require much else as well to be satisfactory, and it is wrongheaded to expect democracy to deliver those other things. This conception follows from the thought that because power relations form part – but not all – of most collective activities, democracy appropriately conditions those activities, but it does not appropriately displace them. We should aspire to get on with our collective lives in democratic ways on my account, but we should nonetheless aspire to get on with them. The creative political challenge is to devise mechanisms of institutional governance that can make this possible.

Two dimensions of democratic politics

Democrats arc committed to rule by the people. They insist that no aristocrat, monarch, bureaucrat, expert, or religious leader has the right, in virtue of such

---

[5] See Dahl (1970, 140–66), Kaufman (1969), Mansbridge (1980), and Walzer (1989, pp. 112–38).

status, to force people to accept a particular conception of their proper common life. People should decide for themselves, via appropriate procedures of collective decision, what their collective business should be. They may reasonably be required to consult and take account of one another and of others affected by their actions, but beyond this no one may legitimately tell them what to do. The people are sovereign; in all matters of collective life they rule over themselves.

Although this is less often commented on in the academic literature, democracy is as much a theory about opposition to the arbitrary exercise of power as it is a theory about collective self-government. In this connection, Moore (1989, p. 25) remarks that historically democracy has been a weapon "of the poor and the many against the few and the well-to-do." Those who have actively sought democracy in organized political movements "have wanted it as a device to increase their share in political rule and weaken the power and authority of those who actually rule." In the modern world at least, democratic movements have derived much of their energy and purpose from opposition to socioeconomic, legal, and political hierarchies that seemed capricious from a democratic point of view. Rooted in the remnants of feudal and absolutist regimes and shaped by the vicissitudes of conquest and chance, the political orders of eighteenth and nineteenth century Europe and North America seemed to the dispossessed to personify arbitrary hierarchy and domination. It was this reality as much as anything else that motivated working-class and other democratic movements. The English philosophic radicals, the French and American revolutionaries, the nineteenth century Chartists, and the anticolonial movements in the third world after the second world war all wanted to free themselves from arbitrary hierarchical orders for which they could see no rationale or justification. It was to this oppositional dimension of the democratic ideal that Nelson Mandela appealed at his sentencing for treason by a South Africa court in 1961. Conceding that he had disobeyed the law by inciting resistance to the government, he nonetheless wondered whether "the responsibility does not lie on the shoulders of the government which promulgated that law, knowing that my people, who constitute the majority of the population of this country, were opposed to that law, and knowing further that every legal means of demonstrating that opposition had been closed to them by prior legislation, and by government administrative action."[6]

Mandela's formulation might be taken to embody the conventional view that democracy is primarily about collective self-government and only secondarily about opposition. Part of his claim, after all, is that he should not be bound by "a law which neither I nor any of my people had any say in preparing."[7]

---

[6] Mandela quoted in Langley (1979, p. 665). On the Chartists, see Thompson (1984). Generally, see Halévy (1972).

[7] Quoted in Langley (1979, p. 664).

But he also insists that the law lacks legitimacy because every avenue of legal opposition to it has been sealed off. In a world of ideal political institutions a derivative view of the place of opposition in democratic politics might be sustainable. But in the actual world, where social orders come to be what they are in morally arbitrary ways and where all procedures of government turn out on close inspection to be flawed, opposition must enjoy a more independent and exalted status in a persuasive account of just democratic politics. Or so I will argue; but first let us attend to the governance side of the equation.

Collective self-government

If democracy is understood to require that the people be sovereign over their collective goals, it exhibits considerable overlap with liberalism as a political ideology. Both are rooted in antivanguardist conceptions of the good; their proponents resist the idea that values and policies should be imposed on people against their wishes in the name of some greater social good. The reasons for affirming this antivanguardist stance vary: they can range from commitments to variants of philosophical skepticism, pragmatism, and antifoundationalism, to beliefs in the psychological value of critical reflection and contested authority, to the conviction that a degree of pluralism about values is sociologically or politically desirable. Liberals and democrats do not divide predictably over these foundational issues, and many in both groups draw from some combination of them reasons for a principled resistance to moral vanguardism.[8]

Liberals and democrats do divide predictably, however, over the institutional implications they draw from their moral antivanguardism. Liberals, who typically regard individual freedom as the greatest good, characteristically focus on devices to protect the individual from the realm of collective action. Democrats, by contrast, try to structure collective action appropriately to embody the preferences of the governed. Liberals characteristically resist this logic on the grounds that no procedure can fairly embody the preferences of all the governed. For liberals, democratic decision rules all too readily become devices by which phantom majorities – sometimes even manipulative minorities – tyrannize individuals.[9]

Although there is merit to the liberal argument, it rests on flawed assumptions about the nature of politics and about the limits of collective action. Concerning the first, the characteristic liberal mistake is to focus on the forms of tyranny performed by and through government as the only – certainly the principal –

---

[8] Nor do all liberals agree with one another, any more than all democrats do, over which of these reasons, combinations of these reasons, or combinations of these and other reasons they invoke for adhering to antivanguardist conceptions of the good.

[9] For one conventional statement of this view see Riker (1982).

kind of tyranny that should worry political theorists. Liberal commitments to negative freedom, conventional constructions of public/private dichotomies, and arguments for limited government are all shaped by this governmentalist view of politics. Governmental power is one potential site of domination, but there are many others that permeate the different domains of "private" life. Government can be an instrument for mitigating domination as well as a source of its generation. As a result, the choices and trade-offs that can minimize domination throughout society will likely defy such simplifying formulae as "the government that governs least governs best."

The liberal view is flawed also because its proponents tend to think that whether or not our lives should be governed by collective institutions is an intelligible question about politics. Hence Nozick's (1974, p. 4) remark that the fundamental question of political theory "is whether there should be any state at all." This view is misleading because the institutions of private property, contract, and public monopoly of coercive force that the proponents of this view characteristically favor were created and are sustained by the state and partly financed by implicit taxes on those who would prefer an alternative system. In the modern world, Nozick's assertion makes as much sense as would a claim that the fundamental question of astronomy is whether or not there ought to be planets. The characteristic liberal sleight of hand involves trying to naturalize or otherwise obscure the institutional arrangements they prefer in order to disguise this reality. Such subterfuges have received more attention than they deserve in the recent history of political theory; they cannot any longer detain us.[10]

This is not to say that the liberal fear of majority rule is groundless. It is to say that we need a different response to it than the conventional liberal one. We can begin to develop this by noting, first, that there is no reason to think that there is one best rule of collective decision. Different rules will be appropriate in different domains of social life, depending on the nature of the domain in question, the importance of the decision to participants, the potential costs of decisions to third parties, and related contingent factors. Such a plural attitude about decision rules flows naturally out of the view that civil society is made up of domains of social action that differ qualitatively from one another.[11]

Few liberals would deny this last claim, but they usually regard unanimity rule as the best default option, the decision rule most likely to protect individuals against violations of their rights. This is at least partly why liberals so often find markets attractive. Markets embody unanimity rule in that every transaction requires the consent of both parties. On the liberal view, classically advocated in *The Calculus of Consent* (Buchanan and Tullock, 1962), it is always *departures* from unanimity that stand in presumptive need of justification, whether

---

[10] For extensive discussion of the question, see Shapiro (1986; 1990a).
[11] See Walzer (1983, pp. 3–20) and MacIntyre (1984, pp. 181–203).

on efficiency or other grounds. James Buchanan and Gordon Tullock argue in that work that, under conditions of a hypothetical social contract, rational individuals concerned with safeguarding their interests would insist on a hierarchy of decision rules, starting with unanimity rule for constitutional matters. Next come "those possible collective or public decisions which modify or restrict the structure of individual human or property rights after these have once been defined and generally accepted by the community." Foreseeing that collective action may "impose very severe costs on him," the individual will tend "to place a high value on the attainment of his consent, and he may be quite willing to undergo substantial decision-making costs in order to insure that he will, in fact, be reasonably protected against confiscation." He will thus require a decision rule approaching unanimity. Last is the class of collective actions characteristically undertaken by governments. For these "the individual will recognize that private organization will impose some interdependence costs on him, perhaps in significant amount, and he will, by hypothesis, have supported a shift of such activities to the public sector." Examples include provision of public education, enforcement of building and fire codes, and maintenance of adequate police forces. For such "general legislation" an individual at the constitutional stage will support less inclusive decision rules, though not necessarily simple majority rule, and indeed, within this class, different majorities might be agreed on as optimal for different purposes. "The number of categories, and the number of decision making rules chosen, will depend on the situation which the individual expects to prevail and the 'returns to scale' expected to result from using the same rule over many activities" (Buchanan and Tullock, 1962).

This story is intuitively plausible only if we take the contractualist metaphor on which it rests seriously, assuming a prepolitical status quo where there is no collective action and then a series of consensual moves that lead to the creation of what we know as political society. But, as Rae (1969), Barry (1990, pp. 242–55; 312–16), and others have pointed out, once this assumption is jettisoned there is no particular reason to regard unanimity rule as the most appropriate default decision rule.[12] In the real world of ongoing politics, if I assume that I am as likely to oppose a given policy as to support it regardless of whether it is the status quo, then majority rule or something close to it is the logical rule to prefer. Once we move from majority toward unanimity rule, we begin to privilege the status quo. This will rightly seem arbitrary in a world that has not evolved cooperatively from a precollective condition. In short, other things

---

[12] Under Rae's assumptions, when the number of voters is odd the optimal decision rule is majority rule, *n* over two, plus one-half; when *n* is even, the optimal decision rule is either majority rule (*n* over two plus one), or majority rule minus one (simply *n* over two). See also Taylor (1969). Generally, see Mueller (1989, pp. 96–111).

being equal, tyranny of the majority is something that people should rationally fear, but not as much as they should fear tyranny of the minority.[13]

The preceding discussion reinforces the suggestion that there is no single best decision rule for democratic governance. In domains of social life where relations really do tend to approximate the contractualist story – in that they are both created ex nihilo by the participants and are basically cooperative in character – a presumptive commitment to unanimity rule is defensible. One might think of marriage in contemporary America as a paradigm case. It is created consensually, usually with the expectation that in important matters, day-to-day governance will also be consensual. (Indeed, with the advent of no-fault divorce in the 1970s, we see an unusually strong form of the unanimity requirement at work. In most American states, either spouse can insist – subject to a brief waiting period – on a divorce unilaterally: the marriage continues only so long as both parties agree. Far from privileging the status quo, this variant of unanimity rule makes it perpetually vulnerable, because the rule is not defined by reference to the status quo but by fictively recreating the conditions antecedent to it at the wish of either party).[14]

Many social relationships do not approximate the contractualist ideal; they are not created ex nihilo in the sense that contemporary American marriages usually are, and they are to a high degree structured by forces other than the wills of the participants. Even childless marriages involve the generation of reliances and externalities that can undermine their exclusively consensual character. These are questions of degree, however. Many social relations are not contractualist to anything like the extent that marriage is, even when such reliances are taken into account. Most obviously, think of parent–child relations. Constitutional political arrangements are often pointed to as presumptively contractualist because of their foundational character and their place in the social contract tradition. Such arrangements might once have been consented to by the relevant parties, although even in the American founding a narrowly circumscribed class agreed in fact – and then not unanimously. Indeed, adopting the Constitution

---

[13] Even if we accept the contractualist metaphor, the logic of Buchanan's and Tullock's defense of unanimity rule can be shown to break down once time and externalities are taken into account. See Rae (1975).

[14] It might appear that no-fault divorce destroys the marriage contract qua contract entirely, because it is terminable at the will of either party. But such a conclusion (i) ignores the fact that conventional unanimity rule operates in marriages unless and until they reach the point of dissolution, and (ii) conflates the *grounds* for divorce with the *terms* of divorce (and in particular the distribution of costs that courts will impose on divorcing parties). In fact, many countries, and some American states, that embrace some form of no-fault divorce do not go all the way with it. Instead, they insist that the court find that "irretrievable breakdown" has occurred, for which purpose the judge may take various factors including the wishes of both parties into account. See Glendon (1987, pp. 64–81).

involved violating the unanimity condition in the Articles of Confederation. Generations later, whatever contractualist element these arrangements once exhibited has receded into the mists of time. In such circumstances (and no doubt there are others) there is no presumptive reason to regard unanimity rule as best on the grounds that it embodies the consent of the governed.

Nor are there good reasons to think that some alternative decision rule should appropriately govern all relations where a contractualist element is either missing or overdetermined by other factors. As the examples just mentioned indicate, this is a heterogeneous class. In some domains, the sort Rae (1975) evidently has in mind, majority rule is prima facie the best decision rule. These include relations typically characterized by arm's-length transactions, where substantial aspects of the collective action in question are competitive rather than cooperative, and where there are no obvious reasons to countenance paternalistic decision making. There are also often circumstances in which people are either born into structural relations that cannot easily be escaped or, if there is a contractualist element to their participation, it is accompanied by a good deal of what Marxists like to think of as "structural coercion." Whatever the surface appearances, the relations in question are not substantially voluntary. Arguments for workplace democracy in which majority rule plays a substantial role generally appeal to some combination of these characteristics in justifying this appeal; Rae's logic supplies us with reasons for accepting them.[15]

Not every noncontractualist or minimally contractualist form of association should presumptively be governed by majority rule, however. Both Buchanan and Tullock's and Rae's reasoning take it for granted that, *ceteris paribus*, decision making costs should be minimized, for which they have sometimes been criticized by participatory democrats.[16] Rather than follow the participatory democrat's reasoning (which creates difficulties of its own),[17] the argument here is that participation must itself be thought about in a context-sensitive way. In some circumstances, participation is no more than a cost to be minimized, subject to achieving or preventing a particular outcome. Anyone who has sat through enough faculty meetings will know what at least one of those circumstances is. In other situations, institutions may reasonably be structured to maximize participation. Juries are an obvious example. Unanimity is generally required just because it forces discussion and joint deliberation, which, in turn, are believed most likely to lead to discovery of the truth in trial courts, and that is the point of the exercise. Parent–child relations are also noncontractualist relations (because the child does not ask to be born, let alone to be born to the

---

[15] See Dahl (1985a, pp. 111–135).
[16] See Spitz (1984, pp. 134–215).
[17] See Shapiro (1994, pp. 142–44).

parent in question) that do not lend themselves to governance by majority rule, at least not on many questions. In these relations, more flexibility is necessary in delineating the appropriate scope for participation by different parties, because they include the total dependence of young children on their parents, relations among more-or-less equal adults, and relations between adults and their aging parents. And because human beings are developmental creatures for whom decision making has to be learned over time, there has to be space for regimes of domestic governance to adapt to peoples' changing capacities and dependencies. To be appropriate, the decision rules governing domestic relations must be able to respond to this complex reality.

Taking note of such complexities lends credence to the suggestion that when they can be discovered and made to work, local solutions to local problems are to be preferred. The kinds of knowledge that are pertinent to democratizing an activity will often be disproportionately available to insiders because of their hands-on experience and their participants' understanding of the activity in question. Notice, however, that there will be circumstances in which no local decision rule can be made to work effectively from the standpoint of democratic self-government, the most obvious being when the obstacles to exit are insuperable for some yet easily overcome for others. The American history of white flight from inner-city school districts since the 1960s stands as eloquent testimony to that fact. Whether the substantially white middle-class population opts out of the public school system or moves out of the inner city (or both, to avoid both using and paying for the inner-city schools), its ability to leave undermines democracy in educational provision. Local majority rule promotes white flight, but local unanimity rule gives minorities veto power, which enables them to avoid contributing to the provision of public education, regardless of the benefits they or their children derive from it. In this type of circumstance, the presence of collective action problems in the provision of public goods suggests that constraints other than choosing one local decision rule over another should come into play.

The decision rules appropriate to different walks of life vary, then, with the activity in question and the purposes around which it is organized. Yet to say this is to solve one problem by raising another, because these activities and purposes are never fixed and there is usually, perhaps endemically, disagreement about them.[18] How can we say that the nature of the activity in question makes one decision rule more appropriate than another, having conceded that those purposes and activities are inevitably in contention? Whereas most liberals would say that all social relations should be redesigned to approximate the contractualist ideal as much as possible (regardless of how they are currently organized), the subordinate character of the democratic commitment in the present argument

[18]   This is discussed at length in Shapiro (1990b, pp. 252–61).

precludes my defending an analogous claim. Instead, it recommends a more pragmatic approach that is antivanguardist in method as well as substance, because we should neither accept things as they have evolved nor aspire to redesign them tabula rasa. Rather, the goal should be to take social relations as we find them and discover ways to democratize them as we reproduce them. This means that prevailing ways of doing things reasonably make a partial claim on our allegiance, but this claim is conditional and always subject to revision in democratic ways; the inertial legitimacy of existing modes of governance can never achieve a status greater than that of a rebuttable presumption. The creative challenge is to devise methods of governance that both condition existing ways of doing things democratically and open the way to their reevaluation over time.

Although there is no best decision rule for the governance of different domains of civil society, a general constraint for thinking about decision rules follows from what has been said so far: Everyone affected by the operation of a particular domain of civil society should be presumed to have a say in its governance. This follows from the root democratic idea that the people appropriately rule over themselves. To require that everyone affected should have a say is not to require that this presumption be conclusive, or that every say should necessarily be of equal weight. There are often – but not always – good reasons for granting outsiders to a domain (who may be subject to its external effects) less of a say than insiders concerning its governance, and even within a domain there may be compelling reasons to distribute governing authority unequally and perhaps even to disenfranchise some participants in some circumstances. What these circumstances are cannot be specified in general, but we can say that we begin with a presumption of universal inclusion.

We can also say that proposals to undermine universal inclusion reasonably prompt suspicion, whatever their source. In the limiting case, if someone sells himself into slavery, his agreement should be regarded as void ab initio. Most incursions on inclusion are considerably less radical than selling oneself into slavery; nor are such incursions usually self-directed in the way that selling oneself into slavery is. As a consequence, evaluating policies and practices that limit the nature and extent of the governed's participation in decisions that affect them is more difficult (and controversial) than is the case with slavery. In the ongoing world of everyday politics there will often be circumstances in which inclusion is reasonably traded off against other imperatives. But the general argument counsels suspicion of these trade-offs; the burden of persuasion lies with those who advocate them.

This account of collective self-government is causally based. The right to participate comes from one's having an interest that can be expected to be affected by the particular collective action in question. In this respect, the present argument differs from liberal and communitarian views, both of which tend to regard membership in the relevant community as a trump (liberals by assumption, communitarians by express argument).[19] Once the contractualist way of think-ing has been dethroned, it is difficult to see any principled basis for regarding membership as primary. On the view advanced here, the structure of decision rules should follow the contours of power relations, not those of political mem-berships. Adopting this causally based view has implications for a host of issues relating to intergenerational justice and the handling of externalities. In a world in which international military and environmental questions increasingly dom-inate political agendas, whether or not one adopts such a view can be expected to be consequential over an expanding portion of the political landscape.

It will be objected that serious difficulties arise in determining who is affected by a particular decision and who is to determine whose claims about being affected should be accepted. To provide a full defense of the causally based view here would take us too far afield, but two points should be noted. First, although who is affected by a decision is bound to be controversial, this fact scarcely distinguishes causally based arguments from membership-based arguments. Who is to decide, and by what authority, who is to be a member is as fraught with conceptual and ideological baggage as who is to decide, and by what authority, who is causally affected by a particular collective decision. These difficulties should not therefore count as decisive against the causally based view if the membership-based view is seen as the alternative. Second, there is considerable experience with causally based arguments in tort law. Although tort actions are often concerned with the causal effects of individual rather than collective decisions, in dealing with them courts have developed mechanisms for determining whose claims should be heard, for sorting genuine claims from frivolous ones, and for distinguishing weaker claims to have been adversely affected by an action from stronger claims and shaping remedies accordingly. This is not an argument for turning politics into tort law; the point of the comparison is rather to illustrate that in other areas of social life, institutional mechanisms have been developed to assess and manage conflicting claims of being causally affected by actions. They may be imperfect mechanisms, but they should be evaluated by reference to the other imperfect mechanisms of collective decision making that actually prevail in the world, not by comparison to an ideal that prevails nowhere.[20]

---

[19] Liberals take the basic unit of the nation state for granted, treating it as a kind of Lockean voluntary association writ large, as has often been pointed out in criticism of Rawls. See Rawls (1971, pp. 371–82, 1993). No doubt this is often a consequence of the liberal proclivity for thinking in contractualist terms. For an illustration of the communitarian view of membership as the basic trumping good, see Walzer (1983, pp. 29, 31–63).

[20] My contention that the causally based view is more defensible than the going alternatives is compatible with a number of recent arguments whose purpose is to decenter membership-based sovereignty as the decisive determinant of participation, and to replace it with systems of

Institutionalizing opposition

One need not go all the way with Moore (1989, p. 8), for whom the single defining characteristic of a democratic order is "the existence of a legitimate and, to some extent effective, opposition," to hold that the realistic possibility of opposition is essential to democratic life.[21] Institutions that make "loyal" opposition possible perform important functions in democracies. They provide sites for potential alternative leaderships to organize themselves (making it possible for governments to fall without regimes collapsing); they make it possible to direct social dissent and dissatisfaction into the democratic regime rather than at its foundations; and they produce groups and individuals who have an interest in asking awkward questions, shining light in dark places, and exposing abuses of power. The importance of these functional considerations should not be minimized, but there is a more basic reason why the realistic possibility of opposition is an essential requirement of democracy. Unless people can challenge prevailing norms and rules with the realistic hope of altering them, the requirement that the inherited past not bind us unalterably would be empty.

The imperative to make effective opposition possible suggests two types of conditioning constraints for the operation of every domain of civil society, one procedural and one quasi-substantive. Procedurally, the imperative suggests at a minimum that rules of governance should be deemed unacceptable if they render revision of the status quo impossible. There should always be the space and the resources to challenge both existing ways of doing things and the norms governing them, room to argue for innovative change. This constraint reflects two assumptions about politics that I take for granted here: that no decision rule works neutrally to the advantage of all, and that it is reasonable to anticipate enduring disagreement about human ends.[22]

On its own, the permissive procedural requirement is often too weak to make the possibility of effective opposition real. In such circumstances it should be supplemented by other institutional measures. But the permissive requirement is not as toothless as might appear to be the case at first sight. To require that meaningful opposition be tolerated is frequently to require more than dominant groups wedded to the status quo want to accept, because it can weaken their monopoly on the definition of collective values and purposes. Not surprisingly, dominant groups often seek to oppose opposition or render it ineffective. Part of the challenge of democratic theory is to institutionalize ways to stop them.

---

overlapping jurisdiction in which different groups of persons are seen as sovereign over different classes of decisions. See Pogge (1992), Wendt (1994), and Antholis (1993).

[21] See also Foord (1964).

[22] For defense of these assumptions, see Shapiro (1990b, pp. 258–61).

My suggestion for a quasi-substantive constraint is that hierarchies should be presumed suspect. The reason is that although hierarchies can exist for many legitimate purposes, by definition they contain both power inequalities and truncated opportunities for opposition. Power, as Lord Acton said, tends to corrupt. Even, and perhaps especially, when they aquire power legitimately, power holders all too easily convince themselves that their authority should expand in space and time, that critics are ignorant or irresponsible, and that subordinates lack the requisite ability to ascend from inferior roles. The allure of power then diverts power holders within hierarchies from their legitimate goals, leading to the reduction of hierarchies to their power dimensions. The comparatively limited scope for opposition within hierarchies makes it difficult to block or check their atrophy into systems of domination; indeed, as atrophy advances, the possibilities for opposition are likely to be increasingly constrained. It is for this reason that democracts should keep a skeptical eye on all hierarchical arrangements, placing the burden of justification on their defenders. Power need not be abused, but it often is, and it is wise for democrats to guard against that possibility.

To say that hierarchies should be presumed suspect is not to say that all social hierarchies should be eliminated, even if this could be achieved. Hierarchies may be dangerous, but at the same time they can often be useful.[23] Indeed, because most human activity is mediated through language that has to be learned, a degree of hierarchy infuses everything we do. Yet hierarchies come in many kinds. Some hierarchies are inescapable, others are not. Some hierarchies are essential to the pursuit of particular goods, others are contingently related to them. Some hierarchies are chosen by the people affected by them, others are imposed by third parties. Some hierarchies are temporary, others more or less permanent features of peoples' lives. My claim, then, is not that hierarchies should always be eliminated. Rather it is that there are good grounds for suspicion of them, even when they result from democratic collective decisions. Too often escapable hierarchies masquerade as inescapable ones, involuntary subordination is shrouded in the language of agreement, unnecessary hierarchies are held to be essential to the pursuit of common goals, and fixed hierarchies are cloaked in myths about their fluidity. Democrats reasonably maintain an attitude of presumptive mistrust toward prevailing hierarchies; they should look for institutional and other structuring devices to limit hierarchies and to mitigate their unnecessary and corrosive effects. Such devices may be thought of as contributing to the evolving frameworks of democratic constraints within which

---

[23] The quixotic political commitments that follow from the injunction to overthrow all hierarchy everywhere have been explored by Unger (1987). For criticism of his argument, see Shapiro (1989).

people should be free to negotiate and renegotiate the terms of their cooperation and conflict.

To say that hierarchies are presumptively suspect is not to say anything about what is to count as sufficient to rebut the presumption. Nor is it to say anything about what kinds of constraints on hierarchies should be employed in different circumstances, or about how these constraints should be enforced. By itself, the general argument cannot answer these questions. But it does generate a series of appropriate queries about hierarchies, ways of probing them in the name of democracy.

The first concerns the degree to which a given hierarchy is inevitable. Consider the differences between adult domestic relations and parent–child relations. Both have taken a multiplicity of forms, even in the recent history of the Occidental world, yet almost all of these have been explicitly hierarchical in character. It is evident, however, that parent–child relations are inevitably hierarchical in ways that adult domestic relations are not. If a relationship is not inevitably hierarchical, the first question that arises is why should it be hierarchical at all? There may be justifiable reasons for a particular nonessential hierarchy (that it is comparatively efficient, that it has been chosen, that the relevant people like it, or some other reason), but from the democratic standpoint the presumption is against hierarchy, and the proponent of such reasons must shoulder the burden of persuasion.

When relations are inevitably hierarchical, a different class of considerations becomes relevant. We begin by asking: Is it necessary that the relations in question be maintained at all? Parent–child relations of some kind must exist, but not all inevitably hierarchical relations are of this sort. To consider a limiting case once again, history has shown that the institution of slavery need not exist. If an inescapably hierarchical relationship is unnecessary, it immediately becomes suspect. Slavery thus fares badly from this standpoint, quite apart from its incompatibility with the presumption of universal inclusion.

A second class of appropriate inquiries about hierarchies concerns their pertinence to the activity at hand: Are the hierarchical relations that exist appropriately hierarchical? Parent–child relations, for example, may be more hierarchical than they need to be in many instances, and they may include unnecessary kinds of hierarchical authority. They may also be maintained for a variety of reasons, ranging from the convenience of parents to desires to dominate, that have nothing to do with the interests of their charges. Of alterable hierarchies, we should thus always inquire: In whose interests are they sustained? Those who would sustain a hierarchy of a particular kind, or sustain it for longer than necessary, take on the burden of demonstrating that this operates in the interests of those who are subjected to the relevant hierarchy. For this reason, one would be unmoved by the argument advanced by Amish parents in the

Wisconsin v. Yoder litigation, namely, that they should be free not to send their teenage children to school because experience had taught them that this induced in the teenagers the desire to leave the Amish community, which interfered with their (i.e., the parents') rights of free religious exercise.[24]

Democratic commitments also bid us to attend to the degree to which hierarchies are ossified or fluid. We should distinguish self-liquidating hierarchies, as when children become adults or students become teachers, from non-self-liquidating hierarchies such as caste systems and hierarchies constituted by hereditary transmissions of wealth and power. We should also distinguish hierarchical orders in which anyone can in principle ascend to the top from those where that is not so. No woman can aspire to become Pope, a fact that makes the Catholic religion less attractive than some others in a democracy. In general, the argument tells us to prefer fluid hierarchies over ossified ones, other things being equal. Fluid hierarchies may not create permanently subordinated classes, whereas ossified hierarchies will. Of course other things seldom are equal; nonetheless the requirement is a useful starting point. It tells us what the presumption is and by whom the burden of persuasion should be carried.

Similarly, asymmetrical hierarchies are questionable, whereas symmetrical ones are not necessarily so. Polygamous marriages are generally asymmetrical, for example, and as such should be deemed suspect: A husband can have many wives but a wife cannot have many husbands.[25] If these polygamous regimes were symmetrical, or had their members practiced "complex marriage" as did the nineteenth century Oneida Perfectionist community (in which any number of men could marry any number of women), they would not be questionable by reference to this aspect of the argument. Again, there may be other reasons

---

[24] *Wisconsin v. Yoder* 406 U.S. Sup. Ct. 205 (1972). From the standpoint of the present argument *Yoder* was thus wrongly decided, although it would have been a more difficult case had the parents pressed their best understandings of their children's' interests rather than their own.

[25] This is not to say that all polygamous regimes fare equally poorly from the standpoint of democracy. Polygamous regimes from which there is no realistic chance of escape (as when they are enshrined in a country's legal system as the only available form of marriage) fare worse than polygamous regimes that are tolerated but not obligatory and from which escape is legally possible and not prohibitively expensive. Even in these circumstances there is always the possibility that voluntary adherents have been brainwashed, of course, and arguments to this effect cannot be dismissed out of hand. But proponents of these arguments will have to come to grips with the eloquently reasoned denials of their validity that have been put forward by some Mormon women. It has been argued, for instance, that polygamous marriage makes it possible for women to have both a career and a family, so that polygamy "is good for feminism." See Elizabeth Joseph, "My husband's nine wives," *The New York Times*, Thursday May 23, 1991, p. A 16, and "Polygamists emerge from secrecy seeking not just peace but respect," *The New York Times*, Tuesday April 9, 1991, p. A 22.

rooted in democratic theory for objecting to such arrangements, but their symmetry would count in their favor.[26]

Closely related to questions about the relative fluidity and symmetry of hierarchies are questions about the degree to which they are imposed. Did the people who are subjected to them elect to be thus subjected? What were their other realistic options at the time? Whether or not they chose to enter, what degree of freedom to exit now exists? Generally, nonimposed hierarchies fare better than imposed ones, and less imposed hierarchies fare better than more imposed ones. If someone elected to participate at the bottom of an hierarchical relationship when she had alternative nonhierarchical (or less hierarchical) options in front of her, the fact of her choice confers some presumptive legitimacy on the state of affairs. Analogously, if someone remains in an hierarchical order when we are fairly confident that she has the resources to leave, we have less reason to be troubled than when this is not the case.

Finally, the general argument directs us to attend to the relative insularity of hierarchies. To what extent do they consist of self-contained groups of people minding their own business who want to be left alone by outsiders? Withdrawing sects like the Old Order Amish, or migrating groups like the Mormons who went to Utah in the nineteenth century to escape persecution in the East, have at least prima facie valid claims that they should be able to set the terms of their association unimpeded. Such groups do not proselytize, or seek to shape the world outside their communities (as religious fundamentalists, for example, often do). Hierarchical and undemocratic as these groups might be in their internal organization, they are of little consequence to the outside world. By contrast, an hierarchical established church whose influence on outsiders could not be escaped without substantial cost would not enjoy the same prima facie claim to be left alone. Relatively insular groups may be objectionable on some of the other grounds just discussed, but the fact of their insularity diminishes any externality based claim by outsiders to restructure or abolish them.

Three difficulties considered

The preceding elaboration of the two central dimensions of democratic politics is a first installment; as such it raises many questions that it fails to answer. In the space that remains I will say something about what seem to me to be the

---

[26] The Oneida Perfectionists, founded in 1848 in Oneida New York by John Henry Noyes, rejected all forms of private property and extended their belief in community property to community property in persons. Like the Mormon polygamists they were persecuted by the state, eventually abandoning their commitment to complex marriage in 1879. See Weisbrod (1982). In fact, the community was run in an authoritarian manner by Noyes, who decided unilaterally who could marry, suggesting that the community would have been suspect on a number of grounds from the present democratic standpoint. See Klaw (1993).

most important of these questions, having to do with the internal complexity of my argument, tensions between it and other goods, and the appropriate role for the state that is implied by the general argument.

Internal conflicts

Any argument for an internally complex set of principles must confront the possibility that they cannot be satisfied simultaneously. The question then arises: How are conflicts among the different injunctions to be resolved? One response to this question is to come up with a system of metarules for resolving conflicts when they occur. For instance, Rawls's theory of justice consists of a number of principles that, he argues, should be lexically ranked: In the case of conflicts the principles that are higher in his lexical ordering trump those that are lower.[27]

It is evident that my argument exhibits an analogous potential for internal conflict. What the general argument recommends as the appropriate system of governance in a domain may conflict with the presumptive suspicion of hierarchy. People might choose to create a hierarchy by voluntary action or majority rule. Likewise, the various injunctions against hierarchy might produce contradictory prescriptions as far as a particular practice is concerned. The insular character of withdrawing sects, such as Mormons and the Amish, counsels leaving them alone, yet their internally hierarchical practices prompt suspicion from my democratic standpoint. How should conflicts of this kind be resolved?

The two alternatives here are either to try to come up with a system of metaprinciples analogous to Rawls's lexical rules or to supply a principled defense of a more underdetermined view. To try to come up with a complete system of metaprinciples that would resolve every possible tension that could arise out of the complexities of the general argument seems to me to be so demanding a task that it would almost certainly fail.[28] The range of circumstances that can arise is exceedingly large, if not infinite, and the complexity of the social world is such that there will always be challenges to an argument of this kind. This is less troubling than might at first sight appear to be the case. For one thing, the lack of a complete system of metaprinciples does not silence my argument in every circumstance. We can still say, for example, that a practice that runs up against a great many democratic presumptions is correspondingly more suspect for that reason. Slavery is an easy case for just this reason. It violates basic principles of collective self-governance and it is on the wrong side of every presumption about hierarchy that I discussed: it is unnecessary, it is not entered into voluntarily, it is hard or impossible to escape, it is both

---

[27] See Rawls (1971, pp. 42–5, 61–5, 82–9, 151–61) for elaboration.

[28] It is not difficult, for example, to demonstrate the existence of contradictory imperatives flowing from Rawls's lexical rankings. See Scanlon (1975), Hart (1975), and Barber (1975).

asymmetrical and non-self-liquidating, and it has external effects that permeate through the social world. By the same token, a practice that turns out to be on the right side of every presumption will be equally easy to deal with.

The more difficult and interesting cases are those that are less clear-cut. In many of these instances it may be possible to find accommodations among conflicting injunctions. For instance, in the case of the Amish one might take the view that the withdrawing character of the group and the absence of a threat posed by it to the rest of society counsels against any attempt to interfere with its existence, but that the state should nonetheless insist that Amish children be educated so that they have the capacities to function outside the Amish community in the event that they decide to leave. Thus in this view one would not tolerate all their educational practices, but in other respects they would be left alone.[29] Likewise, although the ossified and non-self-liquidating hierarchies in the Catholic Church contravene some democratic presumptions, the history of domination that has accompanied established churches might also counsel that there is wisdom in an especially wide latitude of tolerance as far as religious matters are concerned. A government guided by democratic principles might nonetheless attach some costs to religions that contravene these principle, such as denying tax-exempt status to religions in which some offices are reserved for men, persons of a particular race, or any other group that is defined in a morally arbitrary way. The governing body of the religion in question would then be free to decide whether to live with the sanctions in question or to adjust its practices to avoid them.[30]

These examples indicate that once we recognize that there is a range of possible sanctions and of feasible responses to such sanctions, apparently conflicting imperatives can be managed in a variety of ways that can, over time, be expected to encourage civil institutions to evolve in comparatively democratic ways. To some, even this approach will sound like dangerously radical interference with freedom of religious worship. But reflection on our current laws concerning racially exclusionary organizations and on the distinctions we routinely draw between religions and cults, and between education and brainwashing, should reveal that we routinely make many judgements of this kind, however implicitly. The examples also underline the fact that when we value more than one commitment, we sometimes have to either live with tensions among them or come up with creative solutions to the tensions. This is no less true of the world in which we actually live than it would be in a world in which the principles discussed here furnished the basic charter of governance. The

---

[29] This is the view defended in Arneson and Shapiro (1996).

[30] The U.S. Supreme Court thus reached the right result in *Bob Jones University v. United States* 461 U.S. 574 (1983), when it held that the federal government may legitimately deny tax-exempt status to institutions that would otherwise qualify but that engage in racial discrimination.

imperatives that follow from the constituent parts of the United States Constitution and its amendments generate many tensions, and just as courts and legislatures have to order, rank, and accommodate them in particular contexts, so the same would have to be done in a world governed by the view advocated here. Admittedly, to say this is not to resolve any specific tensions, but it does perhaps indicate the limits of what can reasonably be expected from a general statement of principles.

A different objection to the internally complex character of my recommendations is that they are unnecessarily complex. My claim that freedom to oppose collective outcomes is not derivative of rights to inclusive participation might be granted, but, if this freedom is valued regardless of whether decisions were made democratically, then why value democratic decision making? Is not democracy, on my account, reducible to opposition? My answer is that although inclusive participation and freedom to oppose are valuable independent of one another, the ways in which they are exercised are not without mutual implications. In particular, I propose the following injunction: The more democratically the victors of battles over collective decisions conduct themselves in victory, the stronger is the obligation on the losers to ensure that their opposition is loyal rather than disloyal – and vice versa. Processes of inclusive consultation, meaningful hearings, good-faith consideration of how to mitigate external effects of decisions, and willingness to consider alternatives all build legitimacy for democratic decision making, and they should. No less appropriately, their opposites breed cynicism and mistrust on the part of losers, which erodes democracy's legitimacy in predictable ways. By linking the obligation to make opposition loyal to how democratically those in power conduct themselves, protagonists on all sides are reminded of the imperfection of the rules that give present winners their victories and losers their losses. In addition, if the two are linked, both winners and losers have incentives to search for mechanisms than can diminish the distances between them.

Trade-offs between democracy and other goods

Additional sources of tension arise from my argument being premised on the notion that democracy is a conditioning good – subordinate to the activities whose pursuit it regulates. This means that there can and most likely will be tensions between the requirements of democracy and the activities it is intended to condition. In the limiting case, there will be activities that operate in flat contradiction to the principles I have described. Apart from the case of parent–child relations, to which some attention has already been devoted, there are football teams, armies, and many other organizational forms whose purposes seem to defy democratic governance. No doubt one can always challenge the proposition that such organizational forms must necessarily be undemocratic, and as the rich literature on the governance of the firm indicates, we should always be open to creative possibilities for the democratic management of institutions that seem inherently undemocratic.[31] Yet one has to confront the possibility that there will be circumstances in which there are inescapable trade-offs between democratic control and the pursuit of a particular good, be it efficient firm management, the gathering of military intelligence, the running of a professional sports team, or other valuable activity.

One response is to deal with trade-offs of this kind in the same way that tensions internal to the general argument are handled, by recognizing that when there is more than one thing we value, at times we will have to choose among them. But this should be the last response, not the first. Although there is never a guarantee that trade-offs between democracy and other goods can be avoided, the present argument bids us to try to find ways to avoid them. Consider two of the examples just mentioned. Congress has devised oversight mechanisms that, however imperfectly, ensure some democratic accountability of intelligence agencies consistent with their secret purposes. No doubt we pay a price for the use of these mechanisms and they could be improved upon, but the outcome of the cold war scarcely suggests that our system fared worse than the Soviet system, in which there was virtually no democratic accountability of any sort, or indeed that it fared less well than other systems in the West that until recently have had little or no democratic oversight.[32] As far as professional sports are concerned, there too the situation is less clear-cut than might appear to be the case. Although one would not want everyone on the team voting on plays, there are many areas in professional sports where a measure of democratic control can be achieved without compromise of athletic purpose. Pay and working conditions are the most obvious areas; no doubt there are others. To reiterate, the general point is that the presumption is against undemocratic ways of doing things. It is only a presumption and it can be overcome, but reasons should be demanded and the burden of persuasion should always lie with those who would limit democracy's operation.

Competing demands of different domains

Yet another set of potential tensions arise out of the fact that I am simultaneously concerned with many domains of civil society. It may be the case that pursuing democracy in one domain makes it more difficult, perhaps even impossible, to pursue it in other domains. For instance, participating in governance is part

---

[31] For a useful, though critical, summary of recent literature, see Hansman (1990).

[32] Robert Dahl (1985b, pp. 33–51) has argued that analogous skepticism is in order for claims that democratic control of nuclear arsenals and development interferes with their efficient deployment.

of what democracy requires. Yet there are limits to how much time people have available, so that increased participatory involvement in one domain may mean diminished participation in others. This is what Carmen Sirianni (1993, pp. 283–312) has characterized as the "paradox of participatory pluralism." It arises for anyone who both values democratic participation and embraces a view of politics that ranges throughout civil society. We cannot simultaneously maximize participation over all domains.

The paradox is inescapable for participatory democrats like Sirianni (who offers no solution to it), but my argument suggests avenues for dealing with it. Participation is not valuable for its own sake in my view; rather, it is valuable only as it is pursued in conjunction with the goods that it conditions. Collective self-governance is important in every domain of civil society, but it is never the most important thing; democrats should thus always be open to time-saving and other novel devices to conserve participatory resources. For instance, since the 1970s a number of writers have explored the use of so-called "citizen juries," randomly selected groups that are paid to debate public issues from the selection of presidential candidates to the governance of school districts.[33] Experience with citizen juries suggests that they may provide useful mechanisms for both exerting democratic control and solving the difficulty, pointed to by Sartori (1987, vol. 1, pp. 119–20) and others, that "knowledge – cognitive competence and control – becomes more and more the problem as politics becomes more and more complicated." Randomly selected lay groups, which have no particular vested interest in the outcome in a given area, can invest the time and energy needed to make informed decisions. Such groups can gather data and listen to expert witnesses, making use of esoteric knowledge without being held hostage to it. The decisions they render could be advisory or even binding, at least for certain matters. The possibilities offered by citizen juries are worth exploring because they provide a potential way out of Sirianni's paradox: they combine citizen control with the possibility of sophisticated decision making in a complex world, and they do it in a way that takes into account the economy of time.[34]

Earlier, I suggested that participation should be seen neither in purely instrumental terms nor as the point of the exercise in politics. Such devices as the citizen jury are attractive because they are an example of a creative institutional response to the goal of trying to occupy a middle ground between these two

---

[33] See Fishkin (1991).

[34] Citizen juries must confront the difficulty that whoever sets the agenda may exert disproportionate influence on the outcome, but this is a difficulty that every decision making procedure must confront. It is not the weakness in democratic theory that juries are intended to resolve, though proponents of citizen juries, like proponents of other decision making mechanisms, need to be concerned about it.

views. Everyone might be expected to participate in some citizen juries, just as everyone is expected to sit on some conventional juries. Everyone would know that other randomly selected juries were sitting with no particular agendas or interest groups of their own being advanced. Everyone would also know that no matter how complex and technical decisions were becoming, a meaningful element of lay control would nonetheless be present in all collective decision making. This is essential in a democracy.

The role of the state

Apart from the extremes of limiting cases like slavery, the general argument does not provide conclusive assessments of particular decision rules or mechanisms of opposition. Instead, as we have seen, it generates presumptions and distributes burdens of persuasion in various ways. That is as it should be. Because the general argument is semicontextual, particularities of context are needed to decide when burdens have been appropriately carried and when presumptions should be rebutted. The general argument leads to determinate conclusions in particular contexts only.

To say this is not, however, to deliver on everything that should reasonably be expected of the general argument. Invoking the language of presumptions and burdens of persuasion immediately raises the question: Who is to judge when burdens have been shouldered and presumptions rebutted? Because the evidence will often be inconclusive and opinion about it must be expected to often be divided, just where decision making authority should be located is, and is bound to remain, an important general question. The answer is also partly contextual; different kinds of authoritative judges should be expected to be appropriate in different kinds of circumstances. But the answer is only partly contextual; some general considerations apply.

Antivanguardism and its limits

Whenever anyone claims to know how to get to democracy undemocratically, skepticism is in order for two reasons, one practical and one normative. The practical reason is that it is doubtful that they can know that they are right. Just because democratic reforms are typically reactive responses to particular evils that chart new courses into the future, it is usually difficult to know what their full consequences will be or what new problems the reforms will create. For instance, changes in the structure of American family law, making marriage more of a contract and less of a status, have been motivated by a desire to undermine the patriarchal family. But it has since become evident that one of the net effects of these changes has been to render women increasingly vulnerable to the greater economic power of men in marriage.[35] As this becomes apparent, other ways of democratizing family life will be sought and new experiments tried and modified as and when the obstacles they generate come into view. Democratizing family life will likely require changes in the organization of the economy and perhaps other changes that are yet to be thought of. Likewise, with the debate on democracy in the workplace, there is now considerable disagreement on which are more effective in undermining alienating hierarchy: strategies of worker self-management or plans for employee ownership or part-ownership that leave the structure of management comparatively untouched. Many varieties of both have been tried in different industries. It seems certain that no single model will turn out to be generally applicable and that new possibilities are yet to be tried.[36]

To take a different example from the realm of American institutional governance, during the nineteenth century reasonable salaries and working conditions for politicians were rightly seen as essential to undermining a system in which government was a part-time activity for the wealthy. But these improvements have brought with them new brands of ossified power in the form of professional politicians with lifetime career aspirations in government. Electoral politics have become dependent on money to such a degree that political elites manage to maintain themselves in positions of power for life in ways that are at odds with democracy's hostility toward entrenched hierarchy.[37] As a response to this, new democratic reforms are being called for, geared toward limiting the number of terms politicians can serve and better regulating the role of money in electoral politics.[38]

It defies credulity to suppose that in any of these instances, democratic reformers could have understood social processes profoundly enough, or seen sufficiently far into the future, to have anticipated all the problems and possibilities that lay ahead. Yet these cases are not exceptional; life has more imagination than us, and it will often defeat our best efforts and present unexpected

---

[35] See Okin (1989, pp. 134–69).

[36] See Sabel and Zeitlin (1986) and Archer (1995).

[37] See Alexander (1976) and Sorauf (1992).

[38] In this connection a small but not insignificant victory was achieved for democracy in March 1990 in *Austin v. Michigan State Chamber of Commerce*, 110 Sup. Ct. 1391 (1990), when the Supreme Court cut back on the *Buckley v. Valeo* 424 U.S. 1 (1976) rule, which had held that although contributions to political campaigns may be limited by legislation, limiting expenditures constitutes a violation of the free speech clause of the First Amendment. In *Austin* the Court held that some corporate expenditures on political speech may be regulated. As far as term limits are concerned, there is considerable scholarly debate as to how bad the incumbency problem is and whether or not term limits would be a solution to the problem of the ossification of power in professional hands. They might, for example, lead to a net transfer of power from politicians to bureaucrats, as Fiorina (1992, pp. 53–59) suggests.

obstacles and opportunities. The fabric of social life and the dynamics of historical change are complex and little understood; that is the reality with which we have to live. Designing democratic institutional constraints is thus bound to be a pragmatic business, best pursued in context-sensitive and incremental ways. New activities that come into being, technological change, experience, and the evolution of other causally linked activities all present fresh problems and generate novel possibilities for democratic governance. These are presumptive reasons to be skeptical of anyone who denies this, whether they harbor a hidden agenda that is being obscured by their vanguardist pretensions or they are acting out of misplaced faith in their own prescient abilities.

Means/ends dichotomies are suspect, also, for the normative reason that they undermine the spirit of democracy. Although I have argued that we should resist the participatory democrat's contention that participation is valuable for its own sake, we should be no less wary of purely instrumental conceptions of democracy. Democratic means are never the point of the exercise, but they are usually of more than mere instrumental value. There is value in doing things democratically, and there is value in struggling with how to do things democratically while still achieving one's other goals. Democratic habits of self-restraint and attention to the needs and aspirations of others have to be learned through democratic practice; succumbing to the authoritarianism inherent in means/ends dichotomies is bound to undermine it. In this connection, Dewey penned the right maxim on the eve of the second world war. "Our first defense is to realize that democracy can be served only by the slow day by day adoption and contagious diffusion in every phase of our common life of methods that are identical with the ends to be reached."[39]

The principled refusal to impose solutions from above can provoke the argument that unless this is done solutions will not be implemented at all, and there are, indeed, at least three important classes of exceptions to the initial presumption against vanguardism. The first concerns the provision of public goods. As my earlier discussion of education revealed, when the provision of public goods is at issue and there are differential capacities for exit, no local decision rule will likely be effective in diminishing injustice. This amounts to saying that effective policies will have to be imposed from above.[40] Proponents of "shock therapy" in the transition from communism to capitalism seem often to take an analogous view. Przeworski (1991, pp. 183–4) argues, for example, that during transitions from authoritarianism to democracy, unless economic reforms are rammed through from above, those who are adversely affected by them will mobilize their opposition through the democratic process, scuttling

---

[39] "Democratic ends need democratic methods for their realization," *New Leader*, vol. 22, October 21, 1939. Reprinted in Dewey (1993, p. 206).

[40] For elaboration, see Hochschild (1984).

the reforms. Consequently, fledgling democratic governments "face the choice of either involving a broad range of political forces in the shaping of reforms, thus compromising their economic soundness, or trying to undermine all opposition to the [reform] program." In Przeworski's view, any government "that is resolute must proceed in spite of the clamor of voices that call for softening or slowing down the reform program." Because reformers "know what is good" all political conflicts become no more than a waste of time. Przeworski goes on to point out that every instance of successful market reform during democratic transitions on record was implemented by executive decree, remarking that "[t]his potential is inherent in the very conception of market reforms."[41]

The critical question is whether the reformers really do "know what is good" and in fact pursue it. Much of what is presented by economic reformers as uncontroversially good might in fact be controversial, and many economic reforms that are described as public goods do not meet the technical criteria that require both joint supply and nonexcludability.[42] Whether privatization and stabilization policies lead to the supply of public goods in this sense is debatable. No doubt parts of what is provided are public goods, but other aspects of these policies may amount to little more than mechanisms for the raiding of public treasuries by strategically well-placed groups, generating little or no benefit for anyone else. In such instances, the pursuit of private benefit may be cloaked in the language of public goods, and opposition to the policies that is really a reflection of zero-sum distributive conflict will masquerade as a collective action problem. What is billed as solutions to that problem will actually be partisan policies that help some sectors and hurt others. Democrats who suspect this is the case with substantial parts of postcommunist privatizations are bound to find themselves ambivalent, at least, about the "bitter pill" strategies that depend on "initial brutality, on proceeding as quickly as possible with the most radical measures," and implementing reforms either by administrative fiat or ramming them through legislatures (Przeworski, 1991, pp. 183–4).[43]

In circumstances where one does not doubt that a public good is being supplied, one's democratic moral intuitions are not troubled by decisive action from above. For instance, in the South African constitutional negotiations that led up to the April 1994 elections, it gradually became clear that – desirable as multiparty roundtable negotiations sounded – they were not going to produce agreement on a democratic constitution. Too many groups had too many incentives to pursue private agendas at the expense of ensuring that the public good

[41] See also Kornai (1990), Sachs (1991), and Pleskovic and Sachs (1994).

[42] "A pure public good has two salient characteristics: jointness of supply, and the impossibility or inefficiency of excluding others from its consumption, once it has been supplied by some members of the community." Mueller (1989, p. 11).

[43] For an empirically based critique of the shock-therapy approach, see Orenstein (1996).

was provided. Consequently, it became evident that if a democratic political order was to be put in place, it would have to be hammered out as an elite pact and then imposed on the society. This is what transpired in fact, and the reason that democrats the world over applauded as opponents to the transition were so effectively either marginalized or coopted was that almost no one doubted that what the elites proposed to impose – a democratic constitutional order – was in fact a public good.[44]

Distinguishing the provision of genuine public goods from spurious ones is a difficult and controversial business. Often the two will be mixed, making the distinction even more difficult, as is almost certainly the case with most privatization plans. Even in the case of the South African constitution it seems clear that the elites who committed themselves to providing the public good in question sprinkled in a few benefits for themselves, notably a system of electoral and parliamentary rules that greatly weakens backbenchers vis-à-vis leaderships, as well as bribes to particular interest groups to insulate them from the new political order.[45]

The extent to which policies may legitimately be imposed from above varies with the degree to which genuine public goods are being provided. As the preceding remarks indicate, this will often be hotly disputed and ideologically charged, not least because there will be those who have an interest in obscuring the matter. It may also be genuinely unclear in certain circumstances. When either of these things is the case, what we witness is not a failure in the argument for democracy. Rather, it is a failure in the understanding of, or agreement about, whether or not something constitutes a public good. This is not to diminish the normative importance of the matter, it is only to say that it would be expecting the wrong kind of thing from any political theory to ask that it resolve contentious empirical questions of political economy. The general argument can be expected to counsel what to do when a certain fact pattern obtains, it cannot be expected to tell us whether or not the fact pattern really

---

[44] On the collapse of the roundtable negotiations and the emergence of an elite pact between the National Party and ANC leaderships, see Shapiro (1993).

[45] As far as political elites sprinkling in benefits for themselves is concerned, the new constitution requires that any member of parliament who ceases to be a member of his or her political party also cease to be a member of parliament, and be replaced by someone else from the party's parliamentary list (*Constitution of the Republic of South Africa Bill* [B212B-93(GA)] Chapter 4, sec 43). This provision was retained in the permanent constitution, adopted in May of 1996. It seems hard to overestimate the power that such a system will concentrate in the hands of party elites (who are also the leaders of their parties in the cabinet). As for bribes, all civil service jobs and salaries were guaranteed for at least five years following the transition, and in the last weeks before the election, President de Klerk transferred some three million acres of land to Zulu king Goodwill Zwelitini in order to prevent their falling under the control of the new national government following the April 1994 elections (*The New York Times*, Tuesday May 24, p. A6).

does obtain. The general argument does, however, counsel us to regard claims of providing public goods with suspicion and to subject them to what lawyers think of as "strict scrutiny." American courts typically subject legislative action to this most demanding level of constitutional scrutiny when the proposed action interferes with a "fundamental" liberty, usually a freedom protected by the bill of rights. Strict scrutiny requires a showing that the governmental objective is unusually important – that a "compelling" state interest is at stake – and that it cannot be accomplished in a less intrusive way.[46] By analogy, we might say that the undemocratic imposition of a public good is justified only when the good in question is essential to the operation of a democratic order and cannot be attained in any other way. Those who claim to provide public goods may have ulterior motives, and private goods can often masquerade as public goods. For these reasons, the initial and strong presumption should always be against imposition from above.

A second class of exceptions to the general presumption against vanguardism arises when illegitimate hierarchies are maintained by the state. For example, in the West the disadvantaged status of women in family life was sustained by the common law and other active policies of the state for centuries. One dramatic legacy of this history is that as recently as the 1950s, throughout the United States a husband could not be prosecuted for raping his wife; in England in 1994 he still could not be. By the mid-1990s spousal rape was a prosecutable felony during an ongoing marriage in well over a third of American jurisdictions, the product of a concerted feminist campaign in state legislatures and courts.[47] It would have been impossible for such changes to have come about without the state's active involvement, because it was the policies of the state that were at the root of the injustice in question. Likewise, it took the passage of the married women's property acts (the first wave of which began in the 1840s) to destroy the common-law rule that had given the husband control of, and sometimes title to, the wife's property and possessions during marriage.[48]

In such circumstances it will be necessary, and justifiable, for the state to be centrally involved in dismantling the unjust system it created. Women would have been morally misguided as well as politically shortsighted had they not sought to enlist public institutions in this struggle to refashion the terms of their domestic association. Because the unjust hierarchies to which they had been subjected were direct products of state policies and sustained by the legal order, it was reasonable to require the state to play an active role in dismantling

---

[46] See Tribe (1988, pp. 251–75).
[47] On the changing law of marital rape in the United States, see Freeman (1981), Rhode (1989, pp. 249–51), and Augustine (1991). On the English evolution of the exception, see Bromley and Lowe (1987, pp. 109–12).
[48] See Clark (1988, p. 589).

the injustices in question. Likewise, the effects of the Group Areas Act in South Africa, which led to the forced removal of millions of blacks from viable communities to desolate deserts, are properly responded to by remedial action from a democratic South African state.[49] The general point here is that the more antidemocratic practices have been underwritten by the state, the more powerful is the case for the involvement of state institutions in remedying the unjust status quo.[50]

A third class of exceptions arises when domination within a domain is not a direct product of state action, but is nonetheless sustained by forces external to the domain that can be removed only by state action. This is what Walzer (1983, pp. 3–30) described as "dominance," the transfer of power in one domain of social life where it may be legitimate into another where it is not. Walzer contends, for instance, that economic inequality is not objectionable as such and that it may be justified in the sphere of production for its incentive and other efficiency effects. What is objectionable is that disparities in income and wealth are all too easily translatable into disparities in the political domain, the domestic domain, the educational domain, and other areas where they have no evident rationale. This happens because the resources necessary to exercise power tend to be fungible across domains, and Walzer argues that one of the appropriate tasks of a democratic state is to limit this fungibility. In this view, laws against buying and selling votes for money can be defended, for example, even though such laws are inefficient in the economist's sense. Similarly, refusals by courts to enforce prenuptial agreements that leave divorcing spouses destitute amount to a refusal by the state to allow economic disparities that may be justifiable outside the domestic domain to set the terms of life within it.

Walzer's intuition about this class of cases is defensible, if for different reasons than those he supplies. Whereas for Walzer the reason for trying to prevent domination within a sphere by those who control goods external to it is rooted in shared meanings about which goods are appropriate in which domains, from the present standpoint the justification is rooted in considerations drawn from the political economy of power.[51] I said earlier that the shape of decision rules should follow the contours of power relations. It follows that when obstacles to democracy within a domain are externally sustained, it is appropriate to use state power to remove such obstacles. To deny this would amount to abandoning the commitment to democracy in particular domains to those who have imperial control of fungible resources. In short – *pace* Walzer

---

[49] For an account of the extent and effects of these policies, see Suzman (1993, pp. 65–212).

[50] This says nothing about which state institutions are most appropriate for the purpose, whether it be courts, legislatures, or executive agencies. See below.

[51] I have noted elsewhere that the appeal to shared meanings fails because these are invariably in contention. See Shapiro (1994, pp. 130–35).

– because causal effects rather than shared membership within a domain are decisive in legitimating a right to democratic control, it follows that state action that crosses the boundaries of domains can be justified when this is necessary to advance democracy within a domain.[52]

Action by the state to advance democratic reform can be justified, then, but not as part of any missionary quest on democracy's behalf. There is no secular analog to "Christianizing the infidels" to justify such action, whether by courts, legislatures, or invading armies. Rather, external involvement can be justified by three principal classes of reasons. First, when provision of a public good is at stake, imposed solutions may be justifiable, subject to the caveats I have mentioned. This we might think of as a market-failure justification. Second, the state may often have an affirmative obligation to help foster democracy flowing from its historical culpability in creating and sustaining injustice. Last, when external sources of domination within a domain can be removed only by state action, this can be justified by reference to the argument from causal legitimacy.

Legislatures versus courts

The aspiration to avoid imposed solutions suggests that the presumption should generally be in favor of doing things through representative institutions rather than through courts or other agencies, for the conventional reason that legislatures are comparatively more democratically accountable. There will be exceptions to this, but it is the exceptions that stand in presumptive need of justification. In this connection my argument for democracy exhibits an elective affinity for the approaches to constitutional adjudication that have been defended in recent years by Burt (1992) and Ginsburg (1993), and it will be useful to end with some discussion of their views.

Burt conceives of a constitutional democracy as inescapably committed to two principles – majority rule and equal self-determination – that have the potential to conflict with one another. If majoritarian processes are employed to promote domination of some by others, the contradiction latent in democratic politics becomes manifest. In such circumstances, democracy goes to war with itself and an institutional mechanism is needed to resolve the conflict. This is supplied, in Burt's (1992; p. 29) account, by judicial review, understood as "a coercive instrument extrinsic to the disputants" in a political struggle. Burt sees judicial review as a "logical response to an internal contradiction between majority rule and equal self-determination. It is not a deviation from that theory."

---

[52] It should also be evident from my earlier discussion of public goods and state culpability that I believe Walzer is mistaken in thinking that preventing dominance is the only legitimate basis for the imposition of solutions by the state.

If the court's legitimate role in a democracy is rooted in this logic of preventing domination through democratic process, then in Burt's view it follows that its activities should be limited to dealing with the consequences of the democratic contradiction. And because preventing domination is the goal, it also follows that courts should not take sides in disputes that are byproducts of the democratic contradiction (effectively imposing the wishes of one group on another). Rather, they should declare the domination that has emerged from the democratic process unacceptable and insist that the parties try anew to find an accommodation. Thus in contrast to what many have seen as the altogether too timid approach taken by the U.S. Supreme Court in the school desegregation cases of the 1950s and after, in Burt's view the Court took the right stand. In *Brown v. Board of Education* the Justices declared the doctrine of "separate but equal" to be an unconstitutional violation of the Equal Protection Clause,[53] but they did not describe schooling conditions that would be acceptable. Rather, they turned the problem back to Southern state legislatures, requiring them to fashion acceptable remedies themselves.[54] These remedies came before the court as a result of subsequent litigation, were evaluated when they did, and were often found to be wanting. But the Court avoided designing the remedy itself, and with it avoided the charge that it was usurping the legislative function (Burt, 1992, pp. 271–310).

Ginsburg, too, has made the case that when courts try to step beyond a reactive role, they undermine their legitimacy in a democracy. Although she thinks that it is sometimes necessary for the court to step "ahead" of the political process to achieve reforms that the constitution requires, if it gets too far ahead it can produce a backlash and provoke charges that it is overreaching its appropriate place in a democratic constitutional order (Ginsburg, 1993, pp. 30–38).[55] Ginsburg and Burt both think that the sort of approach adopted by Justice Blackmun in *Roe v. Wade* exemplifies this danger.[56] In contrast to the *Brown* approach, in *Roe* the Court did a good deal more than strike down a Texas abortion statute. The majority opinion laid out a detailed test to determine the conditions under which any abortion statute could be expected to pass muster. In effect, Justice Blackmun authored a federal abortion statute of his own. As Ginsburg (1993, p. 32) put it, the court "invited no dialogue with legislators. Instead, it seemed entirely to remove the ball from the legislators' court" by wiping out virtually every form of abortion regulation then in existence.

---

[53] *Brown v. Board of Education I* 347 U.S. 483 (1954).

[54] *Brown v. Board of Education II* 349 U.S. 294 (1955).

[55] See also "Nomination of Ruth Bader Ginsburg to be an Associate Justice of the United States Supreme Court: Report together with Additional Views," *Exec Report. 103-6 - 93 - 1*, United States Senate.

[56] *Roe v. Wade* 410 U.S. 113 (1973).

In the Burt–Ginsburg view, the sweeping holding in *Roe* diminished the Court's democratic legitimacy at the same time that it polarized opinion about abortion and put paid to various schemes to liberalize abortion laws that were underway in different states. Between 1967 and 1973, statutes were passed in nineteen states liberalizing the permissible grounds for abortion. Many feminists had been dissatisfied with the pace and extent of this reform. This is why they mounted the campaign that resulted in *Roe*. Burt (1992, pp. 348–52) concedes that in 1973 it was "not clear whether the recently enacted state laws signified the beginning of a national trend toward abolishing all abortion restrictions or even whether in the so-called liberalized states, the new enactments would significantly increase access to abortion for anyone." Nonetheless, he points out that "the abortion issue was openly, avidly, controverted in a substantial number of public forums, and unlike the regimen extant as recently as 1967, it was no longer clear who was winning the battle." Following the *Brown* model, the Court might have struck down the Texas abortion statute in *Roe* and remanded the matter for further action at the state level, thereby setting limits on what legislatures might do in the matter of regulating abortion without involving the Court directly in designing that regulation. In the Burt–Ginsburg view, this would have left space for democratic resolution of the conflict that would have ensured the survival of the right to abortion while at the same time preserving the legitimacy of the Court's role in a democracy.

Although the tensions that arise within the present account differ from those that motivate Burt and Ginsburg, in three important respects their view of the role of courts in a democratic order fit comfortably within the general argument developed here. First, they articulate an appropriate institutional response to the injunction that rather than imposing democracy on collective activities the goal should be to try to structure things so that people will find ways to democratize things for themselves. By placing themselves in a nay-saying stance, that is, ruling out practices as unacceptable when they violate democracy's strictures, courts can force legislatures and the conflicting parties they represent to seek creative solutions to their conflicts that can pass constitutional muster. Second, the Burt–Ginsburg view is attractive because it is reactive but directed; it exemplifies the creative pragmatism that motivates the present argument. It involves accepting that there is an important – if circumscribed – role for courts in a democracy, yet it does not make the unmanageable administrative demands on courts that accompany more proactive views of adjudication. In this view a court might reasonably hold that a given policy should be rejected without stating (indeed, perhaps without having decided) what policy would pass muster. "This is unacceptable for reasons *a*, *b*, *c* . . .; find a better way" is seen as an appropriate stance for a constitutional court. Finally, by recognizing the relatively greater legitimacy of legislatures and treating courts as institutional mechanisms for coping with legislative failure, the Ginsburg–Burt view takes into account the fact that no decision making mechanism is flawless. Yet it does so in a way that is rooted in the idea that democratic procedures should be made to operate as well as possible, and, when they fail, remedies should be no more intrusive on the democratic process than is necessary for repair.

Some will object to this as too minimal a role for courts, but democrats have to concern themselves not only with courts that aspire to advance the cause of democracy, as they might reasonably be thought to have done in *Brown* and *Roe*, but also with courts that do not, as was the case in *Dred Scott, The Civil Rights Cases*, and *Lochner v. New York*.[57] Insulated from any further review and lacking, at least in the American context, in democratic accountability, courts can put decisions of this kind in place that may not be reversed for decades or even generations. Although it is thus wise for democrats to embrace an activist role for a constitutional court, it is equally wise to limit courts to a circumscribed and negationist activism.

References

Alexander, H. 1976. *Financing Politics: Money, Elections and Political Reform*, Congressional Quarterly Press, Washington D.C.

Antholis, W. 1993. Liberal Democratic Theory and the Transformation of Sovereignty, Ph.D. dissertation, Yale University, New Haven, Conn.

Archer, R. 1995. *Economic Democracy: The Politics of Feasible Socialism*, Clarendon Press, Oxford.

Arneson, R. and I. Shapiro. 1996. Democracy and religious freedom: A critique of *Wisconsin v. Yoder*, in *NOMOS XXXVIII: Political Order*. I. Shapiro and R. Hardin, eds., New York University Press, New York, pp. 365–411.

Arrow, K. J. 1951. *Social Choice and Individual Values*. John Wiley and Sons, New York (rev. ed., 1963).

Augustine, R. I. 1991. Marriage: The safe haven for rapists, *Journal of Family Law*, **29**(3), 599–90.

Barber, B. 1975. Justifying justice: Problems of psychology, politics and measurement in Rawls, in *Reading Rawls*, N. Daniels, ed., pp. 292–318, Basil Blackwell, Bristol, Eng.

1979. *Strong Democracy*, University of California Press, Berkeley, Calif.

Barry B. 1990. *Political Argument*, 2nd ed, Harvester Wheatsheaf, Hertfordshire.

Beitz, C. 1988. Equal opportunity in political representation, in *Equal Opportunity*, N. Bowie, ed., pp. 155–74, Westview, Boulder, Colo.

Bromley, P. M., and N.V. Lowe. 1987. *Family Law*, Butterworths, London.

Buchanan, J. and G. Tullock. 1962. *The Calculus of Consent: Logical Foundations of Constitutional Democracy*, Ann Arbor Paperbacks, Michigan.

Burt, R. A. 1992. *The Constitution in Conflict*, Harvard University Press, Cambridge, Mass.

---

[57] *Dred Scott v Sandford* 60 U.S. 393 (1856), *In re Civil Rights Cases*, 109 U.S. 3 (1883) and *Lochner v. New York* 198 U.S. 45 (1905).

Clark, H. H. 1988. *The Law of Domestic Relations in the United States*, 2d. ed., West Publishers, St. Paul, Minnesota.

Cohen, J., and J. Rogers. 1983. *On Democracy*, Pelican, Harmondsworth, England.

Dahl, R. 1970. *After the Revolution*, Yale University Press, New Haven, Conn.

  1985a. *A Preface to Economic Democracy*, University of California Press, Berkeley, Calif.

  1985b. *Controlling Nuclear Weapons: Democracy versus Guardianship*, Syracuse University Press, Syracuse, New York.

  1986. Procedural democracy in: R. Dahl, *Democracy, Liberty, and Equality*. Norvegian University Press, Oslo, pp. 191–225.

Dewey, J. 1993. Democratic ends need democratic methods for their realization. Reprint, John Dewey, *The Political Writings*. D. Morris and I. Shapiro, eds., Hackett, Indianapolis, Ind.

Downs, A. 1957. *An Economic Theory of Democracy*, Harper and Row, New York.

Ely, J. H. 1980. *Democracy and Distrust: A Theory of Judicial Review*, Harvard University Press, Cambridge, Mass.

Fiorina, M. 1992. *Divided Government*, Macmillan, London.

Fishkin, J. 1991. *Democracy and Deliberation: New Directions for Democratic Reform*. Yale University Press, New Haven, Conn.

Foord, A. S. 1964. *His Majesty's Opposition 1714–1830*, Oxford University Press, Oxford.

Freeman, M. 1981. If you can't rape your wife, who[m] can you rape? The marital rape exception reexamined, *Family Law Quarterly*, **15**(1), 1–29.

Ginsburg, R. B. 1993. Speaking in a Judicial Voice. *Madison Lecture*, New York University Law School, March 9, 1993. New York University, New York.

Glendon, M. A. 1987. *Abortion and Divorce in Western Law*, Harvard University Press, Cambridge, Mass.

Halévy, E. 1972. *The Growth of Philosophic Radicalism*, Augustus Kelley, New York.

Hansman, H. 1990. When does worker ownership work? *Yale Law Journal*, **99**(8), 1749–1816.

Hart, H. L. A. 1975. Rawls on liberty and its priority, in *Reading Rawls*, N. Daniels, ed., pp. 230–252, Basil Blackwell, Bristol, Eng.

Hochschild, J. 1984. *The New American Dilemma: Liberal Democracy and School Desegregation*, Yale University Press, New Haven, Conn.

Kaufman, A. 1969. Human nature and participatory democracy, in *The Bias of Pluralism*, William Connolly, ed., pp. 201–12, Lieber-Atherton.

Kitto, H. D. F. 1973. *The Greeks*, Pelican, Harmondsworth, England.

Klaw, S. 1993. *Without Sin*, Allen Lane, New York.

Kornai, J. 1990. *The Road to a Free Economy: Shifting from a Socialist System*, W.W. Norton, New York.

Langley, J. A. ed., 1979. *Ideologies of Liberation in Black Africa 1856–1970*, Rex Collins, London.

MacIntyre, A. 1984. *After Virtue*. Indiana University Press, Notre Dame, Indiana.

Mansbridge, J. 1980. *Beyond Adversary Democracy*, Basic Books, New York.

Moore, B. Jr. 1989. *Liberal Prospects Under Soviet Socialism: A Comparative Historical Perspective*, Averell Harriman Institute, New York.

Mueller, D. C. 1989. *Public Choice II*, Cambridge University Press, New York and Cambridge.

Nozick, R. 1974. *Anarchy, State, and Utopia*, Basic Books, New York.

Okin, S. M. 1989. *Justice, Gender, and the Family*, Basic Books, New York.

Orenstein, M. 1996. Out of the Red: Building Capitalism and Democracy in Post-Communist East Europe. Ph.D. dissertation, Yale University, New Haven, Conn.

Pateman, C. 1970. *Participation and Democratic Theory*, Cambridge University Press, Cambridge.

Plescovic, B., and J. Sachs, 1994. Political Independence and economic reform in Slovenia, in *The Transition in Eastern Europe*, edited by O. Blanchard, K. Froot, and J. Sachs. University of Chicago Press, Chicago. Vol. I, pp. 191–220.

Pogge, T. 1992. Cosmopolitanism and sovereignty, *Ethics*, **103**, 48–75.

Przeworski, A. 1991. *Democracy and the Market*, Cambridge University Press, Cambridge and New York.

Rae, D. W. 1969. Decision rules and individual values in constitutional choice, *American Political Science Review*, **63**(1), 40–56.

　　1975. The limits of consensual decision, *American Political Science Review*, **69**(4), 1270–94.

Rawls, J. 1971. *A Theory of Justice*, Harvard University Press, Cambridge, Mass.

　　1973. Fairness to goodness, *Philosophical Review*, **38**, 218–31.

　　1985. Justice as fairness: Political not metaphysical, *Philosophy and Public Affairs*, **14**(3), 223–51.

　　1993. The law of peoples, *Critical Inquiry*, **20**, 36–68.

Rhode, D. 1989. *Justice and Gender*, Harvard University Press, Cambridge, Mass.

Riker, W. 1982. *Liberalism Against Populism*, Waveland Press, Illinois.

Rousseau, J.-J. 1972. *The Social Contract*, Pelican, Harmondsworth, England.

Sabel, C. and J. Zeitlin. 1986. Historical alternatives to mass production, *Past and Present*, **108**, 133–176.

Sachs, J. 1991. The Transformation of Eastern Europe: The Case of Poland. The Frank E. Seidman Lecture, Rhodes College, Memphis, Tenn., September 26, 1991.

Sartori, G. 1987. *The Theory of Democracy Revisited*, 2 vols, Chatham House, N. J.

Scanlon, T. M. 1975. Rawl's theory of justice, in *Reading Rawls*, N. Daniels, ed., pp. 169–205, Basil Blackwell, Bristol, Eng.

Schumpeter, J. 1942. *Capitalism, Socialism and Democracy*, Harper and Row, New York.

Shapiro, I. 1986. *The Evolution of Rights in Liberal Theory*, Cambridge University Press, New York.

　　1989. Constructing politics, *Political Theory*, **17**(3), 475–82.

　　1990a. Three fallacies concerning majorities, minorities, and democratic politics, in *NOMOS XXXII: Majorities and Minorities*, J. Chapman and A. Wertheimer, eds., pp. 79–125, New York University Press, New York.

　　1990b. *Political Criticism*. University of California Press, Berkeley, Calif.

　　1993. Democratic innovation: South Africa in comparative context, *World Politics*, **46**(1), 138–41.

　　1994. Three ways to be a democrat, *Political Theory* **22**(1), 124–51.

Sirriani, C. 1993. Learning pluralism: Democracy and diversity in feminist organization, in *NOMOS XXXV: Democratic Community*, J. Chapman and I. Shapiro, eds., New York University Press, New York.

Sorauf, F. J. 1992. *Inside Campaign Finance*, Yale University Press, New Haven, Conn.

Spitz, E. 1984. *Majority Rule*, Chatham House, New Jersey.

Sunstein, C. 1995. On legal theory and legal practice, in *NOMOS XXXVII: Theory and Practice*, I. Shapiro and J. W. DeCew, eds., pp. 267–87, New York University Press, New York.

Suzman, H. 1993. *In No Uncertain Terms*, Knopf, New York.

Taylor, M. 1969. Proof of a theorem on majority rule, *Behavioral Science*, **14**, 228–31.

Thompson, D. 1984. *The Chartists*, Temple Smith, London.

Tocqueville, A. de. 1969. *Democracy in America*. Reprint, edited by J. P. Mayer, translated by G. Lawrence, Doubleday, Garden City, New York.

Tribe, L. H. 1988. *American Constitutional Law*, 2d ed., Foundation Press, New York.

Unger, R. 1987. *Politics*. 3 vols. Cambridge University Press, Cambridge and New York.

Walzer, M. 1983. *Spheres of Justice: A Defense of Pluralism and Equality*, Basic Books, New York.

　　1987. *Interpretation and Social Criticism*. Harvard University Press, Cambridge, Mass.

　　1989. A day in the life of a socialist citizen, in *Radical Principles*, Basic Books, New York.

Weisbrod, C. 1982. On the breakup of Oneida, *Connecticut Law Review*, **14**(4), 717–32.

Wendt, A. 1994. Collective identity-formation and the international state, *American Political Science Review*, **88**(2), 384–96.

CHAPTER 12

Democracy on the margin

Russell Hardin

Democracy and group census

Because it faces severe limits on its workability, democracy is not a panacea for politics. It works only on the margins of great issues. The few big issues it can handle are those on which there is broad consensus – such as the consensuses in the United Kingdom, Canada, and the United States on fighting World War II. Most forms of government could handle such issues roughly as well. Indeed, the United Kingdom handled World War II by ceasing to be democratically accountable for the duration of the war. For conflictual issues, democracy can work only against a background of rough coordination on order. Without that essentially prior coordination, democracy is trammeled or irrelevant. And even with the relevant coordination on order, if precise theoretical claims are at issue, democracy works only in the sense that it reaches a result – but not in the sense that it gets the right result. Often, indeed, a democrat would want decisions to not be made democratically.

Democracy is essentially a member of the mutual-benefit class of theories. If political divisions cut very much deeper than the marginal issues on which we can democratically compromise, democracy may no longer seem to produce mutual benefits. It then produces major – not marginal – winners and losers. Big disagreements bring us down. For example, democracy could not handle conflict over slavery in the United States, it was very shaky in handling socialism in the postwar United Kingdom, and it could not even get off the ground in independent Burundi with its first democratic election pilloried as merely an ethnic census. It is when democratic outcomes merely mirror a simple

Presented to the Villa Colombella Group meeting, Dijon, France, September 1994. This paper has benefitted from discussions at that meeting and in the seminar series on Emerging Trends in Political Science, Department of Political Science, Rutgers University (September 1994), and from a written commentary by Ayse D. Özkan.

census – of ethnicity or other group membership – that they begin to be too conflictual for compromise and too disruptive for continued order.

Electing a government by ethnic census need not be a disaster. The government might turn out to be reasonable and relatively equitable. Or no census group might be able to dominate the government. For example, an election that turned into a group or ethnic census in former Yugoslavia might not have been a problem, because no group could have won big – Serbs at about a third of the total were the largest group. Ethnic censuses in Croatia, Serbia, Kosovo, and Macedonia, however, would have produced huge majorities for one group over others – as they have done in both Croatia and Serbia under the lethal leadership of, respectively, Franjo Tudjman and Slobodan Milosevic.

Commonly, however, election by group census is disastrous. The 1993 elections in Burundi that democratically brought the first Hutu president to office by a nearly two-to-one margin was reviled by Tutsis as de facto an ethnic census. The Hutu victory set off the current civil war in Burundi. Recent elections in Sri Lanka have been ethnic censuses that have deepened conflict. India threatens to slide into ethnic census to replace its shaky democracy. Canada and Belgium might eventually be taken apart by ethnic census. Lani Guinier and others have proposed a territorially contrived ethnic census to allow the election of more blacks in the United States. Government has often been based on group membership censuses of other kinds, such as corporatist government by guilds, estates, or other corporate groups, including worker and industry groups.

There are at least two conspicuous conceptual problems with group census voting. First, such a system may run aground on *changing structures of the relevant groups*. For example, ethnic censuses in Yugoslavia and other nations miss the large fraction of the population who are the product of intermarriage. And the fixing of shares of representation economically is entirely misguided if there is economic change. Luddites and related groups might often win restrictions that would hobble generally beneficial economic change. Allotting fixed numbers or percentages of seats in a representative body to a particular group – something that might initially be grounded in claims of democratic representativeness – can lead to severely antidemocratic results if the relative size of the group changes. Oddly, if the government must periodically or eventually reconsider the weight of seats assigned to a declining group, the reconsideration must lead to direct conflict with the group.

Second, a group census makes sense at all only to the extent that the issues at stake in government decisions are *issues on which one's position systematically correlates very strongly with one's group membership*. Typically, this will be true only for certain classes of matters. In particular, group membership and policy position correlate when government is in a position to allocate resources to various groups and might do so on the basis of the groups' support. But for such issues, government is not a matter of providing for the mutual advantage of all unless it is blind to group membership in its allocations or is carefully neutral in allocating according to percentage of total population or workforce. Then, a group census might be necessary for determining allocation percentages, but not for electing a government.

One might argue that group membership and policy position could correlate strongly on certain other policies, such as those concerning religious beliefs. For example, in the United States there is a relatively strong correlation between being Catholic and opposing the legality of abortion. Here, it is implausible to suppose government serves mutual advantage unless the divisive issue is considered *less important* than the value of generalized order with democratic decision making. In general, this is a likely view, although Hobbes, Locke, and many others struggled through eras in which religion was seemingly the most important issue and was deeply divisive. Today, religious visions have destroyed the prospects of democracy for the foreseeable future in Iran and threaten to do so as well in Algeria and Egypt. It would be astonishing if religious opposition to abortion, homosexuality, science, and other issues were deep-seated enough to destroy democratic governments in the North Atlantic community.

Interests and democracy

Following Aristotle and many others, Talcott Parsons (1949, pp. 247–49) insisted that it is coincidence of values that makes a society cohere. He supposed that nothing else could possibly bring about this result and he considered it a sociological fact that shared norms are a necessary part of the explanation of social order. But consider the possibility that mere interests could produce coherence. The way to secure the bulk of my interests is the way simultaneously to secure yours. A set of laws that covers all of us in the same way is what we both want. We might quibble a bit about particular laws, but we agree in general on the set of them. Similarly, on many major policy issues, we share interests to some extent, often to a great extent. Of course, I might like to have specially contrived laws that exempt just me from some burdens or hindrances – but only monarchs and senators can expect to get such treatment. Next best for me is a fairly extensive set of laws that cover me as well as everyone else. On this, I and virtually everyone else have interest in coordinating.

Parsons cast his position in opposition to the views of Thomas Hobbes (1651). Although he argued in favor of autocracy as the best form of government, Hobbes' theory of government can also be read to support democracy (democracy is merely the third best form of government, after autocracy and oligarchy). The first problem of government is to achieve order so that we may individually be safe in our daily efforts to live with others and to work for our own benefit. If this interest is great enough and common enough, its protection is the background necessary for the marginal workings of democracy – as it is for any constructive form of government.

Hobbes's theory is essentially a mutual-advantage theory of government.[1] In the conditions of his time in England, he supposed it true that virtually everyone would be a loser from any effort at revolution to create a different or a different kind of government. Therefore he concluded that it was best to be loyal to the current government, almost independently of what that government happened to be. This conclusion obviously requires major empirical claims. But these claims seem superficially plausible, at least for most of the plausible current forms of government, although they do not seem plausible for rule by mullahs in Iran or by the military in Myanmar.

If democracy depends on a generalized background coordination on order, what can elicit coordination from all of us? Democracy works especially well when there is a large capital stock that is at risk if order breaks down, especially if the capital stock is spread fairly broadly through the society, as it is in contemporary industrial states. In such a case, if rebuilding the capital stock would take enormous effort and a long time, then all those who share sufficiently in it have an interest in maintaining order.[2] The distressing scenes of people weeping in the ruins or returning to their destroyed homes and lost belongings in the wars of Yugoslavia and even of impoverished Rwanda and Burundi exemplify the enormity of the interest these people had in order.

It is an old thesis in the politics of the working class that class politics will be denatured by *embourgeoisement* – the growing wealth of workers as they gain stakes in homes and other things. John Goldthorpe et al. (1969) argue that English working-class attitudes toward politics do not show evidence of embourgeoisement.[3] But there may well have been a dramatic and important effect of embourgeoisement that their surveys do not capture. Workers might have been rallied for violent revolutionary activity a century ago or even in the 1930s. Without dramatic economic setbacks, it is hard to believe they could be mobilized for revolution today. Workers in successful industrial states today could not wage revolution without great personal losses to themselves and, most likely, their children. Revolutionary class action is likely past in these nations unless there is a prior economic failure that destroys what revolution might have destroyed.[4]

Revolutions are usually made by those who have relatively little to lose, for whom starting over is not radically inferior to continuing as is. Of course,

---

[1] Russell Hardin (1991b).
[2] Hobbes supposed we must all suffer net losses over our own lifetimes from any revolution – only a subsequent generation might benefit from our effort to change governments.
[3] Adam Przeworski (1980) argues the contrary.
[4] See also Russell Hardin (1991a).

among those for whom starting over is often not a great burden are the young, who have yet to start much of anything. A spate of warfare might be entertaining to many of them and it might be a form of procrastination on deciding on a life. Among those who are older, the wealthy might instigate coups, but they do not often make revolutions. There is a somewhat odd exception to this claim, which is that colonial revolutions against foreign rulers are commonly made by the wealthy. For example, George Washington, Thomas Jefferson, and others were the elite of the colonies that became the United States. Perhaps in part for this reason, many students of revolution do not count such colonial secessions as those of the United States, Kenya, or former Northern Rhodesia among the great revolutions that interest them.

Perhaps Hobbes's insight that even the instigators of rebellion are apt to lose from it requires profound understanding. But it seems more likely that many ordinary people would agree and would fear losses before there could be gains from revolution. They might even expect their losses to outweigh their gains in the long term. Still, ordinary people seem willing to join in revolutionary and civil war conflicts, as in contemporary Yugoslavia and in Rwanda and Burundi.

What could have made Yugoslavs, Burundans, and Rwandans go to self-destructive civil war? Some of them perhaps did not think they shared in material gains and other benefits from order, so that they did not have much to lose – though this could not have been many people. Some of them perhaps did not expect their own material belongings and status to be at risk in attacks on other groups. This, for example, may especially be true of Serbs in Bosnia, who were mostly rural, whereas their war against Croats and Muslims was fought in towns and cities, where more prosperous people lived. Some of them stood to gain by leading violent attacks. Finally, and perhaps most important, in cases in which order had already broken down or seemed very shaky, even though violence would mean losses, these losses could be lessened for any group that attacked preemptively.[5] Insofar as this is true, no group in such a position can be trusted unless it somehow convincingly precommits to being democratic, or there are institutional barriers thwarting the recourse to preemptive attack. Again, for groups, even more than for nations, meaningful precommitment is exceedingly difficult.

Consider the Tutsi-dominated Rwandan rebels, who began their civil war against the Hutu-dominated government about 1990. Three decades ago, most Tutsis and many Hutus hostile to the autocratic Hutu government were expelled from Rwanda and lived in refugee camps just outside Rwanda. Their children are the mainstay of the contemporary rebel force. No matter what happens, they should want to start over, because continuation of the life they have had in

---

[5] Russell Hardin (1995, chap. 6).

refugee camps is dismal. Indeed, they should perhaps want to start over even if the cost of doing so is waging and winning a bloody civil war in Rwanda. The victorious Hutus of 1959–61 won too much for their own good, and they have since had to pay for it.

Constitutional precommitment

Democracy can typically work well only where it serves the mutual advantage of diverse interests to have democratic government. There could be many contexts in which some group – usually a small minority interest in conflict with a large interest – might be supposed to have an interest in blocking or disrupting democratic government. If that is so, then democracy is not mutually advantageous – it serves a majority group well but not a minority group. Even in such cases, there might be, at least in principle, possibilities for compromise because failure to compromise leads to losses that could be avoided. Unfortunately, the in-principle possibilities may not be actual possibilities because neither the larger nor the smaller group may be able to convincingly precommit to abiding by the compromise. This is especially true if the terms of the compromise must necessarily be left somewhat open-ended because, as is often likely to be the case, future conflicts cannot be fully anticipated.

A standard device for securing precommitment to various arrangements under an acceptable compromise is to fix those arrangements in a constitution. Unfortunately, precommitment in these contexts succeeds only to the extent that such precommitment is renewed at every subsequent stage for the good reason that it is still in the interest of relevant parties. If interests or parties change, the initial precommitment is put at risk, perhaps grave risk. If precommitment breaks, democracy might then enable one of the current groups to gain ascendancy, contrary to the terms of the constitution. A constitutional agreement might therefore have the perverse result that, *by empowering government, it eventually empowers a nascent majority to dominate other groups.*

Democracy has run into great risk in the United States on at least three occasions. First, of course, was the period of contest over slavery, second was the period of contest over economic policy during the Great Depression, and last was the period of contest over the Vietnam war. In each of these instances, a very important issue seemed to require a decision one way or the other, with little room for mutual-advantage compromise; and there were large fractions of the population who lined up on each of the two sides. In all three of these periods, significant numbers of the population seemed to think that the divisive issue was the most important issue of the day, important enough to be worth wrecking the government to get the right outcome.

One can see one form of the special difficulty facing democracy in the apparent compromise, from the constitutional era onward, over slavery. At the constitutional convention, Northern opponents of slavery let it be, because they wanted Southern states to join the new nation. And Southerners accepted, as their part of the compromise, the end of the slave trade by 1807. Southerners wanted to count slaves fully in determining their states' populations for the purposes of determining the number of their representatives in the House of Representatives. But Northerners did not want to count them at all because they were property, not citizens. The two groups settled on counting a slave as three-fifths of a person for certain constitutional purposes. This was a matter for plausible compromise because the white men who wrote the constitution had more interest in the economic prosperity to be got from strong economic union than in the details of continued slavery in the South.[6]

What was not foreseen at the time of the constitutional debates was that slavery would become far more important to the Deep South and that the growth of the nation into the western territories would tip the balance against the slave states. The original economic census (pro- and contra-slavery) was therefore undercut by changes in both the commitments of the relevant groups and their memberships. The Supreme Court, faced with difficult fugitive slave cases, held to or even exceeded the compromise on behalf of the Southern states. But the national electorate of 1860, voting democratically with full manhood suffrage for whites, ignored the compromise and elected Abraham Lincoln, an abolitionist, president, giving him enough support in Congress to shake the compromise. Precommitment in the form of various institutional structures to block or impede changes in the original compromise was then inadequate to satisfy Southern leaders. The compromise was shattered, the South seceded and was crushed in the Civil War, and slaves were made citizens under a Northern hegemony that lasted for decades.

In the depression-era crisis over economic policy, democracy may have played a strong role in enabling President Roosevelt and the Congress to alter constitutional arrangements beyond recognition. Irrespective of whether their institutional redesign was well conceived, it plausibly dampened politics from the left at the time and thereby helped enable the nation to move onward from the grim depression. But the end result – massive administrative government with very limited oversight from the legislative, executive, and judical branches – de facto abolished much of the prior constitutional scheme of government, in which there had been no autonomous administrative fourth branch. All of the restructuring was possible only because the president and Congress were in rough agreement on shoving responsibility onto the newly created agencies and because the Supreme Court could be bullied into letting the changes stand as though they were exempt from constitutional review.

---

[6] Russell Hardin (1996).

Finally, political efforts to deal with the Vietnam war eventually flaunted the democracy that wanted the war over. After being democratically elected to end the war, President Nixon then fought half the war, escalating it in may ways, including spreading warfare to Cambodia with horrendous consequences. In keeping with the manner of many presidents, going back at least to Abraham Lincoln, Nixon's actions showed contempt for democracy except when it suited his purposes.

Two of these three episodes produced drastic changes in the Constitution. The Civil War conflict was handled extraconstitutionally and then was patched over extraconstitutionally by the victorious Northern states. The 1930s problem of economic failure was handled more nearly harmoniously but still extraconstitutionally. It is often said that the United Kingdom is virtually unique in having an unwritten constitution. In actual fact, the United States now has an unwritten alteration of its constitution with the creation of the fourth, enormously important administrative branch of government. Why did the new system work? As in the adoption of the original constitution by the thirteen states, the new system was a coordination resolution that built on broad consensus. However, the 1930s coordination was not on the constitution per se but on doing something about the economic malaise. Many critics of the time thought the malaise was itself the product of governmental, constitutional failure and that its resolution required de facto constitutional revision.

Even absolute constitutional barriers to change in the terms of a compromise do not work. Multilingual, multicultural, multiethnic, and multireligious nations such as Belgium have often attempted to fix the terms of representation in government to prevent turning an election into an ethnic census. In the longer run, such constitutional barriers may merely undercut the credibility of a constitution, especially if population shifts in favour of one group over another. For a particularly strenuous case of constitutional engineering, consider Tito's Yugoslavia.

Under Tito, Yugoslavia was carved into quasi-ethnic regions that had constitutional standing to protect certain of their supposed interests – although it would be wrong to claim that the groups had substantial interests in conflict beyond the mere conflict over which group got what share of resources and power. At the same time, in practice, Tito was a nationalist without primary attachment to any of these regions. These two stances fit badly together. A genuine nationalist should have carved up the regions less tendentiously, without the seeming confusion of different ethnic "nations" with geographically specific territories. Yugoslavia generally could not be mapped ethnically onto territories. For example, people of many ethnic backgrounds mingled in its biggest cites and many of its smaller towns. Perversely, however, Tito's system created, almost as though it were a matter of nature, leaders of each of the geographical territories who were themselves ethnically *and* territorially identified. As Yugoslavia neared its demise, the personal careers of certain of these regional leaders depended on their success in mobilizing ethnic support against the Titoist system. Only in Bosnia, which was too nearly evenly split between Croats, Muslims, and Serbs, did Tito's system seem to have natural support – until, of course, Tito's system collapsed nationally with the secessions of Slovenia and Croatia.[7]

Virtually all that has happened in the Yugoslav debacle has been in violation of the constitutional precommitments to a strongly federal system. Milosevic altered the status of Kosovo and Vojvodina in order to gain two more votes in the national council of republics and autonomous regions. With Serbia's and Montenegro's votes already behind him, the addition of the two no-longer autonomous regions gave him half the total vote. The secessions of Slovenia and Croatia then gave him solid control, despite the fact that Serbians were a minority of the population.

Precommitments are splendid – if they are followed by continued commitments to the same arrangements. If commitments waver, precommitments totter. In essence, they are worth nothing except to signal what the present commitments are.

Democracy and economic development

Most modern democratic nations grew relatively slowly into democracy. The Suffrage expanded very slowly in England and France, with occasional retrenchment in France. It spread quickly at first but then moved quite slowly in the United States, with black men brought in only after the Civil War and all women only in 1919. In many colonial nations, democracy was introduced full-blown at independence, as it was in much of Eastern Europe in 1989 or immediately afterward.

It is plausible that, in earlier times, mutual-advantage claims would have failed in, say, England for the entire adult populace except for the smaller set of those eligible to vote. Clearly, mutual-advantage claims would have seemed like nonsense to politically sophisticated slaves in the United States until about the time of the Civil War. It was precisely because the majority was turning too heavily against slavery that the Southern states preemptively seceded from the Union before they lost the slavery issue to democratic decision.

Consider also France at the time of the Revolution. Napoleon created a vast class of small-holding peasants, who were essentially subsistence farmers. Suppose full-scale democracy had been introduced then with suffrage for all adults. Peasant agricultural interests would numerically have overwhelmed all other interests combined. It is hard to imagine that government organized around

---

[7] See also Hardin (1995. chap. 6).

the interests of subsistence agriculture could have brought France to prosperity – at least surely not in the next century or two. Progress depended, rather, on moving people off such subsistence farms, which, as Marx recognized, were the central reason for the depravity of the peasant class. When peasants did vote, as in 1848, they voted stupidly with capitalism against their own interests (in socialism, Marx supposed) because they conservatively defended their way of life and supposed their problems were somehow caused by bad state policy rather then the economic impossibility of organizing production their way.[8] In Marx's view, they might have been much better off if not entitled to vote.

In agrarian nations in our time, land reform may be virtually necessary merely to stop the politics of land reform. Land reform might actually harm everyone, but a very large number expect benefits from it and are willing to engage in substantial political activity to bring it about. One might think this is an implausible, because irrational, result. But it is only partly irrational. At the margin, I would be better off if I get my share of land. But if the way I get it is through a system that gives most farm families their own shares of land, then I might not be better off. The tendency to think of the marginal change is perhaps a mistake, but it is one that many people in many contexts make, for understandable reasons such as their lack of special competence in more general economic or strategic reasoning.

Apart from farm workers, current plantation owners, who are a very small number of people, expect losses from land reform unless they are compensated beyond the capacity of most governments. Naturally, they too are willing to politick, by violent means if necessary. If land reform carries, then ordinary economic trends might drive most of the supposed beneficiaries and their children off the land. As people leave the land, there is typically no loss of productivity, but there may often be grievous initial loss of well-being. The next generation might tend to be much better off than they would have been on the farm, but the current generation might be losers for the remainder of their lives.

Both the reform of ownership patterns involved in land reform and the economic changes that impoverish small farmers and drive them from the land might be called structural changes. But the former comes from an identifiable political action, whereas the latter seems to happen in a decentralized, uncontrolled way. There is, of course, some centralized control, although in many industrial nations the control is exercised with various subsidies and protections to help farmers stay on the land, as in France, Japan, and the United States. The decline of farming as an occupation might once have occasioned strong reactions, as something needing forceful control to keep farmers or peasants on the land. But that position lacks credibility after two centuries of radical movement out of an agricultural economy that was, for the bulk of population,

---

[8] Karl Marx (1963), especially, pp. 118–35.

essentially a subsistence industry into an economy that is diverse and that has only a very small, but highly productive, agricultural sector.

In the traditional cases of movement to greater democracy, piecemeal democratization may have been enormously functional in the long run. Instant democracy with universal suffrage might have been much less successful even at bringing about a working, full-suffrage democracy. How then could instant liberal democracy suddenly work after 1989 in much of Eastern Europe? There had, of course, been a veneer of democracy under Communism, but there was not competitive democracy or genuinely open choice. Rather, there were elections, with strong incentives to vote even when there was no choice available. Hence the peoples of Eastern Europe had the experience and the habit of voting but not the experience of democracy.

So why could Eastern Europeans make democracy work now? Perhaps because that was a unique time when there was relatively wide consensus on how to organize the economy. The prior economic order was widely questioned, even reviled. A major reason for the consensus was the broad evidence of comparative economics and politics. For example, Czech and East German regions, which had once rivaled the wealth of regions of West Germany and France and exceeded that of Italy, had fallen far behind, especially at the level of individual prosperity. And their peoples had far greater restrictions on various freedoms. Many East Europeans knew people or even had relatives who had gone west to thrive personally, professionally, and financially. Many East Europeans did not wish to emigrate in order to thrive. Rather, they wanted to bring the West home.

While there were, and still are, holdouts for a central direction of the economy in all of these nations, the governments that have been elected have virtually all chosen to follow some path to market organization. Yugoslav-Serbia and Romania might not yet find such a path compelling, but Poland, the Czech Republic, Hungary, Slovakia, Slovenia, Croatia, and Bulgaria have taken such a path. And East Germany voted itself instantly into the West German market. Former communists who were elected to succeed previously elected noncommunists in Poland and Hungary, apparently on the strength of their protests that liberalization was being pursued too quickly and harshly, have nevertheless continued the basic pro-market policies.[9] This was a time when consensus was plausibly broad enough that any kind of government might have been expected to make relevant policy.

Of course, it is too early to tell whether the conditions for democracy are adequate in any of these cases, and there is good reason to doubt that Russia and some of the former Soviet Republics are ready for democracy. Beneath the

---

[9] István Deak (1994).

current consensus on the need for economic reform, there may be other conflicts too deep and wide to be bridged by routine democratic compromise. Indeed, in some of these nations, there are ethnic conflicts that cut very deeply, and in others there may still be too great a disagreement about fundamental economic policy, with continuing strong support from some quarters for central control of the economy. There are some clear losers from the move from central command to market economy and, coincidentally, there are losers from changes in economic demand as agriculture continues to be displaced by industry and basic heavy industry is displaced by new electronic, communication, other high-tech, and chemical industries, as well as by service industries that were missing in the old system but that now spring up to fill demand. Both losing groups pose potential opposition to market reforms.

Normative issues in democracy

In Anthony Down's *Economic Theory of Democracy* there are two coordinate theses.[10] The first, the median-voter model, concerns the rational choices of candidates for office: In a two-party system, candidates must locate themselves at the center of the policy space or they will be outflanked, leaving them with only minority support. The second thesis concerns the rational choices of voters. At one level, there is no problem in rationality for voters. Voters should merely vote for the candidate whose positions are nearest their own. The problem comes before this stage. Should rational voters take the trouble to vote at all? And should voters take the trouble to become sufficiently well informed to know which candidate's positions are nearest their own? These are, for Downs, rational questions of self-interest. But they also underlie normative questions of what one more broadly ought to do.

If individuals have no reason to participate, because they cannot affect outcomes, then they have no reason to know enough to participate wisely if they did participate. This fact has several normative implications. First, it implies that the limits to democracy entail limits in individual responsibility in the role of democratic citizen. Second, it affects – perhaps drastically – arguments for the autonomy of democratic participation. And third, it undercuts contractarian claims for the rightness of democratic, ostensibly consensual, results.

Limits on citizen responsibility

Democratic citizens may have responsibilities that are limited in ways that reflect natural limits and constraints on democracy. There are at least two classes of problems: those that follow from systematic actual conflict with majority

---

[10] Anthony Downs (1957).

decisions and those that follow from the nature of democratic participation. The first class represents failures of democracy that follow from applying it to deeper conflicts rather than merely to marginal issues. Such a failure raises questions about the responsibility of citizens to abide by democratic decisions. The second class represents logical implications of the likely mismatch between individual citizen's incentives and the requirements for democratic procedures.

For an example of the first class, consider the 1993 election that democratically brought Hutus to power in Burundi. The Hutus were sure to keep that power indefinitely if democratic majoritarian preferences were followed because, on the evidence of the votes cast, they outnumbered Tutsis by about two to one. Suppose that the democratically elected government imposed discrimination against the minority Tutsis, perhaps gross discrimination.[11] It then would be hard to argue that the mere fact of democratic election of this partially malevolent government commands from Tutsis their loyalty to the government until the next election. Arguably, Tutsis would owe it no allegiance whatever, no more than Hutus might have owed the prior, autocratic Tutsi government.

A similar conclusion may follow for either farm laborers or large plantation owners in many contemporary agrarian states that face or have recently faced land reform. It might also follow for some minority language groups, although not for many others. Many minority language groups gain far more from being quasi-assimilated in a particular society under its government than they could possibly gain from any other option they have. One might argue that they should nevertheless be given linguistic privileges or special consideration, but that would be a matter within the ambit of democratic decision inasmuch as it is a marginal issue against the background of generally beneficial order and even wealth.

Turn to the second class of problems – the mismatch of individual incentives with democratic requirements. The crux of citizen responsibility in a democracy is the causal efficacy of the role of citizen and the individual's justification for acquiring relevant knowledge. If the role is entirely inefficacious, there is no social reason to acquire knowledge. I may have reason to acquire knowledge because it gives me pleasure, but not because it will be useful for causing good public effects through my role as citizen. It is conceivable that we would all be better off if we all participated democratically. We might therefore fine individuals who failed to vote, as many nations have done. But that would be inadequate to guarantee that they vote intelligently or even at all knowledgeably. We might somehow require some evidence of relevant study of the issues. But then we begin to risk having the state decide what counts are relevant knowledge.

---

[11] In fact, Tutsis rebelled preemptively to destroy the government before it could organize well enough to have much power.

Hence although we might overcome the problem of lack of participation, we probably could not overcome the problem of uninformed participation.

Might it be true that we would all be better off if we just invested time in understanding the issues of elections in order to vote intelligently? At the margin, surely, most individuals would not be better off from their own sole efforts to be informed. But perhaps I would be better off from having everyone be better informed. For one perverse reason, I might not be. That perverse reason is that having people be better informed might turn every election into something more nearly like a group census. But that would make politics more divisive and might destroy the possibilities for continuing democratic government.

Apart from this possible perversity, suppose that being informed means, typically, investment of an hour every week day in learning about current politics (not merely the lurid tales of sexual escapades, but the stuff of policy). That hour could come from work time, goofing off time, entertainment time, family time, or sleep time. Most likely there would be real losses to compensate for the redirected effort. Even then, most of the newly informed citizens are pitiful amateurs in comparison to the numerous bureaucrats, elected officials, and specialists, if that were not so, we could change the latter all at will. This discussion is itself amateurish – not least because the problem seems not to have been seriously addressed in the literature on citizen responsibility. In the end, if we are to claim that citizens have a responsibility to know more than they typically do, we will need a justification for the claim. And that justification will have to take into account the likely trade-offs involved in citizens knowing more. *It seems plausible that there will be no justification that stands against such a test.*

It follows that not only we can make at best limited claims for the responsibility of citizens to participate in democratic government but also that democracy cannot be justified by appeal to its grounding in substantial citizen participation. Despite the origins of the word and the way it is typically used in popular and academic discourse, democracy either cannot entail massive citizen participation or it is irrelevant to actual practice in modern polities.

Individual autonomy

Democracy is often supported because it is thought to contribute to the development of individual autonomy or because it is supposed to be the ideal form of government for a society of autonomous individuals. Because prosperity, security, and various other aspects of well-being also play very large roles in developing autonomy, government must secure these things as well as democratic participation. Indeed, government arguably should see to it that these things are secured first and then worry about democratic principles, because these things, and not political participation, are the sine qua non for autonomy for most people. For causal reasons, political participation cannot be a significant part of the autonomy of the vast majority of individuals in a nation as large as the United States – or even Sweden. Hence either autonomy is a repugnantly narrow concept or it does not heavily depend on participation.

One might be committed to democracy independently of whether it works in some sense. Some writers, especially in popular media, occasionally assert commitment to democracy as an absolute value, as though it must trump all other values when it conflicts with them. This is not a credible position nor need it be discussed with great seriousness. Virtually no one insists on democracy even for all political decisions. The standard, trivially obvious examples, are the need for secrecy in making policy during warfare and the preference for justice over opinion or interests in court cases. The form of the Allied invasion of Europe at the end of World War II was not a subject fit for democratic decision. Nor is the question of someone's guilt for a crime a subject fit for such decision.

In addition to these standard examples, it is plausible that the rise of administrative government over the past century is largely a response to the inability of democratic forms to handle vast areas of government policy. In the United States, as in many nations, democracy has been reduced to relatively weak and limited oversight in many contexts. Many critics think this development is a corruption of democratic forms. Libertarians hold it to be normatively wrong because in entails coercion without prior agreement. But almost no one proposes serious alternative ways of handling the relevant problems. The chief practical complaints and recommendations are about marginal problems in the administrative state, such problems as what might generously be read as an agency's going beyond its legislative authority. One might think it a deeper problem that the very existence of the agency goes beyond constitutional authority. Somehow, we seem democratically to have consented to the radical change and dedemocratization of government – although there were no genuine votes on the matter other than such votes as to elect and re-elect the people who underwrote these revisions of the govermental structure.

It is not necessary to argue that there is another *form* of government that beats democracy to show that full-scale democracy is not always the way to go. In general, democracy might be the best form of government under certain circumstances (as outlined above) even though its forms might be better violated on occasion. But under some conditions, relatively limited democracy might be generally, not just occasionally, preferable to full-scale democracy.

The right result

Many democratic theories are themselves deduced from particular moral principles, such as utilitarian or Kantian principles. In these theories, it is possible to pass independent judgment on the rightness of a democratic outcome. A utilitarian, for example, might think it true that the least fallible device for achieving utilitarian outcomes is democratic decision procedures. But the device is merely contingently the least fallible – it is not infallible. Hence the utilitarian might conclude that, in a particular application of such procedures, the wrong result was reached.

In contractarian theories, however, it might actually follow that what we choose is the criterion of the right – there is no independent criterion.[12] In many discussions of democracy there is the seeming assumption or implication that whatever we democratically choose is therefore right. Perhaps these conclusions derive from an implicitly contractarian view. Often, however, they may be grounded in little more than an intuitive sense that democracy is good and therefore what it accomplishes is the measure of the good.

Unfortunately, any contractarian theory that sets agreement as the criterion of the right or good is on very shaky ground for a modern polity. In a nation of even modest size, there is little or no chance that typical citizens have sufficient reason to master the issues open to democratic decisions well enough to contribute intelligently to their resolution. And even if they do master the issues, they have little or no prospect of using their mastery to influence the democratic choice. The odds against their votes ever making a difference are overwhelming. There was a tie vote in a local election in New Jersey in 1994 – this otherwise trivial vote became national news because it was the exceedingly rare case of a tie in which one more vote could have made a difference. There have also been votes that were de facto ties in larger elections in which the counting error is too great to know who really has won in a very close count, as recently happened in a New Hampshire election to the United States Senate. One more vote is unlikely to make a difference in such an election. The individual voter essentially does not count.

Hence if responsible citizens who have mastered the issues wish to influence policy, they will not do it by voting, which is almost the whole story of the participation of many citizens. Rather, they will have to undertake actions to influence those who have been elected, those who might run for office, or those who might not vote the right way without efforts to mobilize them. These are relatively demanding and costly efforts. Most people do not ever undertake such efforts at any serious level. A large proportion of those who do undertake them may be intending to build political careers, so that these efforts are investments toward a future benefit and not merely a public-spirited contribution to some greater good. Perversely, then, for the democratic theorist who measures the good by the results of participation, personal career interests must often – even typically – be more important than regard for the outcomes of democratic choice. (The historian William L. O'Neill finds this a distressing aspect of American politics during World War II.[13] Alas, it was merely politics as usual.)

[12] Russell Hardin (1990).
[13] William L. O'Neill (1993).

One might argue for an ideal conception of democracy, in which all or most citizens knowledgeably participate. But that ideal cannot be used to justify or practically criticize the results of an actual democracy in which participation is heavily subject to the accidental whims of individual interest. Indeed, one might argue for the goodness of a democratic system that has denatured participation, a system that fundamentally violates the ideal. Such a system may also denature many potential conflicts, the very conflicts that, if acute, make democracy unworkable. *What makes democracy work makes it fail the test of the ideal conception.*

It does not follow that citizen ignorance per se is good. What is good is the background fact that most individuals can see their interests as being elsewhere than in politics. Hence they are not motivated to participate with intensity and are therefore not motivated to know enough to participate well. Politics might enrich or impoverish us, might elevate or demolish us – it has done all of these things to a single generation of Germans now living, but we generally have insufficient interest to try to affect these results. Moreover, we should be glad of that fact, because we cannot suppose a democracy of millions, even 280 million, should take up a great part of the lives of those millions. Everyone should be able to specialize substantially, and high or even chief among our specializations should be our own lives. With specialization, we achieve the division of labor that is necessary for substantial creation and well-being.

In a sense, our individual lives are marginal to the larger political result. We want our lives to be against a relatively good and stable background of government and order, of economy and society, and we want all of these to leave us scope for individual creativity, pleasure, family, or even personal involvement in politics. But personal involvement in politics cannot be the sine quo non of life unless most people are to have no life or unless politics is disastrously intrusive. For most of us, sufficiently intense participation in politics over a long time guarantees the dismal result that we lose our individual lives, we become diminished in the name of a nation, a party, an ethnic group, or a cause. The 1930s memoirs and letters of Europeans who were not specialists in politics or journalism often provoke sadness at the extent to which the person was submerged in the politics of the day, often down to the level of the most tedious specific issues.

Concluding remarks

Democracy is inherently a marginal device for regulating political conflicts. That it works when it does is evidence of lack of deeply divisive conflicts that trump the value of general order. It does not work well if it is grounded in group census, and, indeed, the claim for group census is implicitly a claim that conflicts are too grievous and broad for democracy. Democracy is in Hobbe's family of mutual-advantage devices. An extant government that takes the form of a mutual-advantage device merits our coordination on it to the extent that it serves our interests better than moving to an alternative would. Other strong claims for the normative value of democracy are not compelling – except, perhaps, causal claims that democracy achieves some good better than other forms of government could, as in Millian defenses of liberal democracy. Finally, if mutual advantage is the normative ground for democracy, individuals or groups whose mutual advantage is not served have little normative reason for adhering to democratic principles unless, for causal reasons, their adherence would help to effect some good, such as the general welfare.

References

Deak, I. 1994. Post-Post-Communist Hungary, *New York Review of Books*, **11**, 33–8.

Downs, A. 1957. *An Economic Theory of Democracy*, Harper and Row, New York.

Goldthorpe, J. H., D. Lockwood, F. Bechhofer, and J. Platt. 1969. *The Affluent Worker in the Class Structure*, Cambridge University Press, Cambridge.

Hardin, R. 1990. Contractarianism: Wistful thinking, *Constitutional Political Economy*, **1**, 35–52.

    1991a. Acting together, contributing together, *Rationality and Society*, **3**, 365–80.

    1991b. Hobbesian political order, *Political Theory*, **19**, 156–80.

    1995. *One for All: The Logic of Group Conflict*, Princeton University Press, Princeton, N.J.

    1996. *Liberalisation, Constitutionalism, and Democracy*, Oxford University Press, Oxford (in press).

Hobbes, T. 1651. *Leviathan*, Reprint Penguin Books, Harmondsworth, England, 1968.

Marx, K. 1963. *The 18th Brumaire of Louis Bonaprate*. Reprint, World Publishing, New York.

O'Neill, W. L. 1993. *A Democracy at War: America's Fight at Home and Abroad in World War II*, Free Press, New York.

Parsons, T. 1949. *The Structure of Social Action*. 2nd edition, Free Press, New York.

Przeworski, A. 1980. Material interests, class compromise, and the transition to socialism, *Politics and Society*, **10**, 125–153.

Index